THE VIDEO DETECTIVE'S

1997

GUIDE TO THE

TOP
1000

FILMS OF ALL TIME

THE VIDEO DETECTIVE'S

1997

GUIDE TO THE

TOP 1000

FILMS OF ALL TIME

BY JIM RIFFEL

*Contributing Editor,
Jacqui Brownstein*

THE ECCO PRESS

THE ECCO PRESS
100 West Broad Street
Hopewell, New Jersey 08525

Published simultaneously in Canada by
Penguin Books Canada Ltd., Ontario
Printed in the United States of America

Library of Congress Cataloging-in-Publication Data

Riffel, Jim.
    The video detective's 1997 guide to the top 1000 films of
all time / by Jim Riffel ; additional material and editing by
Jacqui Brownstein. — 1st Ecco ed.
        p.   cm.
    Includes index.
    ISBN 0-88001-542-X
    1. Motion pictures—Catalogs. 2. Video recordings—
Catalogs. I. Brownstein, Jacqui. II. Title.
PN1998.R518   1997
016.79143'75—dc21   96-53493

9 8 9 7 6 5 4 3 2 1

FIRST EDITION

There are a lot of bad movies out there and I don't want to see them. Chances are, you don't want to see them either. So what I've done is compiled a list of over 1000 of the best films ever made, divided them up into 19 different categories, and put it all into a handy, pocket-size guide just for you. I've even added a checklist at the back of the book so you can keep track of what you've seen.

You may be surprised to find films in this "best of" book that you've never even heard of before. Besides the classics like Citizen Kane and *2001: A Space Odyssey* there's plenty of lesser known but just as "classic" pics like *Lady Jane*, *Birdy*, *Hearts of Darkness*, and *The Lady Eve*.

So take my advice, "use this book and never rent a bad movie again."

Your Pal,
The Video Detective

Special thanks to Dorothy Riffel, Kathy Passucci, Traci and Charlie DeAngelis, D. Adam Young, Dave Myers, Anthony DeLuca, Mark Miller, Don Calabrese, Alan Ferraro, Tim Keyes, Craig Smith, Scott Blair, Dave Stone, Ken Pew, Brad Hickman, Laurie Suk, Alan Grobert, Walt Gollender, Wayne Novelli, and Phil and Joe.

CONTENTS

THE VIDEO DETECTIVE'S

1997

GUIDE TO THE

TOP 1000

FILMS OF ALL TIME

THE ADDICTION *1995 81m/C* HORROR

This is not the best vampire movie ever made, but it's certainly the weirdest and contains bizarre symbolism and dialogue referring to, among others, Kierkegaard and Nietzsche. Taylor is a graduate student who gets bit by Sciorra and sees life (or death if you prefer) through new eyes. Ferrara lays on the symbolism when Taylor and her toothy pals decide to feed on the philosophy faculty of her school. Some great moments.

C: Lili Taylor, Paul Calderon, Christopher Walken, Annabella Sciorra, Edie Falco   D: Abel Ferrara

THE ADVENTURES OF PINOCCHIO *1996 96m/C (G)* CHILDREN/FAMILY

Amazing special effects make this live action version of the Disney animated classic really work. The story of a puppet coming to life has music by Stevie Wonder.

C: Martin Landau, Jonathan Taylor Thomas   D: Steve Barron

AMERICAN BUFFALO *1996 100m/C (R)* SLEEPER

Franz and Hoffman star with Nelson as a group of inept thieves who decide to try to change their lives in one fell swoop: they're going to rob a coin collection. Overlooked, interesting film based on David Mamet's play.

C: Dennis Franz, Dustin Hoffman, Sean Nelson   D: Michael Corrente

ANGELS AND INSECTS *1995 118m/C (R)* DRAMA

A penniless young entomologist returns from the Amazon and is boarded at the estate of a sympathetic philanthropist. There he finds himself becoming involved with two ladies of the household, marrying one and embarking on a project to record the yearly life cycle of an ant colony with the other.

Insect references and imagery abound.

C: Mark Rylance, Patsy Kensit, Kristin Scott Thomas, Saskia Wickham, Jeremy Kemp   D: Philip Haas

ANGUS *1995 87m/C (PG-13)* CHILDREN/FAMILY

A solid coming-of-age story about an overweight high school freshman who doesn't fit in. His mother wants to transfer him to a private school. His grandfather's attitude is "screw 'em, who cares what everybody else thinks?" And the high school quarterback, who's been bugging Angus since kindergarten, has the ultimate plan to make a fool of him.

C: Charlie Talbert, George C. Scott, Kathy Bates, Rita Moreno, Chris Owen   D: Patrick Read Johnson

ANTONIA'S LINE *1995 93m/C (R)* FOREIGN

This film from Holland is a touching fairy tale about the major events which distinguish the passage of time (birth, love, and death) in the human condition, as seen through the eyes of a strong-willed dying ninety-year-old woman reminiscing in her final hours.

C: Willeke Van Ammelrooy, Jan Decleir, Els Dottermans, Dora Van Der Groen   D: Marleen Gorris

AUGUST *1995 99m/C (PG)* DRAMA

Based on Chekhov's *Uncle Vanya* this version, set in Wales, has Hopkins as a bachelor living on a family estate pondering how life has passed him by. There's hilarious trouble when he's rebuffed by a beautiful guest at his idyllic country estate.

C: Anthony Hopkins, Kate Burton, Gawn Grainger   D: Anthony Hopkins

BASQUIAT *1996 106m/C (R)* FOREIGN

The fast life and early death of Jean-Michel Basquiat (he died at 27) are brought to the screen by real life artist Julian Schnabel, a friend of Basquiat. Basquiat, who lived on the streets of New York in a cardboard box, shot to the top of the art world after being championed by Andy Warhol. Instead of success making his life better it made it worse and Basquiat became addicted to heroin. Big cast was gotten by Schnabel by giving some of them his own valuable paintings.

C: Jeffrey Wright, David Bowie, Dennis Hopper, Gary Oldman, Christopher Walken, Willem Dafoe, Tatum O'Neal, Parker Posey, Courtney Love   D: Julian Schnabel

BIG NIGHT *1996 108m/C (R)* SLEEPER

At the Jersey shore in the '50s two immigrant brothers own a restaurant, one concerned with making a profit, the other concerned with making gourmet dishes the customers will remember forever. When their business is in trouble, they decide to try saving it by putting on a feast for one big night. The story runs the gamut of emotions from A to Z and is easily one of the best films of 1996.

C: Stanley Tucci, Tony Shalhoub, Minnie Driver, Ian Holm, Isabella Rossellini   D: Stanley Tucci, Campbell Scott

THE BIRDCAGE *1996 118m/C (R)* COMEDY

Hilarious remake of the French film *La Cage Aux Folles*, updated for the '90s. Life partners, nightclub owner Armand and his club's star attraction, female impersonator Albert, have to play it straight when Armand's son announces his engagement to the daughter of a very conservative politician and has invited them for a family dinner.

C: Robin Williams, Nathan Lane, Gene Hackman, Dianne Wiest   D: Mike Nichols

BOTTLE ROCKET *1996 91m/C (R)* SLEEPER

Dignan, Bob, and Anthony are three suburban twentysomethings who decide on a life of crime. Unfortunately, none have a killer instinct, which makes for a major roadblock. Dignan apologizes as he's taking the money, Anthony doesn't want to rob anymore because he's fallen in love with a Spanish-speaking chambermaid, and Bob, who's wealthy, only joined the gang because Dignan and Anthony are his friends. Owen C. Wilson, who makes an awesome acting debut, also co-wrote the hilarious screenplay.

C: Owen C. Wilson, Luke Wilson, Robert Musgrave, James Caan
D: Wes Anderson

BOUND 1996 108m/C (R) SLEEPER

Violet (Tilly) and Corky (Gershon) are lovers. They love each other and they also love money. Violet's boyfriend is a mobster who has a couple million bucks lying around. The girls decide they would be happier if the money was theirs. This leads to mayhem.

C: Jennifer Tilly, Gina Gershon, Joe Pantoliano, John P. Ryan
D: Larry and Andy Wachowski

BREAKING THE WAVES 1996 158m/C FOREIGN

An innocent young lady from a small village in Scotland suffers a severe tragedy when an accident leaves her husband in a state of paralysis. But she now believes, by performing a certain act, she can rescue him.

C: Emily Watson, Stellan Skarsgard, Katrin Cartlidge, Jean-Marc Barr, Udo Kier   D: Lars Von Trier

BRIAN WILSON: I JUST WASN'T MADE FOR THESE TIMES 1995 75m/B&W DOCUMENTARY

Well made study of Beach Boys' leader Brian Wilson and how he took his band to the top of the charts. Unfortunately Wilson couldn't handle the fame. His band split up, Wilson spent ten years in various states of mental distress, softening the blow with drugs and alcohol. In the film historians and music legends like Linda Ronstadt, Tom Petty, David Crosby, and Graham Nash refer to him as a genius and one of the greatest songwriters of the 1900s. It's interesting to hear Wilson talk about his future in the music business.

D: Don Was

THE BROTHERS MCMULLEN 1995 98m/C (R)
DRAMA

Three Irish Catholic brothers from Long Island, New York, grapple with love, temptation, and commitment in this delightfully sweet romantic comedy.

C: Edward Burns, Mike McGlone, Shari Albert, Jack Mulcahy, Connie Britton, Elizabeth P. McKay D: Edward Burns

CARRIED AWAY 1996 104m/C (R) SLEEPER

Hopper plays a school teacher in a small country town who feels he's never had an adventure, never been "carried away." That all changes when 18-year-old Locane moves to town and enrolls for her senior year. Irving plays Hopper's longtime girlfriend who helplessly watches their lives unravel. The movie could easily have become a sex farce but instead is an excellent, realistic bittersweet love story.

C: Dennis Hopper, Gary Busey, Amy Irving, Amy Locane   D: Bruno Barreto

CARRINGTON 1995 120m/C (R) DRAMA

Sensuous period piece about the painter Dora Carrington's unorthodox relationship with homosexual writer Lytton Strachey from their meeting in 1915 to his death (and her suicide) in 1932.

C: Emma Thompson, Jonathan Pryce, Steven Waddington, Samuel West   D: Christopher Hampton

CITY OF LOST CHILDREN 1995 111m/C (R)
FOREIGN

A circus strongman sets out on a strange journey to find Denree, his little brother who has been kidnaped. Along the way he encounters a roving band of dangerous orphans, a dream-stealing evil scientist named Krank, Siamese twins known as the Octopus, and a brain in a tank. Like Terry Gilliam's *Brazil*, this movie is of the "I'm concentrating too much on bizarre images and not enough on story" school of film making. But the images are some of the most amazing ever put on screen.

C: Ron Perlman, Daniel Emilfork, Joseph Lucien, Judith Vittet, Genevieve Brunet   D: Marc Caro, Jean-Pierre Jeunet

DEAD MAN WALKING *1995 122m/C (R)* BIOGRAPHY

Based on a true story about a nun who forges a deep and revealing relationship with a death row inmate. Excellent performances by Sarandon and Penn.

C: Susan Sarandon, Sean Penn, Robert Prosky   D: Tim Robbins
AA: '95 Best Actress (Sarandon), Nom: Best Actor (Penn)

DEVIL IN A BLUE DRESS *1995 101m/C (R)* DRAMA

It's 1940s Los Angeles and an out-of-work veteran is hired to find a woman, but finds himself entangled in a web of murder instead.

C: Denzel Washington, Tom Sizemore, Don Cheadle, Jennifer Beals
D: Carl Franklin

THE ENGLISH PATIENT *1996 159m/C (R)* DRAMA

The North African desert is the setting for this heart wrenching romantic epic in which the love between an Hungarian count and a British married woman is tested against the tragedies of life and World War II.

C: Ralph Fiennes, Kristin Scott Thomas, Juliette Binoche, Willem Dafoe   D: Anthony Minghella

FARGO *1996 100m/C (R)* DRAMA

The true story of a Minnesota car salesman with money problems who hires two thugs to kidnap his wife, hoping her wealthy father will quickly pay the ransom. A simple plan turns into a nightmare as the Coen brothers, who are the kings of style, turn out another four star film.

C: Steve Buscemi, Frances McDormand, William H. Macy, Harve Presnell   D: Joel Coen

THE FUNERAL *1996 90m/C (R)* DRAMA
Crime drama set in New York City in the '30s. Three racketeering brothers and the women in their lives.

C: Chris Penn, Christopher Walken, Vincent Galeo, Isabella Rossellini, Annabella Sciorra, Benicio Del Toro   D: Abel Ferrara

GEORGIA *1995 117m/C (R)* DRAMA
Two sisters, one a very successful singer/songwriter and the other an aspiring rock star who's a junkie. They find the toughest act to follow were their dreams.

C: Jennifer Jason Leigh, Mare Winningham, Ted Levine, John Doe D: Ulu Grosbard   AA: '95 Nom: Best Actress (Winningham)

GET ON THE BUS *1996 122m/C (R)* DRAMA
Lee tends to make films which deal with the problems between blacks and whites. With this film he deals with the problems between blacks and blacks. The plot revolves around a young black film maker interviewing (and getting feedback from) African-Americans on their way to Louis Farrakhan's Million Man March.

C: Ossie Davis, Gabriel Casseus, Hill Harper, Roger Smith, Andre Braugher, Richard Belzer   D: Spike Lee

HATE (LA HAINE) *1995 97m/B&W* (FOREIGN)
SLEEPER
Three youths roam the streets of riot-ridden France with a gun one of them has stolen from the police. He vows to kill an officer if his friend, who lies in a coma from a police beating,

dies. Just before dawn the friends stumble into an empty mall and watch on a big screen the news that their friend is dead. It's now the moment of truth. A gritty powerful statement of a society on a locomotive to hell.

C: Vincent Cassel, Hubert Kunde, Said Taghmoui, Karim Belkhadra
D: Mathieu Kassovitz

HEAVEN'S PRISONERS *1996 132m/C (R)* SLEEPER

Baldwin is a "retired" police officer down in the bayou. A plane crash near his home sets a series of events in motion that pull him back into the world of crime and all the evil that goes with it. Roberts gives a solid performance as the bad guy.

C: Alec Baldwin, Eric Roberts, Teri Hatcher, Mary Stuart Masterson, Kelly Lynch   D: Phil Janeau

I SHOT ANDY WARHOL *1996 104m/C (R)* DRAMA

Taylor stars as Valerie Solanas, a '60s feminist/writer with a genius IQ who became obsessed with Andy Warhol. Solanas started S.C.U.M. (The Society of Cutting Up Men), relentlessly pursued Warhol to produce one of her plays, and slowly slipped into madness, putting both hers and Warhol's life in jeopardy. It's all true. Harris gives a brilliant portrayal of Warhol and Dorf is excellent as Candy Darling.

C: Lili Taylor, Jared Harris, Stephen Dorff, Lothaire Bluteau, Martha Plimpton   D: Mary Harron

IL POSTINO (THE POSTMAN) *1995 110m/C (PG)* IT FOREIGN

Bittersweet story of a shy, almost illiterate postman who strikes up a friendship with an exiled Chilean poet on a remote Italian island. The postman gets the poet to write verse so he can woo a local beauty.

C: Philippe Noiret, Massimo Troisi, Maria Grazia Cucinotta
D: Michael Radford   AA: '95 Nom: Best Picture, Actor, Director

INDEPENDENCE DAY *1996 135m/C (PG-13)*
ACTION/ADVENTURE

The feel good movie of 1996. An alien armada arrives unin-vited and proceeds to lay waste to our cities, killing billions of people. That is until July 4th when some guys decide it's time to take our planet back. So under the leadership of the Presi-dent of the United States they fire the shot heard 'round the universe.'

C: Will Smith, Bill Pullman, Jeff Goldblum, Mary McDonnell, Judd Hirsch, Randy Quaid   D: Roland Emmerich

JAMES AND THE GIANT PEACH *1996 80m/C (PG)*
CHILDREN/FAMILY

First a young boy's parents are stolen by black rhinoceroses, then a strange man gives him a bag of alligator tongues. Soon after the alligator tongues make a dead tree bear a peach the size of a house. The boy, James, takes off in the fruit with an army of wacky insect pals battling bizarre pirates and other assorted foes. Based on Roald Dahl's book, it's fun entertainment for the kids.

D: Henry Selick

JANE EYRE *1996 112m/C (PG)* DRAMA

Charlotte Bronte's tale of a girl from childhood in a loveless foster family and Lowood School, until a decade later she be-comes the governess at Thornfield Hall. Once at Thornfield she meets the dark, brooding Mr. Rochester, her employer, where they fall in love but a mysterious, dark, secret keep them from marrying. If the story intrigues you rent the 1944 version with Orson Welles, a much better version.

C: Charlotte Gainsbourg, William Hurt, Anna Paquin, Joan Plowright
D: Franco Zeffirelli

JOURNEY *1995 100m/C* DRAMA

This made-for-TV film focuses on a boy whose restless mother abandons him and his sister. He is brought up by his grandparents who attempt to create a sense of family and family history for him.

C: Jason Robards, Jr., Brenda Fricker, Max Pomerance, Meg Tilly
D: Tom McLoughlin

JOURNEY OF THE AUGUST KING *1995 95m/C (PG-13)* DRAMA

A widowed farmer assists a vulnerable female slave who has run away in 1815 North Carolina.

C: Jason Patric, Sam Waterson, Thandie Newton, Larry Drake, Sara-Jane Wylde   D: John Duigan

JUDE *1996 122m/C (R)* DRAMA

This was Thomas Hardy's final novel. It's about an idealistic villager's Job-like rein of misery in 1880s England. This is a crushingly sad story of obsession and doom, but a beautiful film.

C: Christopher Eccleston, Kate Winslet, Liam Cunningham, Rachel Griffiths   D: Michael Winterbottom

JUPITER'S WIFE *1994 78m/C* DOCUMENTARY

An encounter in Central Park with Homeless Maggie who claims she has ESP, is the wife of the god Jupiter, and the daughter of the late actor Robert Ryan.

D: Michel Negroponte

THE LATE SHIFT *1996 95m/C (R)* BIOGRAPHY

In this made-for-HBO movie you are taken behind the scenes to see the infighting for Johnny Carson's hosting job on *The Tonight Show*. Leno and Letterman both want the job and think they deserve it. Bates gives a stand-out performance.

C: John Michael Higgins, Daniel Roebuck, Kathy Bates, Bob Balaban, Treat Williams   D: Betty Thomas

LLOYDS OF LONDON *1936 115m/B&W* DRAMA

For the first time on video this is the engrossing, often exciting story of the famous English insurance and banking firm. You see the early history of Lloyds and its rise to prominence around the time of the battle of Trafalgar. Of course, a fictional love story is thrown in for good measure.

C: Tyrone Power, Madeleine Carroll, Freddie Bartholomew, George Sanders, C. Aubrey Smith   D: Henry King

LONE STAR *1996 137m/C (R)* DRAMA

A skeleton of a sheriff who disappeared forty years ago is dug up in a Texas desert. The present sheriff decides to open the investigation of what caused the disappearance, setting in motion a series of events he may not be happy he started. Considered one of Sayles' best.

C: Chris Cooper, Kris Kristofferson, Joe Morton, Elizabeth Pena, Matthew McConaughey   D: John Sayles

MAD DOG TIME *1996 93m/C (R)* ACTION/ ADVENTURE

Dreyfuss plays Vic, a crime boss who's just been released from a mental institution. While in the asylum, his underlings have been wreaking havoc and setting record numbers in the murder department. Is Vic's release going to make things better or worse? This is the kind of film where the sound of gun fire is heard more than dialogue, and you leave the theater ducking when a car backfires. Take note of the cast below.

C: Gabriel Byrne, Jeff Goldblum, Richard Dreyfuss, Diane Lane, Ellen Barkin, Gregory Hines, Burt Reynolds, Rob Reiner, Billy Idol, Richard Pryor   D: Larry Bishop

MARTHA + ETHEL *1995 80m/C (G)* DOCUMENTARY

Jyll Johnstone and Barbara Ettinger show the effect that their names, Martha and Ethel, had on their lives. Martha, a strict disciplinarian from Germany, ruled the Johnstone children, and Ethel, a caring southern black woman, took care of the Ettingers.

D: Jyll Johnstone

A MONTH BY THE LAKE *1995 94m/C (PG)* DRAMA

A middle-aged English woman (Redgrave) seeks romance at an Italian resort on the threshold of World War II.

C: Vanessa Redgrave, Edward Fox, Uma Thurman, Alessandro Gassman   D: John Irvin

MR. AND MRS. LOVING *1996 95m/C* DRAMA

This made-for-television pic is a true story about a 1960s interracial couple who refuse to accept the law that they can't marry.

C: Timothy Hutton, Lela Rochon, Ruby Dee, Bill Nunn, Corey Parker
D: Dick Friedenberg

MR. HOLLAND'S OPUS *1995 143m/C (PG-13)* DRAMA

A frustrated music composer becomes a high-school music teacher and finds his true calling in life is to inspire his students.

C: Richard Dreyfuss, Glenne Headly, Jay Thomas, Olympia Dukakis
D: Stephen Herek   AA: '95 Nom: Best Actor (Dreyfuss)

MUPPET TREASURE ISLAND *1996 100m/C (G)* CHILDREN/FAMILY

In the Muppets' first action-adventure pic you learn a new meaning for "swashbuckling" as they sing and sword fight their way through this remake of the Robert Louis Stevenson classic.

C: Kermit the Frog, Miss Piggy, Tim Curry, Harvey Korman   D: Brian Henson

NIXON 1995 191m/C (R) BIOGRAPHY

Oliver Stone, one of the most controversial directors, tells the story of Richard Nixon, one of the most controversial presidents. As was the case with his film *JFK*, *Nixon* gets into select government misinformation and the personal side of the public life.

C: Anthony Hopkins, Joan Allen, Powers Boothe, Ed Harris, Bob Hoskins   D: Oliver Stone   AA: '95 Nom: Best Supporting Actress (Allen)

THE NUTTY PROFESSOR 1996 95m/C (PG-13) COMEDY

A remake of the Jerry Lewis classic, this proves to be a better movie. Love-struck nebbish and overweight professor Sherman Klump invents a potion that transforms him into an oily lounge lizard, Buddy Love. Murphy pulls off a tour de farce playing a total of seven roles.

C: Eddie Murphy, Jada Pinkett, James Coburn, Larry Miller   D: Tom Shadyac

101 DALMATIANS 1996 103m/C (G) CHILDREN/ FAMILY

Almost all of the Disney films which deal with fairy tales and other classic stories are animated. This one originally was in 1961, but now a live action version, also by Disney, has come along. Close plays the kooky criminal Cruella de Vil, an evil nemesis with a dastardly plan for the dogs.

C: Glenn Close, Jeff Daniels, Joely Richardson, lots of dogs
D: Stephen Herek

PALOOKAVILLE 1996 92m/C (R) SLEEPER

Sid, Russ, and Jerry would like to be successful criminals but they haven't the intelligence, the guts, or the drive. They're sort of a cross between the three musketeers and the three stooges. Though they dream of better days, they're ultimately stuck with themselves. Unlike the slew of crime movies that have been released since Tarantino gave the genre an adrenaline shot with *Reservoir Dogs*, this movie has a heart and pulse that makes it real.

C: William Forsythe, Vincent Gallo, Adam Trese, Frances McDormand   D: Alan Taylor

PARADISE LOST: THE CHILD MURDERS AT ROBIN HOOD HILLS *1996 135m/C* DOCUMENTARY

Two children are found dead in the woods, victims of a bizarre satanic sacrifice. Three high school friends are taken into custody and charged with the murder. Could these seemingly normal teenagers, who are now facing the death penalty, have committed such a horrendous crime? This documentary is a gripping, true story.

D: Joe Berlinger and Bruce Sinofsky

THE PREACHER'S WIFE *1996 124m/C (PG)* HOLIDAY

The problems of a preacher and his wife begin to disappear after they get a visit from, a well, an angel. Washington plays the heavenly creature in this crowd pleasing holiday pic. A remake of the 1947 classic *The Bishop's Wife*.

C: Denzel Washington, Whitney Houston, Courtney B. Vance, Gregory Hines   D: Penny Marshall

RICHARD III *1995 105m/C (R)* DRAMA

Shakespeare's historical drama is transplanted to 1930s London, mostly as an excuse for great jazzy costumes and great jazz music. But the story is the same, with Richard having a great time being evil and so does the viewer watching him.

C: Ian McKellen, Robert Downey, Jr., Annette Bening, Maggie Smith,

Jim Broadbent, Nigel Hawthorne   D: Richard Loncraine

RIDICULE *1996 104m/C (R)* FOREIGN

How much power do words have? To find out the answer go back to the court of Louis XVI and watch as a few good lines in the right places can save your life and kill someone else. A dark comedy of morals.

C: Charles Berling, Jean Rochefort, Fanny Ardant, Judith Godreche
D: Patrice Leconte

THE ROAD TO GALVESTON *1996 93m/C (PG-13)* DRAMA

Based on a true story, a widowed woman takes three home-less Alzheimer patients on a rejuvenating trip that will change their lives forever. Keep the hankie nearby.

C: Cicely Tyson, Piper Laurie, Tess Harper, Clarence Williams III
D: Michael Toshiyuki Uno

THE ROCK *1996 129m/C (R)* ACTION/ADVENTURE

Psycho Harris and his band of merry maniacs take a group of tourists hostage on Alcatraz Island, "The Rock," and demand big bucks for their release. Enter Connery, a mysterious su-perman who the government releases from prison to rescue the innocent victims. He gets help from Cage, one of the only chemical-weapons experts who can defuse Harris' missiles which are aimed at San Francisco.

C: Sean Connery, Nicolas Cage, Ed Harris, Michael Biehn, William Forsythe, David Morse   D: Michael Bay

SABRINA, THE TEENAGE WITCH *1996 90m/C* CHILDREN/FAMILY

From the *Archie Comics* Sabrina learns of her spell-casting heritage during the first full moon after her 16th birthday and struggles with love and rivals all while learning how to control her new powers.

C: Melissa Joan Hart, Sherry Miller, Charlene Fernetz   D: Tibor Takacs

THE SCARLET LETTER *1995 135m/C (R)* DRAMA

Hawthorne's classic tale of adulteress Hester Prynne is re-told here in a steamy version. Don't think you know how this one ends—Moore felt no one would remember how the book ended, so . . .

C: Demi Moore, Gary Oldman, Robert Duvall   D: Roland Joffe

SEARCH FOR ONE-EYE JIMMY *1996   m/C (R)* COMEDY

A west coast film student comes back east to shoot a documentary about his old neighborhood. But he stumbles onto a real story when a local character goes missing. He then interviews the grieving family and neighborhood miscreants.

C: Steve Buscemi, Jennifer Beals, Samuel L. Jackson, Holt McCallany, Nick Turturro, Anne Meara   D: Sam Henry Kass

THE SECRET OF ROAN INISH *1995 103m/C (PG)* CHILDREN/FAMILY

An Irish fable involving a magical creature, who is part seal and part woman. The myth suggests this special creature may be the ancestral mother of an entire family. A delightful, whimsical story.

C: Mike Lally, Eileen Colgan, Jeni Courtney   D: John Sayles

SECRETS AND LIES *1996 142m/C (R)* SLEEPER

A young black woman finds her biological mother, who turns out to be white. The conflict their relationship causes to those around them makes for a powerful story about truth and love. Winner of the top prize at the 1996 Cannes Film Festival and Los Angeles Film Critics Association.

C: Brenda Blethyn, Marianne Jean-Baptiste, Claire Rushbrook, Timothy Spall   D: Mike Leigh

SHINE *1996 105m/C (PG-13)* BIOGRAPHY

Gripping true story details the life of Australian pianist David Helfgott and how he overcame the brutal relationship with his father and how it almost destroyed his career.

C: Armin Mueller-Stahl, Noah Taylor, Geoffrey Rush, Lynn Redgrave, John Gielgud   D: Scott Hicks

STEALING BEAUTY *1996 119m/C (R)* DRAMA

A 19-year-old ingenue goes to Tuscany to read her mother's poetry and lose her virginity. At a villa she meets an aging, dying writer (Irons) and a young smarmy sculptor.

C: Liv Tyler, Jeremy Irons, Donal McCann   D: Bernardo Bertolucci

THE SUBSTITUTE *1996 115m/C (R)* DRAMA

Berenger as a mercenary soldier turned substitute teacher to avenge his teacher girlfriend who is hospitalized by the inner-city high school toughs he is now teaching.

C: Tom Berenger, Diane Venora, Cliff DeYoung, Ernie Hudson
D: Robert Mandel

SWINGERS *1996 94m/C (R)* DRAMA

Mike has been heartbroken for six months and can't get his act together. Trent saves the day by taking him to Vegas and then to the retro-forties cocktail clubs of L.A. Like Barry Levinson's *Diner*, this solid story of a group of friends relies less on a plot and more on character study to breeze to its satisfying end.

C: John Favreau, Vince Vaughn, Ron Livingston, Patrick Van Horn, Alex Desert   D: Doug Liman

THINGS TO DO IN DENVER WHEN YOU'RE DEAD
1995 124m/C (R) COMEDY

Garcia is "Jimmy the Saint," a reformed thug who's forced back into the bad business by "The Man with a Plan" (Walken). Garcia recruits "Critical Bill" (Williams), "Franchise"

(Forsythe), and "Pieces" (Lloyd). The easy "situation" they need to take care of goes awry and "The Man with a Plan" calls in "Mr. Shhh" (Buscemi) to kill 'em all. Great cast, great names, great film.

C: Andy Garcia, Treat Williams, William Forsythe, Christopher Walken, Steve Buscemi, Christopher Lloyd, Gabrielle Anwar
D: Gary Fleder

TIN CUP *1996 129m/C (R)* COMEDY

Shelton tries to do for golf what he did for baseball in *Bull Durham*. Costner runs a broken down golf driving range because he doesn't have the discipline it takes on the PGA circuit. Along comes his old friend and rival (Johnson) with a psychologist girlfriend (Russo) and Costner is ready to hit the pro circuit again for love and money. But does he have the discipline this time around?

C: Kevin Costner, Rene Russo, Don Johnson, Cheech Marin
D: Ron Shelton

TRAINSPOTTING *1996 94m/C (R)* DRAMA

When this pic first opened the press focused exclusively on the scenes of heroin addiction. A marketing angle, I guess, because the five Edinburgh losers of the film portrayed are not addicted to drugs as much as they are to wasting time and going nowhere. That is until one makes the dangerous decision of doing what he has to do to get out.

C: Ewan McGregor, Ewen Bremmer, Johnny Lee Miller, Kevin McKidd, Robert Carlyle, Kelly MacDonald, Peter Mullan, James Cosmo   D: Danny Boyle

TREES LOUNGE *1996 94m/C (R)* DRAMA

Buscemi, who made his first critical mark playing a homosexual dying with AIDS in *Parting Glances*, and is now the hero of offbeat cinema, makes his directorial debut with this semi-autobiography of a man in his 30s looking for direction. When he's not in the Tree Lounge, the local bar, he's driving an ice cream truck and getting in trouble with his friend's 17-year-old daughter. The film asks the question, "How long can this pointless life last?" The ending answers it perfectly.

C: Steve Buscemi, Mimi Rodgers, Debi Mazar, Seymour Cassel, Anthony LaPaglia, Carol Kane   D: Steve Buscemi

WELCOME TO THE DOLLHOUSE *1996 87m/C (R)*
SLEEPER

If you've ever felt like an outsider while you were in grade school this film is for you. Dawn "Wiener dog" Weiner is a shy twelve-year-old who has an unrequited crush on the school stud, can't find a friendly seat in the school cafeteria, and returns home every day to find just as unfriendly an atmosphere. A tragic comedy that's one of the most realistic coming-of-age films of the last ten years.

C: Heather Maturizzo, Daria Kalinina, Matthew Faber, Angela Pietropinto   D: Todd Solondz

WHEN WE WERE KINGS *1996 100m/C*
DOCUMENTARY

In 1974 Muhammad Ali and George Foreman were to meet in South Africa for a championship fight billed as the "Rumble in the Jungle." Promoter Don King hired film maker Leon Gast to document the musical extravaganza which was to precede the battle and star James Brown. The festival was a bizarre muddled disaster but Gast's film, which eventually concentrated on Ali, Foreman, and the fight, is excellent.

D: Leon Gast

THE AFRICAN QUEEN *1951 113m/C*

Katharine Hepburn plays a missionary in Africa who needs a ride to safety and is offered one by an alcoholic sea captain (Bogart). As they slowly make their way down the river, they must battle the elements and each other, and their struggles give birth to a stubborn love. One of the all-time greats.

C: Humphrey Bogart, Katharine Hepburn, Robert Morley, Theodore Bikel, Peter Bull **D:** John Huston **AA:** '51 Best Actor (Bogart), Nom: Best Director, Actress (Hepburn)

ALL ABOUT EVE *1950 138m/B&W*

An all-time classic about a seemingly innocent young actress who becomes secretary to a veteran star (Bette Davis) and begins to use every connection available to quickly and shamelessly rise to the top, leaving the star flabbergasted. Razor sharp satire on the theater world.

C: Bette Davis, Anne Baxter, George Sanders, Celeste Holm, Thelma Ritter **D:** Joseph L. Mankiewicz **AA:** '50 Best Director, Picture, Supporting Actor (Sanders), Nom: Best Actress (Baxter, Davis), Supporting Actress (Holm, Ritter)

AMADEUS *1984 158m/C (PG)*

The rivalry between composers Antonio Salieri and Wolfgang Mozart is brought to the screen with stunning brilliance. Salieri, who desired the same admiration and respect bestowed on Mozart, must face the brutal realization that although he was talented, Mozart was a genius.

C: F. Murray Abraham, Tom Hulce, Elizabeth Berridge, Simon Callow **D:** Milos Forman **AA:** '84 Best Actor (Abraham), Adapted Screenplay, Director, Picture, Nom: Best Actor (Hulce)

AN AMERICAN IN PARIS *1951 113m/C*

An incredible 17 minute dance number (the longest ever

filmed) is one of the highlights of this story about a soldier who stays in Paris after the war to paint and try to win the heart of a lovely girl. Lavishly produced. Songs include "I Got Rhythm" and "Embraceable You."

C: Gene Kelly, Leslie Caron, Oscar Levant, Nina Foch, Georges Guetary   D: Vincente Minnelli   AA: '51 Best Picture, Screenplay, Nom: Best Director

ANNIE HALL *1977 94m/C (PG)*
Woody Allen's favorite topic, the trials and tribulations of love and relationships, is taken to hilarious and poignant heights in this semi-autobiographical film about his union with Diane Keaton. Crammed with cameos from Paul Simon, Jeff Goldblum, Christopher Walken, Carol Kane, Sigourney Weaver, and others.

C: Woody Allen, Diane Keaton, Tony Roberts, Shelley Duvall   D: Woody Allen   AA: '77 Best Actress (Keaton), Director, Picture, Screenplay, Nom: Best Actor (Allen)

APOCALYPSE NOW *1979 153m/C (R)*
An almost surreal account of a captain's journey into the depths of the Vietnam jungle to assassinate a demented, decorated AWOL officer who started his own loyal tribe. Filled with stunning visuals, incredible battle scenes and the famous helicopter raid.

C: Marlon Brando, Martin Sheen, Robert Duvall, Frederic Forrest, Sam Bottoms   D: Francis Ford Coppola   AA: '79 Nom: Best Director, Picture

BAD DAY AT BLACK ROCK *1954 81m/C*
Tracy gives one of his best performances as a stranger who drifts into town and uncovers a brutal secret. Marvin and Borgnine shine as two ruthless cronies.

C: Spencer Tracy, Lee Marvin, Ernest Borgnine, Robert Ryan, Anne Francis   D: John Sturges   AA: '54 Nom: Best Director, Actor (Tracy)

BEN HUR *1959 212m/C*

A tyrannical Roman Governor reduces his wealthy childhood friend to a galley slave and imprisons his family. Years later the man returns seeking vengeance against the ruler. Includes one of the most famous scenes in the history of motion pictures, the "Roman Chariot Race."

C: Charlton Heston, Jack Hawkins, Stephen Boyd, Haya Harareet, Hugh Griffith   D: William Wyler   AA: '59 Best Actor (Heston), Director (Wyler), Picture, Supporting Actor (Griffith)

THE BEST YEARS OF OUR LIVES *1946 170m/B&W*

The classic story of three veterans who return home, face a number of emotional conflicts, and try to put their lives back together. Released just after WWII ended, helping many deal with the massive problems the bloodshed caused. Russell is the only person ever to win two Oscars for the same role, being awarded an additional statue for the valor he brought to his wartime colleagues.

C: Frederic March, Myrna Loy, Teresa Wright, Dana Andrews, Harold Russell, Virginia Mayo   D: William Wyler   AA: '46 Best Actor (March), Director, Picture, Supporting Actor (Russell)

THE BIG SLEEP *1946 114m/B&W*

Private detective is hired by a young lady, falls in love with her sultry, older sister and gets knee deep in murder and mayhem. Stunning in its mood and feel, responsible for setting the "noir" style, and considered one of the best films ever made.

C: Humphrey Bogart, Lauren Bacall, John Ridgely, Martha Vickers, Louis Jean Heydt   D: Howard Hawks

BONNIE AND CLYDE *1967 111m/C*

The fast, vicious lives of the infamous Bonnie Parker and Clyde Barrow are detailed, from their first meeting through the string of bank hold-ups and cop shootouts to the gruesome violent ending. Warren Beatty produced and starred.

C: Warren Beatty, Faye Dunaway, Michael J. Pollard, Gene Hackman, Estelle Parsons D: Arthur Penn AA: '67 Best Supporting Actress (Parsons), Nom: Best Actor (Beatty, Hackman), Supporting Actor (Pollard), Actress (Dunaway), Director, Picture

BRIDGE ON THE RIVER KWAI *1957 161m/C*

Great war film about American and English prisoners who are ordered to build a bridge for Japanese Colonel Sessue Hayakawa. The British officer in charge uses this exercise to show the Japanese as inferior humans and soldiers. Holden plays an escaped POW who plans to level the bridge.

C: William Holden, Alec Guinness, Jack Hawkins, Sessue Hayakawa, James Donald D: David Lean AA: '57 Best Actor (Guinness), Director, Picture, Nom: Best Supporting Actor (Hayakawa)

BUTCH CASSIDY AND THE SUNDANCE KID *1969 110m/C (PG)*

Based on the true story of the two legendary outlaws who robbed banks and trains, evaded the law, and their final confrontation in South America. Great screen chemistry between leads Newman and Redford.

C: Paul Newman, Robert Redford, Katherine Ross, Strother Martin, Cloris Leachman D: George Roy Hill AA: '69 Nom: Best Director, Picture

THE CAINE MUTINY *1954 125m/C*

The boat Captain Queeg commands is rocking and it's not because of the water. He's losing his mind and dishes his mental dirt out to his men. They've had enough, revolt, and a powerful court martial ensues.

C: Humphrey Bogart, Jose Ferrer, Fred MacMurray, Van Johnson, Lee Marvin, Tom Tully D: Edward Dymtryk AA: '54 Nom: Best Picture, Actor (Bogart), Supporting Actor (Tully)

CASABLANCA *1942 102m/B&W (PG)*

One of the most famous films of all time has Bogart running a bar in Nazi-occupied Morocco. In walks old love Ingrid Bergman ("of all the gin joints . . .") and a bittersweet romantic tale unwinds. Beautifully engrossing with one of the best endings ever caught on film.

C: Humphrey Bogart, Ingrid Bergman, Claude Rains, Peter Lorre D: Michael Curtiz   AA: '43 Best Director, Picture, Screenplay, Nom: Best Actor (Bogart)

CHINATOWN *1974 131m/C (R)*

Jack Nicholson plays a private detective hired for what appears to be a routine infidelity (that's his specialty) case. Before long he's thrown into a chaotic world of deception, greed, and murder, spiraling through twists and turns, culminating in a thrilling shootout in Chinatown.

C: Jack Nicholson, Faye Dunaway, John Huston, Diane Ladd, John Hillerman   D: Roman Polanski   AA: '74 Best Adapted Screenplay, Nom: Best Picture, Director, Actor (Nicholson), Actress (Dunaway)

CITIZEN KANE *1941 119m/B&W*

Orson Welles was 25 years old when he co-wrote, directed, and starred in this masterpiece which is based on the life of William Randolph Hearst (a fact denied but assumed). The film traces the newspaper tycoon from his simple beginnings to his ruthless peak and back down to his cold and lonely end. Hailed by most critics as the greatest film ever made.

C: Orson Welles, Joseph Cotten, Everett Sloane, Dorothy Comingore, Ruth Warrick D: Orson Welles AA: '41 Best Original Screenplay, Nom: Best Picture, Director, Actor (Welles)

CITY LIGHTS *1931 86m/B&W*

Chaplin, in his "Little Tramp" character, falls in love with a blind girl who sells flowers on the street corner. He later befriends a rich drunk and uses this connection to illegally get the money the girl needs for an eye operation. When he's thrown in jail, all seems headed for tragedy. Beautiful comic/drama.

C: Charlie Chaplin, Virginia Cherrill, Florence Lee, Hank Mann, Harry Myers, Jean Harlow   D: Charlie Chaplin

A CLOCKWORK ORANGE *1971 137m/C (R)*

It's sometime in the future. A young violent gang member wreaks "ultraviolence" until he is imprisoned. He is released after undergoing an experimental peace-inducing treatment. On the outside he meets some of his victims, who serve up their own form of justice. A true masterpiece from Stanley Kubrick.

C: Malcolm McDowell, Patrick Magee, Adrienne Corri, Michael Bates, Warren Clarke   D: Stanley Kubrick   AA: '71 Nom: Best Adapted Screenplay, Director, Picture

COOL HAND LUKE *1967 126m/C*

Paul Newman, in what some consider his greatest role, plays Luke, a young man sentenced to a long prison term on a southern chain gang. The more the ruthless warden comes down on him, the harder he tries to escape.

C: Paul Newman, George Kennedy, J. D. Cannon, Strother Martin, Dennis Hopper   D: Stuart Rosenberg   AA: '67 Best Supporting Actor (Kennedy), Nom: Best Actor (Newman), Screenplay

CRIMES AND MISDEMEANORS *1989 104m/C (PG-13)*

The moral dilemmas of two men are intertwined with a skillful mix of comedy and drama. One man, a documentary film-maker, can't handle his displeasure at chronicling the life of a conceited television star. The other, a highly respected doctor, must decide whether to have his family and career ruined or murder his mistress.

C: Martin Landau, Woody Allen, Alan Alda, Mia Farrow, Joanna Gleason, Anjelica Huston   D: Woody Allen   AA: '89 Nom: Best Director

THE DEER HUNTER *1978 183m/C (R)*

Powerful story of three men (Walken, DeNiro, Savage) from a poor steel town who go off to Vietnam and the devastating impact it has on their lives. DeNiro is classic as the force that gets them out of a sadistic Vietnamese riverside prison and as a loyal friend returning to Vietnam to try to rescue Walken.

C: Robert DeNiro, Christopher Walken, Meryl Streep, John Savage D: Michael Cimino AA: '78 Best Director, Picture, Supporting Actor (Walken), Nom: Best Actor (DeNiro), Supporting Actress (Streep)

DELIVERANCE *1972 109m/C (R)*

Four "city boys" decide to spend their vacation tackling the treacherous waters of a wild river. Their exciting outing turns nightmarish when the river destroys their canoes and they're left to defend themselves against a few backwoodsmen. Realistically horrifying. Contains famous "bow and arrow" scene.

C: Jon Voight, Burt Reynolds, Ronny Cox, Ned Beatty, James Dickey D: John Boorman

DOG DAY AFTERNOON *1975 124m/C (R)*

A homosexual (Pacino) stages a daring bank robbery in order to pay for his lover's sex change operation. The heist is bungled, he's trapped inside with hostages, the media begins its field day, and his chances for a clean getaway fade with every passing minute. Based on a true story.

C: Al Pacino, John Cazale, Charles Durning, James Broderick, Chris Sarandon D: Sidney Lumet

DOUBLE INDEMNITY *1944 107m/B&W*

A thriller in every sense of the word, this pic centers around a woman and her lover who murder her husband to collect the insurance money. The policy states that if he dies accidentally from a moving train, the payout is doubled. They kill him and place the body on the tracks, thinking they've committed the perfect crime. They're wrong. Critically acclaimed, considered one of the best pictures ever made.

C: Fred MacMurray, Barbara Stanwyck, Edward G. Robinson
D: Billy Wilder   AA: '44 Nom: Best Picture, Director, Actress (Stanwyck)

DR. STRANGELOVE OR HOW I LEARNED TO STOP WORRYING AND LOVE THE BOMB 1964 93m/B&W

Stanley Kubrick's brilliant satire on nuclear war centers around the government's crazed actions after a deranged general sends an A-bomb toward Russia. Contains some of the funniest scenes ever filmed.

C: Peter Sellers, George C. Scott, Sterling Hayden, Keenan Wynn, Slim Pickens   D: Stanley Kubrick   AA: '64 Nom: Best Actor (Sellers), Director, Picture

DUCK SOUP 1933 70m/B&W

Groucho Marx plays the leader of a wacky country, Freedonia, and takes along his brothers, Chico and Harpo, employing them as spies. An endless stream of gags follows. One of the Marx Brothers' best.

C: Groucho Marx, Harpo Marx, Chico Marx, Zeppo Marx, Louis Calhern   D: Leo McCarey

E.T.: THE EXTRA-TERRESTRIAL 1982 115m/C (PG)

One of the most financially successful films ever made about a helpless alien who is stranded on Earth and taken in by a group of caring kids who hide the alien from their parents and try to help him find his way home. Debra Winger provides the friendly visitor's voice.

C: Henry Thomas, Dee Wallace Stone, Drew Barrymore, Robert MacNaughton, Peter Coyote   D: Steven Spielberg   AA: '82 Nom: Best Director (Spielberg), Picture

EAST OF EDEN *1954 115m/C*

Dean delivers an unforgettable performance in this adaptation of John Steinbeck's classic novel about a strained communication between a father and son. Powerful, moving, and timeless.

C: James Dean, Julie Harris, Richard Davalos, Raymond Massey, Jo Van Fleet   D: Elia Kazan   AA: '54 Best Supporting Actress (Van Fleet), Nom: Best Director, Actor (Dean), Screenplay

THE EXORCIST *1973 120m/C (R)*

The first big-budget Hollywood horror film has Linda Blair as an innocent 11-year-old possessed by the devil. When a priest comes to perform an exorcism, her head spins around like a radar dish, she spews green slime, and begins to wreak havoc of biblical proportions.

C: Ellen Burstyn, Linda Blair, Jason Miller, Max Von Sydow, Jack MacGowran   D: William Friedkin   AA: '73 Best Adapted Screenplay, Nom: Best Actress (Burstyn), Director (Friedkin), Supporting Actor (Miller), Supporting Actress (Blair)

FIVE EASY PIECES *1970 98m/C (R)*

Jack Nicholson gives a brilliant performance as a pianist who once showed great promise but chose to work in the oil fields. He returns home for one final attempt to reconcile with his father and comes to term with his demons. Known for the famous "chicken sandwich in the diner" scene.

C: Jack Nicholson, Karen Black, Susan Anspach, Lois Smith, Billy Green Bush   D: Bob Rafelson   AA: '70 Nom: Best Actor (Nicholson), Picture, Story and Screenplay, Actress (Black)

FRANKENSTEIN *1931 71m/B&W*

A scientist and his assistant dig up graves, store the cadavers in their lab, and plan a ghoulish experiment of building a creature from different body parts. The experiment is a success ("It's Alive. . .It's Alive!") with only one problem; they gave the creature a criminal's brain. A classic among classics.

C: Boris Karloff, Colin Clive, Mae Clarke, John Boles, Dwight Frye
D: James Whale

THE FRENCH CONNECTION *1971 102m/C (R)*

Two New York City narcotics detectives discover what could be the biggest drug ring of all time. This four star action film is based on a true story and contains one of the most famous car chases ever filmed.

C: Gene Hackman, Roy Scheider, Fernando Rey, Tony LoBianco, Eddie Egan   D: William Friedkin   AA: '71 Best Actor (Hackman), Director, Picture, Adapted Screenplay. Nom: Best Supporting Actor (Scheider)

GANDHI *1982 188m/C (PG)*

The life of lawyer turned spiritual leader, Mahatma Ghandi, is brought to the screen with awe-inspiring results. From his humble beginning to his tragic assassination, the film magnificently shows how one man truly changed the world.

C: Ben Kingsley, Edward Fox, Candice Bergen, John Gielgud, John Mills   D: Richard Attenborough   AA: '82 Best Actor (Kingsley), Director, Original Screenplay, Picture

THE GENERAL *1927 78m/B&W*

Comedy genius Buster Keaton plays a locomotive engineer whose train has been stolen. The humor begins when he tries to get it back. Based on a true incident during the Civil War. Keaton amazingly did his own stunts.

C: Buster Keaton, Marion Mack, Glen Cavender, Jim Farley, Joe Keaton   D: Buster Keaton, Clyde Bruckman

THE GODFATHER *1972 171m/C (R)*

Francis Ford Coppola's gripping portrait of a 1940s mafia family is considered one of the greatest films ever made and deservedly so. The horror, rage, violence, and paranoia of being in the thick of organized crime is told with brutal realism. Includes the famous "horse's head" scene.

C: Marlon Brando, Al Pacino, Robert Duvall, James Caan, Diane Keaton   D: Francis Ford Coppola   AA: '72 Best Actor (Brando), Picture, Adapted Screenplay, Nom: Best Director, Supporting Actor (Pacino, Caan, Duvall)

GODFATHER II *1974 200m/C (R)*

This sequel is just as effective as its predecessor as it intertwines and compares the lives of its present day leader (Pacino) with the "don" of old (DeNiro), while continuing the story of the original.

C: Al Pacino, Robert DeNiro, Diane Keaton, Robert Duvall, James Caan, Michael Gazzo, Lee Strasberg, Talia Shire   D: Francis Ford Coppola   AA: '74 Best Picture, Director, Supporting Actor (DeNiro), Adapted Screenplay, Nom: Best Supporting Actress (Shire), Actor (Pacino), Supporting Actor (Gazzo, Strasberg)

THE GOLD RUSH *1925 85m/B&W*

It's the mid 1800's and Charlie Chaplin is looking for a fortune in gold and love in the Klondikes. One of Chaplin's best, containing the famous "shoe for dinner" and "dinner roll two step" scenes.

C: Charlie Chaplin, Mack Swain, Tom Murray, Georgina Hale   D: Charlie Chaplin

GONE WITH THE WIND *1939 231m/C*

Sweeping epic masterpiece follows the turbulent life of pretty Southern belle Scarlett O'Hara as she journeys through a beautiful upbringing on a sprawling plantation to the tragedy of the Civil War and her torrid love affairs with Rhett Butler and Ashley Wilkes. Filled with technically complicated scenes, like the burning of Atlanta which was amazingly done on the MGM lot. One of the all-time greats.

C: Clark Gable, Viven Leigh, Olivia de Havilland, Leslie Howard, Thomas Mitchell D: Victor Fleming AA: '39 Best Picture, Actress (Leigh), Director, Supporting Actress (Hattie McDaniels), Screenplay, Nom: Best Actor (Gable), Supporting Actress (de Havilland)

THE GRADUATE 1967 106m/C (PG)

A lethargic, confused college graduate is snapped into action by an older woman's desire to seduce him and his own desire for the woman's daughter. His rescue of the daughter from her wedding is a classic scene.

C: Dustin Hoffman, Anne Bancroft, Katherine Ross, Murray Hamilton D: Mike Nichols

THE GRAPES OF WRATH 1940 129m/B&W

The poverty stricken Joad family leaves the Dust Bowl of Oklahoma and heads out west to find a better life in the grape fields of California. John Steinbeck's classic novel on the Great Depression contains great acting and an epic scale production.

C: Henry Fonda, Jane Darwell, John Carradine, Charley Grapewin, Zeffie Tilbury D: John Ford AA: '40 Best Director, Supporting Actress (Darwell), Director, Nom: Best Picture, Actor (Fonda), Adapted Screenplay

HAROLD AND MAUDE 1971 92m/C (PG)

Classic story of Harold, an 18-year-old obsessed with death, who makes a habit of attending strangers' funerals. While viewing a burial he meets Maude, an 87-year-old eccentric woman, who also frequents funerals of people she never knew. The two begin a relationship and Maude, whose own philosophy of life and death is far from morbid, changes Harold's life forever.

C: Ruth Gordon, Bud Cort, Cyril Cusack, Vivian Pickles, Charles Tyner D: Hal Ashby

HIGH NOON 1952 85m/B&W

Classic tale has Gary Cooper playing a sheriff who is getting married and retiring on the same day. It's also the day that the ruthless leader of a band of outlaws is coming to town to seek revenge against the sheriff. Told in real time with clocks in scenes counting down the minutes to the final confrontation.

C: Gary Cooper, Grace Kelly, Lloyd Bridges, Lon Chaney, Jr., Thomas Mitchell D: Fred Zimmerman AA: '52 Best Actor (Cooper), Director, Picture

HOW GREEN WAS MY VALLEY 1941 118m/C

Considered to be John Ford's masterpiece, this tells fifty years in the life of a family of miners and follows their hopes, dreams, and disappointments as mining goes from a hard but honest way of making a living to a big, complicated unionized business.

C: Walter Pidgeon, Maureen O'Hara, Donald Crisp, Sara Allgood D: John Ford AA: '41 Best Picture, Director, Supporting Actor (Donald Crisp), Nom: Best Supporting Actress (Allgood)

IT HAPPENED ONE NIGHT 1934 104m/B&W

Gable is a newspaper reporter who meets Colbert, a rich young lady who is trying to escape her wealthy life to find true happiness. A steamy battle of the sexes begins as both try to teach each other about life. Along the way they fall in love. Classic Capra movie magic and one of the few films ever to sweep all the major categories at the Academy Awards.

C: Clark Gable. Claudette Colbert, Roscoe Karns, Walter Connolly, Alan Hale D: Frank Capra AA: '34 Best Picture, Director, Actor (Gable), Actress (Colbert), Adapted Screenplay

IT'S A WONDERFUL LIFE 1946 125m/B&W

American classic about an average man in an average town

who feels his life is worthless and decides to jump off a bridge. He's saved from the choppy water below by his guardian angel who shows him just how important he is to all the people around him. An uplifting magical film, worth all of the praise it's received. Based on a story which appeared on a Christmas card.

C: Jimmy Stewart, Donna Reed, Lionel Barrymore, Henry Travers
D: Frank Capra   AA: '46 Nom: Best Picture, Director, Actor (Stewart)

THE KING AND I *1956 133m/C*

A woman takes a job teaching the children of the King of Siam. She soon locks horns with the ruler, only to later fall in love with him. Based on Margaret Landon's novel *Anna And The King Of Siam*. Songs include "Getting To Know You" and "I Have Dreamed."

C: Deborah Kerr, Yul Brynner, Rita Moreno, Martin Benson, Terry Saunders   D: Walter Lang   AA: '56 Best Actor (Brynner), Nom: Best Actress (Kerr), Director, Picture

THE LADY EVE *1941 93m/B&W*

A Preston Sturges masterpiece about a hapless, snake-loving beer tycoon, and the conlady who believes he's a simple-minded easy mark. Unforgettable performances by leads Fonda and Stanwyck.

C: Henry Fonda, Barbara Stanwyck, Charles Coburn, Eugene Pallette   D: Preston Sturges

LAURA *1944 85m/B&W*

A detective assigned to the murder case of a New York City female executive interviews her friends, and comes up with a long list of likely suspects. He also sees a portrait of the deceased and begins to fall in love, leading to a strange, classic thriller.

C: Gene Tierney, Dana Andrews, Clifton Webb, Lane Chandler, Vincent Price, Judith Anderson   D: Otto Preminger

LAWRENCE OF ARABIA *1962 221m/C (PG)*

A lavish biography of T. E. Lawrence, the complex English military leader who helped the Arabs revolt against Turkey in World War I. Stunning in its scope with absolutely awesome photography. A film with *no* women.

C: Peter O'Toole, Omar Sharif, Anthony Quinn, Alec Guinness, Jack Hawkins D: David Lean AA: '62 Best Picture, Director, Nom: Best Actor (O'Toole), Supporting Actor (Sharif), Adapted Screenplay

THE MAGNIFICENT AMBERSONS *1942 88m/B&W*

The second film by Orson Welles, about a wealthy Midwestern family that disintegrates under the wheels of progress, is a masterpiece. Beautifully shot and acted with the legendary controversy still surrounding the happy ending stuck on by the studio against Welles' wishes.

C: Joseph Cotten, Anne Baxter, Tim Holt, Richard Bennett, Dolores Costello, Agnes Moorehead D: Orson Welles AA: '42 Nom: Best Picture, Supporting Actress (Moorehead)

THE MALTESE FALCON *1941 101m/B&W*

Considered by many critics to be one of the greatest detective films ever made, Huston was only 29 years old when he helmed this classic. He also wrote the screenplay which was based on the Dashiel Hammett novel and revolves around Sam Spade's (Bogart) complicated search for a priceless statuette.

C: Humphrey Bogart, Mary Astor, Peter Lorre, Sidney Greenstreet, Ward Bond D: John Huston AA: '41 Nom: Best Picture, Supporting Actor (Greenstreet)

THE MANCHURIAN CANDIDATE *1961 126m/B&W*

Rumored to have been secretly banned and buried after its completion, this film is just getting its due. The political thriller revolves around a Korean war officer who believes that he and his platoon were used in a secret communist plot involving brainwashing techniques and assassination. Full of gripping twists and turns.

C: Frank Sinatra, Laurence Harvey, Angela Lansbury, Janet Leigh, James Gregory   D: John Frankenheimer   AA: '61 Nom: Best Supporting Actress (Lansbury)

MANHATTAN *1979 96m/B&W (R)*

Often hilarious, often poignant, story of a middle-aged writer who's desperately trying to move into more serious writing. His life is further complicated by his inability to choose between two women, one his own age, the other a high school senior.

C: Woody Allen, Diane Keaton, Meryl Streep, Mariel Hemingway, Michael Murphy   D: Woody Allen   AA: '79 Nom: Best Supporting Actress (Hemingway)

M*A*S*H *1970 116m/C (R)*

A group of surgeons and nurses at a Mobile Army Surgical Hospital in Korea combat the psychological damage the war is doing to them by throwing endless parties and playing bizarre practical jokes.

C: Donald Sutherland, Elliott Gould, Tom Skerritt, Sally Kellerman, JoAnn Pflug, Robert Duvall   D: Robert Altman   AA: '70 Nom: Best Director, Picture, Supporting Actress (Kellerman)

MIDNIGHT COWBOY *1969 113m/C (R)*

Gritty story about a young Texan who arrives in New York City with dreams of becoming a gigolo. Hanging in the 42nd Street district he's befriended by a sleazy con man who works as his "manager" and both are dragged to the depths of life. The only X-rated film ever to win a Best Picture Oscar.

C: Dustin Hoffman, Jon Voight, Sylvia Miles, Brenda Vaccaro, John McGiver   D: John Schlesinger   AA: '69 Best Director, Picture, Adapted Screenplay, Nom: Best Actor (Voight, Hoffman)

MIRACLE ON 34TH STREET *1947 97m/B&W*

A jolly old man who's hired as the Santa Claus for the Macy's Thanksgiving Day parade feels he's perfect for the job since he is, in fact, the real Kris Kringle. He tries to spread his holiday cheer and no one takes him seriously, including a little girl (Wood) who needs to see a miracle to truly believe in him.

C: Maureen O'Hara, Edmund Gwenn, Natalie Wood, John Payne D: George Seaton   AA: '47 Best Supporting Actor (Gwenn), Story and Screenplay, Nom: Best Picture

MODERN TIMES *1936 87m/B&W*

A factory worker is driven to the edge of sanity by his monotonous job, his slave driving boss, and the oncoming technological revolution. A Chaplin masterpiece.

C: Charlie Chaplin, Paulette Goddard, Henry Bergman   D: Charlie Chaplin

MR. SMITH GOES TO WASHINGTON *1939 130m/B&W*

Stewart plays an innocent young man who is picked to stand in for an ill senator. Once in Washington, he is besieged by corrupt politicians and forced to take a stand. Some classic screen moments result.

C: James Stewart, Jean Arthur, Edward Arnold, Harry Carey, Claude Rains   D: Frank Capra   AA: '39 Best Story, Nom: Best Picture, Director, Actor (Stewart), Supporting Actor (Carey)

MUTINY ON THE BOUNTY *1935 132m/B&W*

Unforgettable picture about a needed rebellion, led by Gable, against a truly despicable sadistic Captain Bligh (Laughton). Not to be missed.

C: Clark Gable, Franchot Tone, Charles Laughton, Donald Crisp   D: Frank Lloyd   AA: '35 Best Picture, Nom: Best Director, Actor (Gable, Tone, Laughton)

MY FAIR LADY *1964 170m/C (G)*

Professor Henry Higgins makes a bet with a friend that he can turn a lowly, unrefined flower girl into a sophisticated, elite woman. Audrey Hepburn plays the female in question. Lushly produced. Terrific tunes include "I Could Have Danced All Night" and "Wouldn't It Be Lovely."

C: Audrey Hepburn, Rex Harrison, Stanley Holloway, Wilfrid Hyde-White, Gladys Cooper D: George Cukor AA: '64 Best Actor (Harrison), Director, Picture, Nom: Best Supporting Actor (Holloway), Supporting Actress (Cooper)

NORTH BY NORTHWEST *1959 136m/C*

Grant plays a New York ad executive who is mistaken for a spy and must run for his life. As if that's not a big enough problem, he's then framed for murder. Pic contains one of Hitchcock's most famous scenes, Grant getting frantically chased by a machine-gun firing crop duster through a corn field. Considered by many to be Hitchcock's best picture.

C: Cary Grant, Eva Marie Saint, James Mason, Leo G. Carroll, Martin Landau D: Alfred Hitchcock

ON THE WATERFRONT *1954 108m/B&W*

Marlon Brando gives one of his most famous performances as the brother of a corrupt mob lawyer who gets reluctantly caught up in union violence, greed, and deceit. Powerful, gripping drama.

C: Marlon Brando, Rod Steiger, Eva Marie Saint, Lee J. Cobb, Karl Malden D: Elia Kazan AA: '54 Best Actor (Brando), Director, Picture, Supporting Actress (Saint), Story and Screenplay, Nom: Best Supporting Actor (Cobb, Malden, Steiger)

ONE FLEW OVER THE CUCKOO'S NEST *1975 129m/C (R)*

Incredible story of a man convicted of statutory rape who chooses an asylum over prison, and then must call on all his emotional resources to stay sane inside insanity. One of the best films ever made, with endless classic scenes.

C: Jack Nicholson, Brad Dourif, Louise Fletcher, Will Sampson, William Redfield, Danny DeVito D: Milos Forman AA: '75 Best Actor (Nicholson), Actress (Fletcher), Director (Forman), Picture, Adapted Screenplay, Nom: Best Supporting Actor (Dourif)

ORDINARY PEOPLE 1980 124m/C (R)

Sutherland and Moore play parents whose one son dies in a swimming accident and whose other son fights a guilt-ridden suicidal desire. Their struggle in this emotional battlefield is heartfelt, moving, and extremely powerful.

C: Mary Tyler Moore, Donald Sutherland, Timothy Hutton, Judd Hirsch, Elizabeth McGovern D: Robert Redford AA: '80 Best Picture, Director, Adapted Screenplay, Supporting Actor (Hutton), Nom: Best Actress (Moore), Supporting Actor (Hirsch)

PAPILLON 1973 150m/C (PG)

Steve McQueen portrays Henri Charriere, a man whose spirit cannot be broken as he relentlessly breaks out of prison after prison until he arrives at "escape-proof" Devil's Island, where he attempts his most daring attempt for freedom.

C: Steve McQueen, Dustin Hoffman, Victor Jory, George Coulouris, Anthony Zerbe D: Franklin J. Schaffner

PATHS OF GLORY 1957 86m/B&W

Engrossing pic based on the true story of a French officer who strategized an absurd attack which failed miserably. Unable to accept his mistake, he picked out three soldiers, blamed them for the disaster, and had them tried for execution. Kirk Douglas plays an officer who is aware of the whole ugly affair and tries to stop it. One of the best war films ever made.

C: Kirk Douglas, Adolphe Menjou, George Macready, Ralph Meeker, Richard Anderson D: Stanley Kubrick

PATTON 1970 171m/C (PG)

The military career of controversial General George S. Patton is brought to the screen with stunning results. Patton, a brilliant strategist, won battle after battle but lost a large amount of men. Scott won the Oscar but refused it. Written by Francis Ford Coppola.

C: George C. Scott, Karl Malden, Stephen Young, Michael Strong, Frank Latimore D: Franklin J. Schappner AA: '70 Best Actor (Scott), Director, Picture, Screenplay

THE PHILADELPHIA STORY 1940 112m/B&W

Classic comedy with Hepburn playing a once married socialite who plans to do it again but is interrupted by her suave ex-husband (Cary Grant) and a goofy reporter. One of the all-time great romantic comedies.

C: Katharine Hepburn, Cary Grant, James Stewart, Ruth Hussey, Roland Young D: George Cukor AA: '40 Best Actor (Stewart), Screenplay, Nom: Best Picture, Director, Actress (Hepburn), Supporting Actress (Hussey)

PSYCHO 1960 109m/B&W

A woman running from the law checks in at the Bates Motel, meets the mentally disturbed owner, and never checks out. Considered by many to be the greatest horror film ever made.

C: Anthony Perkins, Janet Leigh, Vera Miles, John Gavin, John McIntire D: Alfred Hitchcock AA: '60 Nom: Best Director, Supporting Actress (Leigh)

RAGING BULL 1980 128m/B&W (R)

Robert DeNiro gives one of his greatest performances as fighter Jake LaMotta in this brilliant biography of a man whose only true emotional outlet was fighting. Beautifully photographed in rich black and white, and containing some of the most intense fight scenes ever filmed.

C: Robert DeNiro, Cathy Moriarty, Joe Pesci, Frank Vincent, Nicholas

Colasanto   D: Martin Scorsese   AA: '80 Best Actor (DeNiro), Nom: Best Director, Supporting Actor (Pesci), Supporting Actress (Moriarty)

RAIDERS OF THE LOST ARK *1981 115m/C (PG)*

Archeologist Indiana Jones' search for the Ark of The Covenant brings him up against runaway boulders, seas of snakes, evil swordsman, and more in this fast-paced action/adventure flick from legend Steven Spielberg.

C: Harrison Ford, Karen Allen, Wolf Kahler, Paul Freeman, John Rhys-Davies   D: Steven Spielberg   AA: '81 Nom: Best Picture, Director

REAR WINDOW *1954 112m/C*

A photographer who's laid up with a broken leg passes the time sitting at his window watching his neighbors. When he witnesses what he believes to be a man killing his wife, he decides to try to catch the fiend himself. Tense script, excellent direction, occasional Hitchcockian gallow humor.

C: James Stewart, Grace Kelly, Thelma Ritter, Wendell Corey, Raymond Burr   D: Alfred Hitchcock   AA: '54 Nom: Best Director, Screenplay

ROOM WITH A VIEW *1986 117m/C (R)*

A young lady, soon to be a victim of an arranged marriage, meets a free-thinking passionate man who changes her life forever. A beautiful cinematic achievement brought to the screen by the same people who made *Howards End.*

C: Helena Bonham Carter, Julian Sands, Denholm Elliott, Maggie Smith, Judi Dench   D: James Ivory   AA: '86 Best Adapted Screenplay, Nom: Best Picture, Director, Supporting Actor (Elliott), Supporting Actress (Smith)

THE SEARCHERS *1956 119m/C*

An ex-soldier spends five grueling years looking for his niece, who was kidnapped by Comanche Indians. As his journey becomes more and more involved the viewer is not sure whether his reason for trying to find the girl is to help her or hurt her.

C: John Wayne, Jeffrey Hunter, Vera Miles, Natalie Wood, Ward Bond
D: John Ford

SHADOW OF A DOUBT 1943 108m/B&W

Uncle Charley travels to California to visit some relatives. All's well until his niece comes to the realization that he's the notorious serial killer, the "Merry Widow Murderer." Hitchcock's own favorite.

C: Joseph Cotten, Teresa Wright, Macdonald Carey, Hume Cronyn, Henry Travers   D: Alfred Hitchcock

SHANE 1953 117m/C

A drifter who was once a great gunfighter comes to the rescue of a poor family who are being manhandled by a wealthy, corrupt land baron and his hired strong arm. Jack Palance gives a devilishly perfect performance as the bankrolled bad man.

C: Alan Ladd, Jean Arthur, Van Heflin, Brandon de Wilde, Jack Palance   D: George Stevens   AA: '53 Nom: Best Director, Picture, Supporting Actor (de Wilde, Palance)

SILENCE OF THE LAMBS 1991 118m/C (R)

Incredibly suspenseful story about a female FBI agent trying to track down a horrific mass murderer with the help of an imprisoned legendary serial killer known as Hannibal "The Cannibal" Lector. (He earned the nickname from turning his victims into meals.) Anthony Hopkins' incredible performance turned the twisted character into a cult figure.

C: Jodie Foster, Anthony Hopkins, Scott Glenn, Ted Levine, Brooks Smith   D: Jonathan Demme   AA: '91 Best Picture, Actor (Hopkins), Actress (Foster), Director, Adapted Screenplay

SINGIN' IN THE RAIN *1952 103m/C*

A satire on the panic that gripped tinseltown when the motion picture industry changed from silent films to sound. Contains one of the most famous scenes ever filmed, Gene Kelly singing and dancing around lightposts in the rain. One of the all-time top musicals. Songs includes the title track and "All I Do Is Dream Of You."

C: Gene Kelly, Donald O'Connor, Jean Hagen, Debbie Reynolds, Rita Moreno   D: Gene Kelly, Stanley Donen   AA: '52 Nom: Best Supporting Actress (Hager)

SNOW WHITE AND THE SEVEN DWARFS *1937 83m/C*

Classic fairy tale became the first animated feature ever made and Disney was given a special Oscar: one large statue and seven little ones. The beautiful Snow White, the evil queen, the princess, and the seven little guys are all present in this marvelous adaptation of the famous story.

D: David Hand

SOME LIKE IT HOT *1959 120m/B&W*

Jack Lemmon and Tony Curtis play a couple musicians who unwittingly become witnesses to the infamous St. Valentine's Day Massacre. Afraid of being "eliminated," they dress as women and become members of an all-girl band on its way to Florida. Marilyn Monroe also stars in this much acclaimed pic.

C: Marilyn Monroe, Tony Curtis, Jack Lemmon, George Raft, Pat O'Brien   D: Billy Wilder   AA: '59 Nom: Best Actor (Lemmon), Director

SOUND OF MUSIC *1965 174m/C*

Music, comedy, and drama are woven perfectly into this beautiful film about a young lady who takes a job as governess for a large family, falls in love with the widowed father, and helps the family escape from Austria before the Nazi invasion.

C: Julie Andrews, Christopher Plummer, Eleanor Parker, Peggy Wood, Charmian Carr D: Robert Wise AA: '65 Best Director (Wise), Picture, Nom: Best Actress (Andrews)

STAGECOACH *1939 100m/B&W*

A stagecoach is set upon by a group of murderous bandits. The passengers, strangers with nothing in common except the impending doom, must band together. Brought "The Ringo Kid" character to the world, and the first teaming of Wayne and Ford.

C: John Wayne, Claire Tervor, Thomas Mitchell, George Bancroft, John Carradine D: John Ford AA: '39 Best Supporting Actor (Mitchell), Nom: Best Director, Picture

STAR WARS *1977 121m/C (PG)*

Luke Skywalker and his band of space soldiers battle Darth Vader and the ruthless members of the Galactic Empire in one of the highest grossing sci-fi films of all time. Oddly enough it's also one of the only science fiction films ever nominated for Best Picture. Filled with spectacular special effects.

C: Mark Hamill, Carrie Fisher, Harrison Ford, Alec Guinness, Peter Cushing D: George Lucas AA: '77 Nom: Best Picture, Director, Original Screenplay, Supporting Actor (Guinness)

THE STING *1973 129m/C (PG)*

Redford and Newman are a magical team in this witty pic about two con men who take on a seemingly unbeatable mark in 1930s Chicago.

C: Paul Newman, Robert Redford, Robert Shaw, Charles Durning, Eileen Brennan D: George Roy Hill AA: '73 Best Picture, Director, Story and Screenplay

SULLIVAN'S TRAVELS *1941 90m/B&W*

Preston Sturges' satire on a Hollywood director who is sick of making mindless comedies and dreams of producing a socially aware masterpiece. In order to really get into it, he hits the road with only a few cents in his pocket to travel as a hobo and learn how the other half lives.

C: Joel McCrea, Veronica Lake, William Demarest, Robert Warwick, Franklin Pangborn   D: Preston Sturges

TAXI DRIVER *1976 112m/C (R)*

Insomniac Travis Bickle takes a job in NYC driving a cab "anytime, anywhere." His travels open up his eyes to the underworld of the city, pushes his mind to places it's never been and, after developing a sympathetic relationship with a 13-year-old prostitute, ultimately leads to extreme violence. An all-time classic.

C: Robert DeNiro, Jodie Foster, Harvey Keitel, Cybill Shepherd, Peter Boyle   D: Martin Scorsese   AA: '76 Nom: Best Picture, Actor (DeNiro), Supporting Actress (Foster)

TERMS OF ENDEARMENT *1983 132m/C (PG)*

Debra Winger plays a wife and young mother of two who learns she has irreversible cancer. The film follows the effects of the disease on her family and friends with a simple yet stunningly realistic style. One of the most powerful films of the '80s.

C: Shirley MacLaine, Jack Nicholson, Debra Winger, John Lithgow, Jeff Daniels, Danny DeVito   D: James Brooks   AA: '83 Best Picture, Director, Adapted Screenplay, Actress (MacLaine), Supporting Actor (Nicholson), Nom: Best Actress (Winger), Supporting Actor (Lithgow)

THE THIRD MAN *1949 104m/B&W*

Cotten plays an American writer who travels to post WWII Vienna for a job promised by his friend, Harry Lime. Once in Vienna, he learns that Lime is dead, or is he? Cotten needs to find out. Welles has the role of Lime, a black market drug dealer of the sleaziest nature. The underground sewer scene at the end of the film is considered by some to be a masterpiece.

C: Joseph Cotten, Orson Welles, Alida Valli, Trevor Howard, Bernard Lee   D: Carol Reed   AA: '49 Nom: Best Director

TOP HAT 1935 97m/B&W

Fred Astaire is trying to win the affections of Ginger Rogers but she's under the impression he's already taken by a friend. Probably Ginger and Fred's best pic. Songs include "Cheek to Cheek."

C: Fred Astaire, Ginger Rogers, Erik Rhodes, Helen Broderick, Edward Everett Horton   D: Mark Sandrich

TOUCH OF EVIL 1958 108m/B&W

An incredibly eerie and moody story about a lawman (Welles)who's tracking down some thugs that murdered a wealthy crimelord, using a load of dynamite. Heston plays a Mexican government official who, against the lawman's wishes, gets involved in the investigation that's taking place in a seedy border town. Considered by some critics to be a technical masterpiece.

C: Charlton Heston, Orson Welles, Janet Leigh, Joseph Calleia, Akim Tamiroff   D: Orson Welles

TREASURE OF THE SIERRA MADRE 1948 126m/B&W

Two drifters take a job with a construction boss and meet an old-time gold prospector. The three take their earnings and head into the hills to mine for a fortune. They're doing quite well until a band of Mexicans, a new "partner," and greed cause the plan to unravel. A classic which many critics feel is one of the best films ever made.

C: Humphrey Bogart, Walter Huston, Tim Holt, Bruce Bennett, Barton MacLane D: John Huston AA: '48 Best Director, Supporting Actor (Huston), Screenplay, Nom: Best Picture

TWELVE ANGRY MEN *1957 95m/B&W*

If you're into courtroom drama, this is a great film to see. Eleven members of a jury are sure a young boy murdered his father. One member (Henry Fonda) thinks they've jumped to their conclusion and are convicting an innocent youth. A battle ensues.

C: Henry Fonda, Martin Balsam, Lee J. Cobb, E. G. Marshall, Jack Klugman D: Sidney Lumet AA: '57 Nom: Best Picture, Director

2001: A SPACE ODYSSEY *1968 139m/C*

Man, from prehistoric times to a futuristic space age, is eerily defined in this sci-fi classic. A trip to Mars turns grim when the main computer, HAL 9000, gets a mind of its own. Stunning images and imaginative script create an unforgettable viewing experience.

C: Keir Dullea, Gary Lockwood, William Sylvester, Dan Richter D: Stanley Kubrick AA: '68 Nom: Best Director (Kubrick)

VERTIGO *1958 126m/C (PG)*

Stewart plays a detective whose fear of heights leads to a fatal accident of a partner and, possibly, the girl they were following. A while later, he meets the girl's double and a chain of bizarre, frightening events begin. Considered a masterpiece.

C: James Stewart, Kim Novak, Barbara Bel Geddes D: Alfred Hitchcock

WEST SIDE STORY *1961 151m/C*

Two New York gangs fight and sing amidst the fighting and singing of young lovers Tony and Maria. Four star pic all the way around.

C: Natalie Wood, Richard Beymer, Russ Tamblyn, Rita Moreno

D: Robert Wise   AA: '61 Best Director, Picture, Supporting Actor (George Chakiris), Supporting Actress (Moreno), Nom: Best Screenplay

THE WILD BUNCH *1969 145m/C (R)*

William Holden plays the leader of an aging band of outlaws who are on the run from the law. But they're soon to meet a Mexican general and a brutal experience they'll never forget. One of the best films ever made and instrumental in its introduction of slow motion violence.

C: William Holden, Ernest Borgnine, Robert Ryan, Warren Oates, Strother Martin   D: Sam Peckinpah

THE WIZARD OF OZ *1939 101m/C*

The mother of all family films about a girl whisked away during a tornado to the land of Oz where she's told by munchkins that if she wants to get back home she must follow the yellow brick road and see the wizard. Filled with classic scenes, like the army of flying monkeys, and the trees that come alive. Also crammed with great tunes including "Somewhere Over The Rainbow" and "If I Only Had A Brain."

C: Judy Garland, Margaret Hamilton, Ray Bolger, Jack Haley, Bert Lahr, Frank Morgan   D: Victor Fleming   AA: '30 Nom: Best Picture

WUTHERING HEIGHTS *1939 104m/B&W*

The mesmerizing moody story of ill-fated love on the Yorkshire Moors is brought to the screen in stupendous fashion. Critically hailed.

C: Laurence Olivier, Merle Oberon, David Niven, Geraldine Fitzgerald   D: William Wyler   AA: '39 Nom: Best Picture, Director, Actor (Olivier), Supporting Actress (Fitzgerald)

YANKEE DOODLE DANDY *1942 126m/B&W*

Lavishly produced bio of early show biz icon George M. Cohan, from his first efforts at a songwriting career through his heyday as the King of Broadway. Cagney shines in title role. Tunes include title cut and "Give My Regards To Broadway."

C: James Cagney, Joan Leslie, Walter Huston, Richard Whorf, Irene Manning D: Michael Curtiz AA: '42 Best Actor (Cagney), Nom: Best Director, Picture, Story, Supporting Actor (Huston)

ACTION/ADVENTURE

THE ADVENTURES OF ROBIN HOOD *1938 102m/C*

The daring swashbuckler from Sherwood Forest battles the evil minded Prince John, all the while surrounded by lavish sets and beautiful costumes. One of Flynn's most famous roles (he handled all the stunts himself) with de Havilland as his maid Marian.

C: Errol Flynn, Olivia de Havilland, Basil Rathbone, Alan Hale, Una O'Connor, Claude Rains D: Michael Curtiz AA: '38 Nom: Best Picture

AIRPORT *1970 137m/C (G)*

Chaos and mayhem erupt on a jetliner as a madman with a bomb decides to commit suicide on the flight. A box office blockbuster that paved the way for the '70s disaster flick.

C: Dean Martin, Burt Lancaster, Jean Seberg, Helen Hayes, Jacqueline Bisset, Van Heflin D: George Seaton AA: '70 Best Supporting Actress (Hayes), Nom: Best Picture

ANGELS WITH DIRTY FACES *1938 97m/B&W*

Cagney and O'Brien play two friends who grow up and grow apart, Cagney becoming a gangster, O'Brien a priest. The neighborhood kids look up to Cagney, a tough guy, but O'Brien tries to steer them in the right direction. Classic ending caps off classic gangster movie.

C: James Cagney, Pat O'Brien, Humphrey Bogart, Ann Sheridan, George Bancroft   D: Michael Curtiz   AA: '38 Best Actor (Cagney), Nom: Best Director

AROUND THE WORLD IN 80 DAYS *1956 178m/C (G)*

Niven plays the eccentric adventurer who makes a bet that he can circumnavigate the globe in just 80 days. Cameos by more than 20 stars of the '50s.

C: David Niven, Shirley MacLaine, Cantinflas, Robert Newton, Frank Sinatra, Charles Boyer, Marlene Dietrich, Joe E. Brown   D: Michael Anderson, Sr.   AA: '56 Best Picture, Nom: Best Director

ASSAULT ON PRECINCT 13 *1976 91m/C*

A gang takes over a small L.A. police station, wreaking havoc and forcing a suspenseful violent stand-off. Well-paced thriller, directed by John Carpenter. (*Halloween, Starman*)

C: Austin Stoker, Martin West, Darwin Jaston, Nancy Loomis, Tony Burton   D: John Carpenter

BEN HUR *1959 212m/C*

See "Top 100"

BEVERLY HILLS COP *1984 105m/C (R)*

Solid Eddie Murphy vehicle has the comedian playing a Detroit cop whose best friend is brutally murdered. The trail leads to Beverly Hills, so Murphy heads west and, completely out of his element, must track down the killer. Some great action scenes with a strong Murphy performance.

C: Eddie Murphy, Judge Reinhold, John Ashton, Lisa Eilbacher, Ronny Cox   D: Martin Brest

THE BLACK PIRATE *1926 122m/B&W*

After his father's ship is attacked by a band of cut throat pirates, a young sailor winds up on the shore of a desert island. He vows revenge against the evil mob and dishes it out in rollicking sword fights, amazing stunts and great action sequences. One of Douglas Fairbanks, Sr.'s most famous roles.

C: Douglas Fairbanks, Sr., Donald Crisp, Billie Dove   D: Albert Parker

BLOW UP 1966 111m/C
A photographer taking some photos in the park unknowingly snaps some shots that he later discovers may be a murder in progress. Critically hailed.

C: David Hemmings, Vanessa Redgrave, Sarah Miles, Jane Birkin
D: Michelangelo Antonioni   AA: '66 Nom: Best Director, Story and Screenplay

BRING ME THE HEAD OF ALFREDO GARCIA 1974 112m/C (R)
Any film in which a drunk piano player turned crazed bounty hunter drives around in a convertible with the decapitated head of his victim in the front seat has a solid chance of being an underground favorite. This flick is a sick twisted trip through the backroads of Mexico that has Warren Oates as the man looking for the human score who must constantly steer himself out of danger.

C: Warren Oates, Isela Vega, Gig Young, Kris Kristofferson   D: Sam Peckinpah

BULLITT 1968 104m/C (PG)
Steve McQueen plays a detective assigned to watch over an important informer who is going to be used as a key witness. When the informer is killed in a professional hit, McQueen must track down the killers. Heart pounding action with famous chase scene through the streets of San Francisco in which McQueen did his own driving.

C: Steve McQueen, Robert Vaughn, Jacqueline Bisset, Don Gordon, Robert Duvall   D: Peter Yates

CAPRICORN ONE *1978 123m/C (R)*

After a NASA slip up, three astronauts are forced to fake a moon landing and then, after another NASA slip up, are hunted down for their efforts. Fast paced.

C: Elliott Gould, James Brolin, Brenda Vaccaro, O. J. Simpson, Hal Holbrook   D: Peter Hyams

CAPTAIN BLOOD *1935 120m/B&W*

A doctor is ostracized by a corrupt governor and exiled into slavery. He fights his way back, becoming a pirate, and ultimately being pardoned for a crime he didn't commit. Considered by many critics to be the greatest pirate film ever made.

C: Errol Flynn, Olivia de Havilland, Basil Rathbone, J. Carroll Naish, Guy Kibbee   D: Michael Curtiz   AA: '35 Nom: Best Picture

CHARLEY VARRICK *1973 111m/C (PG)*

In one of his best roles, Walter Matthau plays a bank robber who, after successfully knocking over one of his marks, finds out that its biggest depositor is the mob. Soon he's being chased by a ruthless hit man who wants the money back and him dead. Great action flick.

C: Walter Matthau, Joe Don Baker, Felicia Farr   D: Don Siegel

CRIMSON PIRATE *1952 105m/C*

Burt Lancaster takes to the high seas in the swashbuckling extravaganza that has him clanking swords with Spanish royalty.

C: Burt Lancaster, Eva Bartok, Torin Thatcher, Nick Cravat, Christopher Lee   D: Robert Siodmak

DEATH WISH *1974 93m/C (R)*

Bronson plays an architect whose wife is killed and daughter is raped by some street slime. He can't deal with the inept police work and disgusting criminal element, and so he begins nightly walks where he takes the law into his own hands. Fast moving box office smash spawned four sequels.

C: Charles Bronson, Vincent Gardenia, William Redfield, Hope Lange, Jeff Goldblum   D: Michael Winner

DIAMONDS ARE FOREVER *1971 120m/C (PG)*

One of the best James Bond flicks has 007 (Sean Connery) trying to save Washington from being wiped off the map by a space satellite laser. Attractive "babes," in your face action scenes, and Connery's famous "wild ride" through Vegas speed this pic along.

C: Sean Connery, Jill St. John, Charles Gray, Bruce Cabot, Jimmy Dean   D: Guy Hamilton

DIE HARD *1988 114m/C (R)*

Willis plays a New York City cop who takes on a ruthless gang of terrorists who have taken over a Los Angeles high rise, complete with dozens of hostages including his wife. Stunning special effects and action sequences along with a fast paced script raises this a level above the normal big-budget fare.

C: Bruce Willis, Bonnie Bedelia, Alan Rickman, Alexander Godunov, Paul Gleason   D: John McTiernan

DIRTY HARRY *1971 103m/C (R)*

Clint Eastwood is Harry Calahan, a detective always given the dirty jobs no one else wants. He has a penchant for playing by his own rules and uses that style to go after a creep who's kidnapped a girl and is demanding a ransom from the city of San Francisco. "Do you feel lucky?"

C: Clint Eastwood, Harry Guardino, John Larch, Andrew Robinson, Reni Santoni   D: Don Siegel

DIRTY MARY, CRAZY LARRY *1974 93m/C (PG)*

A race car driver, his mechanic, and a wild girl are chased by the law after scoring a nice sum of cash in a daring robbery. A low budget, engrossing pic with a stupefying ending.

C: Peter Fonda, Susan George, Adam Roarke, Vic Morrow, Roddy McDowell   D: John Hough

DON JUAN 1926 90m/B&W

John Barrymore puts on a rollicking show as the Italian royalty who romances the ladies and battles the bad guys. Great action sequences (Barrymore refused a stunt double) and the first film to use music and sound effects.

C: John Barrymore, Mary Astor, Estelle Taylor, Willard Louis   D: Alan Crosland

DR. NO 1962 111m/C (PG)

A mad scientist, operating from his evil headquarters in Jamaica, is wreaking havoc on government space testing. It's up to 007 to stop the madness. The first and one of the best Bond flicks with the prototype for future Bond girls (Andress).

C: Sean Connery, Ursula Andress, Joseph Wiseman, Jack Lord D: Terence Young

EL MARIACHI 1993 84m/C (R)

A drifting Mariachi player wanders into a Mexican border town and is mistaken for a ruthless killer who's just escaped from prison. Needless to say, he's violently hunted by a psychotic drug lord seeking revenge. Excellent editing adds immensely to this pic, which was reportedly made for $7,000.

C: Carlos Gallardo, Peter Marquardt, Consuelo Gomez, Jaime de Hoyos   D: Robert Rodriguez

ELECTRA GLIDE IN BLUE 1978 115m/C (R)

Robert Blake is an Arizona cop who makes up for physical shortcomings by using his brains to get the edge over countless criminals. Fast paced action.

C: Robert Blake, Mitchell Ryan, Billy Green Bush, Jeannine Riley, Elisha Cook, Jr. D: James Guercio

ENTER THE DRAGON *1973 98m/C (R)*

Bruce Lee becomes a British agent sent to infiltrate a Hong Kong drug ring using wit, intelligence, and, of course, his amazing fighting abilities. Some of the best hand-to-hand combat ever put on screen. This is the film that turned Bruce Lee into a world wide phenomenon.

C: Bruce Lee, John Saxon, Jim Kelly D: Robert Clouse

FALL OF THE ROMAN EMPIRE *1964 187m/C*

A Hollywood spectacle that delivers high drama with plenty of action sequences and some incredible battle photography. The story centers around Marcus Aurelius's son plotting the murder of his dad, and the ensuing chaos.

C: Sophia Loren, Alec Guinness, James Mason, Stephen Boyd, John Ireland D: Anthony Mann

FIRST BLOOD *1982 96m/C (R)*

Vietnam vet John Rambo (Stallone) drifts into a small town and is immediately singled out for abuse by the sheriff (Dennehy) who locks him up. Rambo breaks out of jail and heads for the mountains. What follows is an action packed manhunt that turned Stallone into one of the biggest action stars of all time.

C: Sylvester Stallone, Richard Crenna, Brian Dennehy, Jack Starrett, David Caruso D: Ted Kotcheff

48 HRS. *1982 97m/C (R)*

One of the great action directors, Walter Hill, brings us this extremely popular pic about a gruffy cop (Nolte) who pulls an inmate (Murphy) out of prison to help him hunt down a killer.

C: Nick Nolte, Eddie Murphy, James Remar, Annette O'Toole, David Patrick Kelly D: Walter Hill

THE FRENCH CONNECTION *1971 102m/C (R)*
See "Top 100"

FROM DUSK TILL DAWN *1996 108m/C (R)*
Clooney and Tarantino play brothers in crime. Clooney likes to rob and beat people but he won't kill them without good reason. Tarantino likes to rob and beat people and would kill someone if they pronounced his name wrong. They steal some booty, take a family hostage and head to Mexico. Unfortunately they make the mistake of meeting their bad guy partners at a bar frequented by vampires. Enough blood is spilled, sucked, and sprayed to float an ocean liner, but hey, isn't that what movies are all about?

C: George Clooney, Quentin Tarantino, Harvey Keitel, Juliette Lewis
D: Robert Rodriquez

THE FUGITIVE *1993 127m/C (PG-13)*
Based on the '50s TV show about Dr. Kimble, a man wrongfully charged with murdering his wife. He escapes during his transport to prison and begins his search for the real killer, the infamous one-armed man. Slick, fast paced, high tension film with an incredibly realistic train crash that begins the picture.

C: Harrison Ford, Tommy Lee Jones, Jeroen Krabbe, Julianne Moore, Sela Ward   D: Andrew Davis   AA: '93 Best Supporting Actor (Jones), Nom: Best Picture

THE GETAWAY *1972 123m/C (PG)*
McQueen is at his best as a just released convict double-crossed by a corrupt politician who's had him pull off a bank job. McQueen decides to run with the cash so one of the politician's henchmen takes off after him. Al Lettieri's performance as the left-for-dead hitman adds a wallop to an already tension filled pic.

C: Steve McQueen, Ali MacGraw, Ben Johnson, Sally Struthers,

Al Lettieri D: Sam Peckinpah

GOLDFINGER 1964 117m/C (PG)

Bond goes up against the ruthless villain Goldfinger and his voluptuous assistant Pussy Galore as they try to pull a major heist at Fort Knox. This is the pic that includes the infamous bad guy "Odd Job" and his murderous bowler cap. Considered one of Bond's best.

C: Sean Connery, Honor Blackman, Gert Frobe, Shirley Eaton, Tania Mallet D: Guy Hamilton

HARD TIMES 1975 92m/C (PG)

Bronson plays a Depression era drifter who witnesses an empty warehouse "controlled" street fight where gamblers bet high stakes on the outcome. He decides he can handle himself against any of them and teams up with flashy con man/promoter Coburn, and the two try to rise to the top of the profession. Great climax with Bronson taking on a street fighting legend.

C: Charles Bronson, James Coburn, Jill Ireland, Strother Martin D: Walter Hill

HATARI 1962 155m/C

Much loved pic about a group of adventurous hunters, led by John Wayne, who take a trip to Africa to score some big game for elite zoos around the world. Amazing on location photography of the African wild and its animals.

C: John Wayne, Elsa Martinelli, Hardy Kruger, Red Buttons D: Howard Hawks

HEAT 1995 171m/C (R)

DeNiro is a new age thief who does high end jobs that require expensive techno-gadgets and computer wizards. Pacino is the incorruptible cop who's after him. The film contains an awesome shoot-out in the streets of L.A. that is choreographed like a violent ballet.

C: Al Pacino, Robert DeNiro, Val Kilmer, Amy Brenneman, Ashley Judd, Jon Voight   D: Michael Mann

HIGH SIERRA *1941 96m/B&W*

Bogart plays a veteran thief who bungles a big heist and hides out in the Sierra Mountains. Unique characters and wild plot twists made this a high cut above the normal "thug on the run" flicks.

C: Humphrey Bogart, Ida Lupino, Arthur Kennedy, Joan Leslie, Cornel Wilde   D: Raoul Walsh

IN THE LINE OF FIRE *1993 128m/C (R)*

Eastwood plays an aging Secret Service Agent who's assigned to protect the President. When a psycho-killer begins making eerie phone calls revolving around his plan to murder the prez, he takes it to heart to track down the madman. Malkovich, as the ex-CIA lunatic/hitman, gives a chilling performance.

C: Clint Eastwood, John Malkovich, Rene Russo, Dylan McDermott, Gary Cole   D: Wolfgang Petersen   AA: '93 Nom: Best Supporting Actor (Malkovich)

IVANHOE *1952 106m/C*

Sir Walter Scott's classic story about the capture of Richard The Lion Hearted and the brave knight Ivanhoe's battle to release him. Complete with thrashing battles and fair maidens.

C: Robert Taylor, Joan Fontaine, Elizabeth Taylor, George Sanders   D: Richard Thorpe

KING KONG *1933 105m/B&W*

A couple of adventurers/entrepreneurs cage a giant ape in Africa and bring him to the U.S. for "freak show" purposes. The hairy terror falls for one of his captors, gets loose, and wreaks havoc in the Big Apple, culminating in one of the most famous scenes ever filmed, the battle on the Empire State Building.

C: Fay Wray, Bruce Cabot, Robert Armstrong, Noble Johnson, Frank Reicher D: Ernest B. Schoedsauk

KING SOLOMON'S MINES *1950 102m/C*

A safari team forges into the jungle in search of the famous treasures of King Solomon, and comes up against constant terrifying and life threatening situations.

C: Stewart Granger, Deborah Kerr, Richard Carlson, Hugo Haas, Lowell Gilmore D: Compton Bennett AA: '50 Nom: Best Picture

LETHAL WEAPON *1987 110m/C (R)*

The first and best of the series has two cops (one mellow and near retirement, the other gunho and hyper), discovering a ruthless drug ring run by crazed ex-soldiers. Non-stop action and a great chemistry between Gibson and Glover make this a top notch effort.

C: Mel Gibson, Danny Glover, Gary Busey, Mitchell Ryan, Tom Atkins, Darlene Love D: Richard Donner

LONELY ARE THE BRAVE *1962 107m/B&W*

It's the old way versus progress in this fast paced flick that has Douglas playing a traditional cowboy who breaks his friend out of prison and then is diligently pursued by a state-of-the-art, high tech police team, with "modern" equipment like walkie-talkies and a helicopter.

C: Kirk Douglas, Walter Matthau, Carroll O'Connor, Gena Rowlands, George Kennedy D: David Miller

THE LONG GOOD FRIDAY *1979 109m/C*

Bob Hoskins plays a London crime boss who, in the course of a weekend, experiences a series of bombings and murders against his reign. He believes he knows who's behind the acts of terror only to find out he's gravely mistaken. Classic ending.

C: Bob Hoskins, Helen Mirren, Dave King, Bryan Marshall, George

Coulouris, Pierce Brosnan   D: John Mackenzie

THE MAN WHO WOULD BE KING 1975 129m/C (PG)

An exciting tale of two soldiers who decide to travel to Kafiristan, overthrow the throne, and implant themselves in the role of kings. Engaging grand scale production.

C: Sean Connery, Michael Caine, Christopher Plummer, Saeed Jaffrey, Shakira Caine   D: John Huston

THE MARK OF ZORRO 1940 93m/B&W

By day he's your average aristocrat but by night he's a swashbuckling super hero to the oppressed. Who is "he"? He's "Zorro," the masked man fighting the wicked corrupt powers of the kingdom and still having time to woo a beautiful girl. Culminates with one of the most famous, flashy swordfights ever put on screen.

C: Tyrone Power, Linda Darnell, Basil Rathbone, Gale Sondergaard, Eugene Pallette   D: Rouben Mamoulian

MIDNIGHT RUN 1988 125m/C (R)

Grodin gives a perfectly low key performance as an accountant who's embezzled a huge sum of cash from his mob employers. DeNiro is a bounty hunter who's bringing his valuable catch from New York to LA and must deal with the mob and a rival bounty hunter who want Grodin before he reaches the west coast. Farina delivers a classic performance as a mafioso with a temper that rivals Attilla the Hun.

C: Robert DeNiro, Charles Grodin, Yaphet Kotto, John Ashton, Dennis Farina   D: Martin Brest

MOBY DICK 1956 116m/C

Gregory Peck plays Captain Ahab in this fine re-telling of the crusty sailor who leads a crew of men into a war with the killer whale, Moby Dick. Sci-fi writer Ray Bradbury co-wrote the script.

C: Gregory Peck, Orson Welles, Richard Basehart, Leo Genn, Friedrich Ledebur   D: John Huston

THE MOST DANGEROUS GAME *1932 78m/B&W*

A man becomes shipwrecked on an island inhabited by a demented "hunter" who decides that this unexpected guest will be the object of his next hunt. Great thrills, fast paced, and the dated look only adds to the eerie atmosphere.

C: Joel McCrea, Fay Wray, Leslie Banks, Robert Armstrong
D: Ernest B. Schoedsack

MUTINY ON THE BOUNTY *1935 132m/B&W*

See "Top 100"

NAKED PREY *1966 96m/C*

Great pic has a safari group taken prisoners by a jungle tribe of warriors. They brutally kill all the members (a horrifying, disturbing scene which must be seen to be believed) except for the safari leader, who they strip and set free so he can be hunted by the tribe's most skilled warriors. Compelling from the first frame to the end credits.

C: Cornel Wilde, Gertrude Vander Berger, Ken Gampa   D: Cornel Wilde

THE POSEIDON ADVENTURE *1972 117m/C*

A luxury liner on a New Year's Eve cruise is capsized by a tidal wave wiping out all but ten people who now must make their way out the submerged coffin. One of the first "disaster" flicks.

C: Gene Hackman, Ernest Borgnine, Shelley Winters, Red Buttons, Jack Albertson, Carol Lynley   D: Ronald Neame

THE PROFESSIONAL *1995 109m/C (R)*

A reclusive hitman (Reno) is hired by a 12-year-old girl to hunt down the killer who brutally wiped out her family. Oldman gives a wild performance as one of the bad guys.

C: Jean Reno, Gary Oldman, Danny Aiello, Natalie Portman   D: Luc Besson

THE PROFESSIONALS *1966 117m/C*

A rich cattle rancher employs the services of four wild and ready gun-for-hires to wipe out the Mexicans who have kidnapped his wife. Rock solid pic.

C: Burt Lancaster, Lee Marvin, Claudia Cardinale, Jack Palance, Robert Ryan   D: Richard Brooks   AA: '66 Nom: Best Director

PUBLIC ENEMY *1931 85m/B&W*

Considered by critics to be one of the best crime films ever made, this pic centers around a gangster's rise and fall in 1920s Chicago. It contains Cagney's famous "grapefruit in the face" scene.

C: James Cagney, Edward Woods, Leslie Fenton, Joan Blondell, Mae Clarke, Jean Harlow   D: William A. Wellman

RAIDERS OF THE LOST ARK *1981 115m/C (PG)*

See "Top 100"

RESERVOIR DOGS *1992 100m/C (R)*

A group of criminals hold up a jewelry store. The plan goes off like clockwork until the cops come and blow two of their heads off. Tension mounts as the remaining members regroup in an empty warehouse and try to figure out which one of them tipped off the fuzz. Excellent cast with turbo powered script.

C: Harvey Keitel, Tim Roth, Michael Madsen, Steve Buscemi, Christopher Penn   D: Quentin Tarantino

RIOT IN CELL BLOCK II *1954 80m/B&W*

A group of prisoners attempt a daring escape and, when it fails, riot and demand satisfaction. A gripping, well written character study of prisoners, the people who keep them locked up, and the media. Seigel, responsible for the *Dirty Harry* movies, directed.

C: Neville Brand, Emile Meyer, Leo Gordon, Frank Faylen   D: Don Seigel

THE ROAD WARRIOR 1982 95m/C (R)

The apocalypse has arrived and a futuristic drifter teams up with a colony of outcasts to do battle against a roving gang of bloodthirsty psychopaths. This film became the blueprint for the '80s action picture, has one of the most incredible chase scenes ever filmed, and turned Mel Gibson into an American star.

C: Mel Gibson, Bruce Spence, Emil Minty, Vernon Wells   D: George Miller

SCARFACE 1931 93m/B&W

A powerful and violent film about the rise and fall of a 1930s kingpin. Paul Muni, as the crime lord in question, delivers a first class, viciously inspired performance.

C: Paul Muni, Ann Dorvak, Karen Morley, Osgood Perkins, George Raft   D: Howard Hawks

SCARFACE 1983 170m/C (R)

Like the original 1932 version, this film centers around the violent rise and deadly decline of a gangster. The '80s version updates the story to the present and the power monger's fall is due more to his drug problems than to the politics of crime. Pacino is evil, hot tempered and perfect. Top notch gangster flick.

C: Al Pacino, Steven Bauer, Michelle Pfeiffer, Robert Loggia, F. Murray Abraham   D: Brian DePalma

THE SEA WOLF 1941 90m/C

A ship led by a tyrannical captain (Robinson) picks up two shipwreck victims. There is no special treatment as Robinson attempts to turn the two into galley slaves, leading to big trouble.

C: Edward G. Robinson, John Garfield, Ida Lupino, Alexander Knox
D: Michael Curtiz

SEVEN 1995 127m/C (R)

Pitt is a detective assigned to a city in which the sun never seems to shine. Freeman is the cynical veteran who tells Pitt to give up the gun and get a day job. Together they sink into the demented world of a psycho who's picked seven people to kill seven different ways, illustrating his take on the seven deadly sins of the bible. Brace yourself for the ending.

C: Morgan Freeman, Brad Pitt, Kevin Spacey   D: David Fincher

SHAFT 1971 98m/C (R)

When a Harlem gangster's daughter is kidnapped, the king-pin hires Detective Shaft to get her back. Tense pacing and direction and that famous song that hit the top 10. Classic '70s atmosphere.

C: Richard Roundtree, Moses Gunn, Charles Cioffi   D: Gordon Parks

SOUTHERN COMFORT 1981 106m/C (R)

A company of weekend reserve soldiers hit the Louisiana swamplands for a short "tour of duty." When one of them stupidly fires at a backwoodsman their exercise is turned into a real-life battle and they are hunted down by the relentless cajuns. The final horrific scene, where Carradine and Boothe stumble into a deadly cajun barbecue, is awesome.

C: Powers Boothe, Keith Carradine, Fred Ward, Franklyn Seales, Brion James   D: Walter Hill

SPARTACUS 1960 196m/C (PG-13)

Stanley Kubrick's sweeping, grand scale epic of the famous slave who led a revolt against Rome in 73 B.C. Some of the greatest battle scenes ever filmed and a knockout performance by Douglas make it one of the best pics of the '60s. A recently released "Director's Cut" includes a then-controversial bath scene between Olivier and Curtis.

C: Kirk Douglas, Laurence Olivier, Jean Simmons, Tony Curtis, Charles Laughton, Peter Ustinov D: Stanley Kubrick AA: '60 Nom: Best Supporting Actor (Ustinov)

SPEED *1994 115m/C (R)*

A psycho (Hopper) plants a bomb in a crowded bus that is set to detonate if the vehicle's speed drops under 50 miles an hour. Super cop Reeves and passenger Bullock try to steer the impending disaster through the streets of Los Angeles to safety. Fast-paced.

C: Keanu Reeves, Dennis Hopper, Sandra Bullock, Joe Morton, Jeff Daniels D: Jan DeBont

SUPERMAN *1978 144m/C (PG)*

The classic comic book superhero is brought to the screen, pitted against the evil Lex Luthor (Hackman) and his goofy sidekick (Beatty). Fun pic with lots of tongue-in-cheek humor.

C: Christopher Reeve, Gene Hackman, Valerie Perrine, Marlon Brando, Margot Kidder, Jackie Cooper D: Richard Donner

TARZAN AND HIS MATE *1934 93m/B&W*

The sequel to *Tarzan The Ape Man* is one of those rare occurrences where the second picture is actually better than the first. An unscrupulous businessman and his guide try to get Tarzan to lead them to the elephant graveyard where a fortune in ivory tusks awaits.

C: Johnny Weissmuller, Maureen O'Sullivan, Neil Hamilton, Paul Cavanagh D: Jack Conway

THIEF *1981 126m/C (R)*

James Caan is a very successful high tech burglar, pulling

off million dollar heists. All's well until the mob makes a deal with him on a jewel score and then don't keep up their end of the bargain. Great story and character study of an aging criminal.

C: James Caan, Tuesday Weld, Jim Belushi, Willie Nelson
D: Michael Mann

THREE MUSKETEERS 1974 105m/C (PG)

Classic working of a classic story. Three boisterous charismatic swordsmen and their young protegé dive into battle with an evil cardinal and his plot to take over the kingdom. Lester, the director of *A Hard Day's Night*, combines a perfect mixture of comedy, drama, and action. Considered the best of the dozen or so versions about the swashbuckling trio.

C: Richard Chamberlain, Oliver Reed, Michael York, Raquel Welch, Christopher Lee, Faye Dunaway   D: Richard Lester

THUNDERBOLT AND LIGHTFOOT 1974 115m/C (R)

Eastwood stars as a Vietnam vet/thief being chased by his ex-partners who are convinced he's got the cash from their last job. After much sweating, he finally persuades them that he doesn't have the loot. With the money gone, his partners and a drifter decide to rob the same place again. Bad idea.

C: Clint Eastwood, Jeff Bridges, George Kennedy, Geoffrey Lewis, Gary Busey   D: Michael Cimino

THUNDER ROAD 1958 92m/B&W (PG)

Robert Mitchum wrote, produced, and starred in this high action flick about a Korean war vet who returns home to his Tennessee moonshine operation and is quickly in a bloody war with the mob and the heat. Great slam-bam ending. Mitchum also wrote the movie's hit theme song, "Whippoorwill."

C: Robert Mitchum, Jacques Aubuchon, Keely Smith, Gene Barry, James Mitchum   D: Arthur Ripley

TREASURE OF THE SIERRA MADRE *1948*
126m/B&W

See "Top 100"

TRESPASS *1992 104m/C (R)*

Fast-paced, well directed film about two fireman who learn about a gold treasure hidden in an abandoned warehouse and the resulting hell they go through when a ruthless street gang decides they also want it.

C: Ice Cube, Ice-T; William Sadler, Bill Paxton, Art Evans   D: Walter Hill

TRUE ROMANCE *1993 116m/C (R)*

Slater falls in love with a prostitute who wants to get out of the business. So he visits the pimp's lair, is beaten to near death, but escapes with his life and a suitcase of coke. He and his girl head west to sell it and start a new life. Contains some classic scenes including Dennis Hopper's "are you Sicilian?"

C: Christian Slater, Patricia Arquette, Gary Oldman, Christopher Walken, Brad Pitt, Val Kilmer, Dennis Hopper   D: Tony Scott

THE UNTOUCHABLES *1987 119m/C (R)*

Exciting re-telling of the small war which raged between mobster Al Capone and United States Treasurer Officer Elliot Ness, as Ness tried to put Capone behind bars. Violent shootouts, incredible special effects, and a psychotic performance from DeNiro as the evil deranged crime boss. (Watch for the infamous baseball bat scene.) Great stuff.

C: Kevin Costner, Sean Connery, Robert DeNiro, Andy Garcia, Charles Martin Smith   D: Brian DePalma   AA: '87 Best Supporting Actor (Connery)

THE USUAL SUSPECTS *1995 106m/C (R)*

A master criminal is manipulating other thieves and the police to do his bidding. The plot thickens as the thugs and the law try to catch him at his own sinister game. A Hitchcockian thriller that will keep you guessing.

C: Gabriel Byrne, Kevin Spacey, Stephen Baldwin, Benicio Del Toro, Kevin Pollack, Chazz Palminteri D: Bryan Singer AA: '95 Best Supporting Actor (Spacey)

WHITE HEAT *1949 114m/B&W*

Cagney gives one of his most memorable performances as a demented psychotic criminal who has a strange relationship with his mother. Famous "top of the world, ma" ending. Based loosely on Ma Barker and her son, Arthur.

C: James Cagney, Virginia Mayo, Edward O'Brien, Margaret Wycherly, Steve Cocharn D: Raoul Walsh

WHO'LL STOP THE RAIN *1978 126m/C (R)*

Nolte stars as a Vietnam vet who agrees to help a friend smuggle heroin in from Vietnam. They have no idea they're involved in a set-up and when the deal goes down, all hell breaks loose. Based on the award winning book, *Dog Soldiers*.

C: Nick Nolte, Tuesday Weld, Michael Moriarty, Anthony Zerbe, Richard Masur D: Karel Reisz

BIOGRAPHY

ABE LINCOLN IN ILLINOIS *1940 110m/B&W*

The life of "Honest Abe," beginning with his early years in the log cabin and ending with his White House stay, are expertly handled in this insightful, engaging classic. Includes famous debate between Lincoln and Douglas.

C: Raymond Massey, Gene Lockhart, Ruth Gordon, Mary Howard, Dorothy Tree D: John Cromwell

ALL THAT JAZZ *1979 120m/C (R)*

Autobiographical picture by Bob Fosse shows his neurotic obsessed nature, complete with drug addition, relentless smoking and his amazing output of incredible choreography. An intense, high energy film.

C: Roy Scheider, Jessica Lange, Ann Reinking, Leland Palmer, Cliff Gorman, Ben Vereen D: Bob Fosse AA: Nom: Best Picture, Director, Actor (Scheider), Screenplay

AMADEUS *1984 158m/C (PG)*

See "Top 100"

BACKBEAT *1994 100m/C (R)*

Involving look at the early days of the Beatles before they were thrust to fame and fortune in the U.S. Also examines the strong relationship between John Lennon and Stu Sutcliffe, known as the fifth Beatle, who left the band before they hit it big to attend art school. Compelling and expertly made.

C: Stephen Dorff, Sheryl Lee, Ian Hart, Gary Bakewell, Chris O'Neill D: Ian Softley

BADLANDS *1974 94m/C (PG)*

Every few years a filmmaker comes along who blows everyone away. In 1974 the filmmaker was Terence Malick. *Badlands* is based on the true story of Charles Starkweather (Martin Sheen), an unemployed drifter who, along with his 15-year-old girlfriend, went on a killing spree across the midwest in the 1950s. The film is crammed with unforgettable scenes and has some incredibly haunting music.

C: Martin Sheen, Sissy Spacek, Warren Oates D: Terence Malick

BIRD *1988 160m/C (R)*

An intelligent, compelling story of jazz great Charlie Parker, from his rise to stardom to his tragic demise from heroin. Director Eastwood handles the story with an assured style and Whitaker's portrayal is great.

C: Forest Whitaker, Diane Venora, Michael Zeniker, Samuel E. Wright, Keith David   D: Clint Eastwood

BIRDMAN OF ALCATRAZ *1962 143m/B&W*

The incredible true story of Robert Stroud, a man convicted of two murders and sentenced to life on Alcatraz Island. While his mother relentlessly tried to get her son freed, he became a world famous authority on birds.

C: Burt Lancaster, Karl Malden, Thelma Ritter, Telly Savalas
D: John Frankenheimer

BONNIE AND CLYDE *1967 111m/C*

See "Top 100"

BOUND FOR GLORY *1976 149m/C (PG)*

David Carradine portrays folk legend Woody Guthrie in this pic that concentrates on the musician's life during the Depression, when he rode the rails and translated his feeling of the economy and people through his music.

C: David Carradine, Ronny Cox, Melinda Dillon, Randy Quaid
D: Hal Ashby   AA: '76 Nom: Best Picture

BRAVEHEART *1995 120m/C*

Upon his return to his homeland of Scotland, William Wallace finds the land he left has fallen under the tyrannical rule of the brutal English King Edward. Wallace's wife is ruthlessly murdered, and soon he rallies an army of men to take on the new order. Gibson, who plays Wallace and directs, does an outstanding job, and the film contains some absolutely amazing battle scenes.

C: Mel Gibson, Patrick McGoohan, Catherine McCormack, Sophie Marceau, Brendan Gleeson, James Cosmo   D: Mel Gibson   AA: '95 Best Picture, Director

THE BUDDY HOLLY STORY 1978 113m/C (PG)

The life and times of the man who penned "Peggy Sue" and "That'll Be The Day," from his humble beginnings, to his rise to fame, to his unfortunate early death in a plane crash. Busey's "Holly" is amazing.

C: Gary Busey, Don Stroud, Charles Martin Smith, Conrad Janis, William Jordan   D: Steve Rash   AA: '78 Nom: Best Actor (Busey)

BUGSY 1991 135m/C (R)

Las Vegas, Nevada, was a virtual desert until a gangster named "Bugsy" Siegel (Beatty) decided to build a casino and change the country forever. This is the story of the violence, ambition, love, and death, that went into his dream. Keitel gives a great performance as Siegel's hard-edged partner.

C: Warren Beatty, Annette Bening, Harvey Keitel, Ben Kingsley, Bebe Neuwirth   D: Barry Levinson   AA: '91 Nom: Best Picture, Director, Supporting Actor (Keitel, Kingsley), Original Screenplay

CHAMELEON STREET 1989 95m/C (R)

Engaging look at William Douglas Street, a gentlemen from Detroit who successfully impersonated a surgeon (he performed an operation), a *Time* magazine reporter, a Yale law student, a lawyer (he worked for the Detroit Human Rights Commission), and a few other esteemed characters. Incredibly true.

C: Wendell B. Harris, Jr., Angela Leslie, Amina Fakir, Paul McGee, Richard Kiley   D: Wendell B. Harris, Jr.

COAL MINER'S DAUGHTER 1980 125m/C (PG)

The story of Loretta Lynn, the famed country singer who started as a poor Appalachian girl, was married at 13, and soon after struck gold in Nashville. Spacek gives a beautiful performance as Lynn and sings all the songs herself.

C: Sissy Spacek, Tommy Lee Jones, Levon Helm, Beverly D'Angelo

D: Michael Apted   AA: '80 Best Actress (Spacek), Nom: Best Picture, Adapted Screenplay

DIARY OF ANNE FRANK *1959 150m/B&W*

Moving portrait of the famed young Jewish girl who was killed in a Nazi death camp at the age of 13. Before she entered the camp, she and her parents were hidden in an attic for years by Mrs. Van Daan, who fed and cared for the family.

C: Millie Perkins, Joseph Schildkraut, Shelley Winters, Richard Beymer, Gusti Huber, Ed Wynn   D: George Stevens   AA: '59 Best Supporting Actress (Winters), Nom: Best Picture, Director

ED WOOD *1994 104m/B&W*

Sympathetic portrayal of the cross-dressing film director credited with making the worst film of all time, *Plan 9 From Outer Space*. (Has anyone seen *Natural Born Killers*?) Johnny Depp should have been nominated for an Oscar for his role as Wood, a director who went to insane extremes to get his films made. Martin Landau won the statue for his incredible performance as Wood's friend, Bela Lugosi.

C: Johnny Depp, Sarah Jessica Parker, Martin Landau, Bill Murray, Jim Myers   D: Tim Burton   AA: '94 Best Supporting Actor (Landau)

ELEPHANT MAN *1980 125m/B&W*

A moving biography detailing the life of severely deformed John Merrick, a man who was exploited in freak shows until a caring doctor helped him into the uppercrust of society.

C: Anthony Hopkins, John Hurt, Anne Bancroft, John Gielgud, Wendy Hiller   D: David Lynch   AA: '80 Nom: Best Picture, Director, Actor (Hurt)

FALCON AND THE SNOWMAN *1985 110m/C (R)*

An incredible picture based on the true story of Dalton Lee and Christopher Boyce, two California 20-year-olds who almost sold top secret government information to the Russians.

Sean Penn and Timothy Hutton give the performances of their careers as the leads.

C: Sean Penn, Timothy Hutton, Lori Singer, Pat Hingle, Dorian Harewood   D: John Schlesinger

FRANCES 1982 134m/C

The unforgettable and heartwrenching story of Frances Farmer, a highly acclaimed actress who rose to fame in the '30s and '40s but fell victim to alcohol, drugs, a greedy domineering mother, and ultimately, a nervous breakdown. Director Howard Hawks called Farmer "the best actress I ever worked with."

C: Jessica Lange, Kim Stanley, Sam Shepard   D: Graeme Clifford
AA: '82 Nom: Best Actress (Lange)

GANDHI 1982 188m/C (PG)

See "Top 100"

GENTLEMAN JIM 1942 104m/B&W

Widely appealing story of '20s boxing legend Jim Corbett, told in rowdy style with Errol Flynn giving a tremendously winning performance as the heavyweight champ. (Flynn said it was his favorite role). The film ends with the classic championship bout between Jim Corbett and John L. Sullivan.

C: Errol Flynn, Alan Hale, Alexis Smith, Jack Carson, Ward Bond
D: Raoul Walsh

HENRY & JUNE 1990 136m/C (NC-17)

A few years in the life of author Henry Miller (*Tropic Of Cancer*) directly preceding his fame, where he wandered the streets of Paris and hung out with artists, prostitutes, and his wife, June. Henry then met Anais Nin and a strange affair began, leading to success.

C: Fred Ward, Uma Thurman, Maria De Mederios, Richard E. Grant, Kevin Spacey   D: Philip Kaufman

IMPROMPTU 1990 108m/C (PG-13)

The beginnings of the charmed love affair between acclaimed pianist Franz Liszt and esteemed author George Sand is handled with wit, style, and intelligence as Sand relentlessly pursues Liszt, who has no interest in her. Beautifully produced period piece.

C: Judy Davis, Hugh Grant, Mandy Patinkin, Bernadette Peters, Julian Sands, Emma Thompson D: James Lapine

THE KRAYS 1990 119m/C (R)

The violent life and times of twin brothers Reggie and Ronnie Kray, the English mobsters who wreaked havoc on London's East End during the '60s, giving them lots of money and a twisted aura of fame. The sick pair are portrayed by Gary and Martin Kemp, who rose to fame as the pop group Spandau Ballet.

C: Gary Kemp, Martin Kemp, Billie Whitelaw, Steven Berkoff, Susan Fleetwood D: Peter Medak

LA BAMBA 1987 99m/C (PG-13)

Lou Diamond Phillips gives a winning performance as '50s rock and roll star Ritchie Valens who, already a huge star at the age of 17, died in the plane crash that also took the talented Buddy Holly and The Big Bopper. Unforgettable funeral scene at end where Valens' "Sleepwalk" is played over a slow motion funeral procession.

C: Lou Diamond Phillips, Esai Morales, Danielle von Zernaeck, Joe Pantoliano, Brian Setzer D: Luis Valdez

LADY JANE 1985 140m/C (PG-13)

The incredible story of the 15-year-old queen and her very short reign due to her disdain for the ultra-extravagant lifestyle of the throne and her strong sympathy for the poor. Excellent in every way.

C: Helena Bonham Carter, Cary Elwes, Sara Kestelman, Michael Hordern, Joss Ackland   D: Trevor Nunn

LAST EMPEROR *1987 140m/C (PG-13)*

A true epic detailing the life of Pu Yi, who became Emperor of China at the age of three. Shot on location inside the People's Republic of China, the film has incredible cinematography and lavish production values.

C: John Lone, Peter O'Toole, Joan Chen, Victor Wong, Ryuichi Sakamoto   D: Bernardo Bertolucci   AA: '87 Best Picture, Director

LENNY *1974 111m/B&W (R)*

Hoffman is Lenny Bruce, the comic genius hailed by critics and fans but continually persecuted for his brass, offensive delivery. Hoffman is excellent as the self-destructive comedian and Perrine is perfect as his stripper wife.

C: Dustin Hoffman, Valerie Perrine, Jan Miner, Stanley Beck   D: Bob Fosse   AA: '74 Nom: Best Picture, Director, Actor (Hoffman), Actress (Perrine)

LUST FOR LIFE *1956 122m/C*

Compelling bio of tortured artist Vincent VanGogh, beginning with his troubles with the church, moving through his brilliant output of work, and ending with his sad death. Douglas's portrayal of the struggling artist is inspired, including a classic scene dealing with his romantic obsession with his cousin. Many of Van Gogh's actual work, taken from private collections, are used in the film.

C: Kirk Douglas, Anthony Quinn, James Donald, Pamela Brown, Everett Sloane   D: Vincente Minnelli   AA: '56 Best Supporting Actor (Quinn), Nom: Best Actor (Douglas), Adapted Screenplay

MALCOM X *1992 201m/C (PG-13)*

Washington plays Malcom X, the black activist who, after serving time in prison, led an equal rights movement that opened the world's eyes. Unfortunately, it led to his assassination in 1965. Powerful.

C: Denzel Washington, Angela Bassett, Albert Hall, Al Freeman, Jr., Delroy Lindo D: Spike Lee AA: '92 Nom: Best Actor (Washington)

MAN OF A THOUSAND FACES 1957 122m/B&W
Screen legend James Cagney portrays screen legend Lon Chaney in this touching pic that traces the actor's beginning as a child of deaf, mute parents to his rise to the top of film stardom. Includes re-stagings of classic scenes from *Phantom Of The Opera* and *The Hunchback of Notre Dame*.

C: James Cagney, Dorothy Malone, Jane Greer, Marjorie Rambeau, Jim Backus, Robert Evans, Roger Smith D: Joseph Pevney

THE MIRACLE WORKER 1962 107m/B&W
The moving story of the relationship between young Helen Keller, deaf, dumb, and blind from birth, and Anne Sullivan, the teacher who refused to give up and ultimately helped the girl adjust and live in the extremely difficult world she was born to. A courageous, uplifting viewing experience.

C: Anne Bancroft, Patty Duke, Victor Jory, Inga Swenson, Andrew Prine D: Arthur Penn AA: '62 Best Actress (Bancroft), Supporting Actress (Duke)

MOULIN ROUGE 1950 119m/C
Lushly produced life and times of acclaimed, disfigured painter Henri de Toulouse-Lautrec, whose cynical view of the world led to an incredible body of work and a penchant for the low life, wild side of Paris. The costumes and art direction are visual treats.

C: Jose Ferrer, Zsa Zsa Gabor, Christopher Lee, Peter Cushing, Colette Marchard D: John Huston AA: '50 Nom: Best Actor (Ferrer)

MURDER IN THE FIRST 1994 123m/C (R)
A teenager is sent to Alcatraz Island for the petty theft of food

from a general store to feed his sister. Once there he's brutalized by the warden and the hardcore system until a lawyer tries to save what's left of his life. A riveting, expertly acted pic based on a true story.

C: Kevin Bacon, Christian Slater, Gary Oldman, Embeth Davidtz, R. Lee Ermey   D: Marc Rocco

MY LEFT FOOT 1989 103m/C (R)

Powerful story of writer/artist Christy Brown, who was born with cerebral palsy. Thought of as less than human by everyone but his mother, Brown amazingly taught himself to write and paint with his left foot, the only part of his body he could control. Unsentimental approach, coupled with Lewis' awesome portrayal, makes the film unforgettable.

C: Daniel Day-Lewis, Brenda Fricker, Ray McAnally, Cyril Cusack, Fiona Shaw, Hugh O'Conor   D: Jim Sheridan   AA: '89 Best Actor (Day-Lewis), Supporting Actress (Fricker), Nom: Best Picture, Director, Adapted Screenplay

PAPILLON 1973 150m/C (PG)

See "Top 100"

PRICK UP YOUR EARS 1987 110m/C (R)

Oldman portrays acclaimed gay English playwright Joe Orton, the controversial author who shot to stardom but whose life was tragically cut short when his lover, jealous of his fame and success, murdered him. Oldman and Alfred Molina (as his lover) give amazing performances.

C: Gary Oldman, Alfred Molina, Vanessa Redgrave, Julie Walters, Lindsay Duncan   D: Stephen Frears

PRIDE OF THE YANKEES 1942 128m/B&W

Lou Gehrig was one of the greatest players in the history of baseball and this film does him justice. Begins with the Yankee Clipper joining the club in 1923 and ends with his tearful farewell speech at Yankee Stadium, caused by the disease that took his life.

C: Gary Cooper, Teresa Wright, Babe Ruth, Walter Brennan, Dan Duryea D: Sam Wood AA: '42 Nom: Best Supporting Actress (Wright), Picture, Actor (Cooper)

THE PRIVATE LIFE OF HENRY VIII *1933 97m/B&W*

The amazing psychotic life of Henry VIII, a king who had a nasty habit of having his wives beheaded, is brought to the screen complete with Charles Laughton's incredible portrayal of the dastardly ruler.

C: Charles Laughton, Binnie Barnes, Elsa Lanchester, Robert Donat, Merle Oberon D: Alexander Korda AA: '83 Best Actor (Laughton), Nom: Best Picture

RAGING BULL *1980 128m/B&W (R)*
See "Top 100"

REDS *1981 195m/C (PG)*

The turbulent life of John Reed, a journalist who attempted to start an American Communist Party, is detailed in this three-hour epic.

C: Warren Beatty, Diane Keaton, Jack Nicholson, Edward Herrmann, Maureen Stapleton, Gene Hackman D: Warren Beatty AA: '81 Best Director, Supporting Actress (Stapleton), Nom: Best Picture, Actor (Beatty), Actress (Keaton), Supporting Actor (Nicholson), Original Screenplay

SCHINDLER'S LIST *1993 195m/B&W (R)*

Powerful portrait of Oskar Schindler, the WWII German businessman who forced the Nazis to allow him to employ Jews in his factories. What was first an act motivated by greed later, through self redemption, became an act of human love and resulted in Schindler saving over 1,000 Jews from certain death in concentration camps. Beautifully filmed in black and white with excellent performances by all.

C: Liam Neeson, Ben Kingsley, Ralph Fiennes, Embeth Davidtz, Caroline Goodall   D: Steven Spielberg   AA: Best Director (Spielberg), Picture, Adapted Screenplay, Nom: Best Actor (Neeson), Supporting Actor (Fiennes)

SERPICO *1973 130m/C (R)*

Al Pacino stars as Frank Serpico, the renegade New York City undercover cop who went up against the police force to expose its corruption. Disgusted by the inner-workings of the NYPD, the real-life Serpico left the force and moved to Sweden.

C: Al Pacino, John Randolph, Jack Kehoe, Barbara Eda-Young, Cornelia Sharpe   D: Sidney Lumet   AA: '73 Nom: Best Actor (Pacino)

SHADOWLANDS *1993 130m/C (PG)*

Moving story of Christian theologian C. S. Lewis's relationship with divorced poet Joy Gresham. Gresham developed cancer and C. S. Lewis's deep Christian beliefs were tested.

C: Anthony Hopkins, Debra Winger, Edward Hardwicke, Joseph Mazzello, Michael Denison   D: Richard Attenborough   AA: '93 Nom: Best Actress (Winger)

SID & NANCY *1986 111m/C (R)*

In the late 1970s Sid Vicious and The Sex Pistols stormed onto the music scene and created the first worldwide punk rock success. Vicious couldn't hold on though and the film chronicles his meteoric rise and ferocious downward spiral, culminating with him murdering his girlfriend, Nancy Spungen, and killing himself. You needn't be a fan of punk rock to appreciate this great pic.

C: Gary Oldman, Chloe Webb, Debbie Bishop, David Hayman   D: Alex Cox

SOMEBODY UP THERE LIKES ME *1956 113m/B&W*

Boxing great Rocky Graziano's life, from his poor New York

City upbringing to his stint in prison, to his reign as middleweight world champion, is perfectly portrayed by a young Newman. Considered by many to be one of the greatest boxing films.

C: Paul Newman, Pier Angeli, Everett Sloane, Eileen Heckart, Sal Mineo   D: Robert Wise

STAR 80 *1983 104m/C (R)*

Compelling story of Playmate of the Year Dorothy Stratton, a teenager plucked out of a burger joint by a small-time talent scout who fell in love with her and managed her rise to stardom. She became a Playboy centerfold and a promising movie star but as her success increased, her stormy relationship with her manager-husband, played brilliantly by Roberts, spiraled into despair. The end result was tragic.

C: Mariel Hemingway, Eric Roberts, Cliff Robertson, David Clennon, Josh Mostel, Carroll Baker   D: Bob Fosse

TUCKER: THE MAN AND HIS DREAM *1988 111m/C (PG)*

Stylish, slick, and smooth pic of dream warrior Preston Tucker, a man with a vision in 1946 to build the beautiful car America had been waiting for, complete with new features he'd invented, like the "seat belt" and a third headlight that turns with the steering wheel. The big three auto makers in Detroit didn't want any competition and the war was on. Great performance by Bridges as visionary.

C: Jeff Bridges, Martin Landau, Dean Stockwell, Frederic Forrest, Mako, Christian Slater   D: Francis Ford Coppola   AA: '88 Nom: Best Supporting Actor (Landau)

VINCENT & THEO *1990 138m/C (PG-13)*

Robert Altman's vivid, beautifully photographed portrait of the genius painter centers around his relationship with his brother Theo, an art gallery employee who tried to sell Vincent's paintings to a public that wasn't buying. This created tremendous despair for both brothers and eventually drove Van Gogh to suicide and Theo to madness.

C: Tim Roth, Paul Rhys, Johanna Ter Steege, Wladmir Yordanoff
D: Robert Altman

WHAT'S LOVE GOT TO DO WITH IT? *1993 118m/C (R)*

High energy bio of rock and soul star Tina Turner. Her early success, her brutal relationship with Ike, and her ambitious comeback are all detailed and brought to life by the amazing performances of Bassett as Tina and Fishburne as Ike.

C: Angela Bassett, Laurence "Larry" Fishburne, Vanessa Bell Calloway, Jennifer Lewis, Phyllis Stickney   D: Brian Gibson   AA: '93 Nom: Best Actor (Fishbourne), Actress (Bassett)

CHILDREN/FAMILY

THE ABSENT-MINDED PROFESSOR *1961 97m/C*

A college professor/scientist stumbles upon a formula that can make objects fly, flubber. The madcap hijinx kick into high gear when a fiendish villain plots to steal the invention. Includes a hilarious scene where the college basketball team uses the airborne magic during a big game. Disney fun for the whole family.

C: Fred MacMurray, Keenan Wynn, Nancy Olsen, Tommy Kirk, Leon Ames   D: Robert Stevenson

THE ADVENTURES OF MILO AND OTIS *1989 89m/C*

Well received pic about two furry friends (a dog and a cat) and the problems that occur when the feline falls in a river, is swept away, and the dog has to go after her. Live action, but no humans appear.

D: Masanori Hata

ALADDIN *1992 90m/C (G)*

A poor but spirited boy hooks up with a magic genie to fight for the heart of a princess stuck with an evil power hungry monger. The part of the genie was expanded after Robin Williams began working his magic, resulting in a classic performance. Songs include "Arabian Nights" and the AA winner "A Whole New World."

D: Ron Clements, John Musker

ALICE IN WONDERLAND *1951 75m/C (G)*

Classic Lewis Carroll story about a young girl who falls down a hole and winds up in a strange wonderful world filled with zany characters like the Mad Hatter and the Cheshire Cat. As effective on adults as it is on children. Songs include "I'm Late," "A Very Merry Un-Birthday."

D: Clyde Geronomi

BABE *1995 91m/C (G)*

A farmer brings home a pig he won at a county fair and his wife immediately eyes it for a festive Christmas dinner. But his swine, who talks and makes friends with the other barnyard animals, has different plans.

C: James Cromwell, Magda Szubanski V: Christine Cavanaugh, Miriam Margolyes, Danny Mann, Hugo Weaving   D: Chris Noonan

BACK TO THE FUTURE *1985 116m/C (PG)*

Goofball scientist Christopher Lloyd (*Taxi*'s "Jim Ignatowski," one of TV's all-time great characters) builds a time machine out of a DeLorean sports car. His young friend (Michael J. Fox) accidentally blasts off into 1955, where he runs into his then unmarried parents, causing what could be a disastrous rewrite of the future. Fox must make sure his parents fall in love and then must get back to 1985. Fast-paced fun.

C: Michael J. Fox, Christopher Lloyd, Lea Thompson, Crispin Glover

Wendie Jo Sperber, Cameo by Huey Lewis   D: Robert Zemeckis
AA: '85 Nom: Best Original Screenplay

THE BAD NEWS BEARS *1976 102m/C (PG)*

Walter Matthau stars as a hapless little league baseball coach who transforms a team of misfits into a team of winners by recruiting a young female with an incredible curve ball. Excellent entertainment for the whole family with a good message.

C: Walter Matthau, Tatum O'Neal, Vic Morrow, Joyce Van Patten, Jackie Earle Haley   D: Michael Ritchie

BAMBI *1942 69m/C (G)*

The classic tale of a baby deer's upbringing and how he and his friends must deal with the ups and downs of the forest and, inevitably, man. A stunning achievement in every sense of the word. Filled with great songs ("Love Is A Song" and "My Little April Shower") and that scene stealing character, Thumper.

D: David Hand

THE BEAR *1989 92m/C (PG)*

Live action, incredibly filmed tale of a cub who is separated from its ma and pa and finds a grown male Kodiak who it latches onto. The two run into trouble when a pair of hunters begin to track the Kodiak. A great adventure for the whole family.

C: Jack Wallace, Tcheky Karyo, Andre Lacombe   D: Jean-Jacques Annaud

BEAUTY AND THE BEAST *1991 84m/C (G)*

Disney classic with a young pretty girl agreeing to become the companion of "the beast" so her father, who "the beast" has sentenced to death, will be set free. Though his appearance is horrific, his heart is gold, and she finally falls in love with him.

Great songs add to the pleasure. The only animated film ever to be nominated for a Best Picture Oscar as of this writing.

D: Kirk Wise, Gary Trousdale   AA: '91 Nom: Best Picture

BENJI 1974 87m/C (G)

The dog that won all the children's hearts stars in this wacky adventure that has him saving a couple young kids from ruthless kidnappers and, of course, finding puppy love. Entertaining family fun.

C: Benji, Peter Breck, Christopher Connelly, Patsy Garrett, Deborah Walley   D: Joe Camp

BIG 1988 98m/C (PG)

A young boy makes a wish at a carnival's fortune teller slot machine. The next morning the 13-year-old wakes up in a 35-year-old body (Tom Hanks). He runs away from home, lands a job in a toy company, meets a pretty woman, and searches for a cure.

C: Tom Hanks, Elizabeth Perkins, John Heard, Robert Loggia, Jared Rushton   D: Penny Marshall   AA: '88 Nom: Best Actor (Hanks)

THE BLACK STALLION 1979 120m/C (PG)

A terrible storm leaves a young boy and a wild Arabian stallion shipwrecked on an island. Their relationship grows and after they are rescued the boy and the horse start training for a big race. Beautifully done.

C: Kelly Reno, Mickey Rooney, Teri Garr, Clarence Muse   D: Carroll Ballard

BORN FREE 1966 95m/C

Engrossing, heartwarming story of two Kenya wardens who raised Elsa, the orphaned lioness. A sure-fire winner for the whole family. The music and title song won Oscars.

C: Virginia McKenna, Bill Travers   D: James Hill

A BOY NAMED CHARLIE BROWN *1970 86m/C*

Charlie Brown rises through the intellectual ranks in a National Spelling Bee championship where he goes up against a very special girl. Good clean fun.

D: Bill Melendez

THE BRAVE LITTLE TOASTER *1987 90m/C*

A group of household appliances that were left in a summer cottage are led by a spunky toaster on a magical journey to the big city to find their owner.

V: Jon Lovitz, Tim Day, Tim Stack D: Jerry Rees

BUGSY MALONE *1978 94m/C (G)*

Great pic has an all children cast in a comedy-musical about a crime war in 1930s Chicago. Some very good song and dance numbers complete with a big grand finale shoot-out where the machine guns unload whipped cream instead of bullets. Lots of fun.

C: Jodie Foster, Scott Baio, Florrie Augger, John Cassisi D: Alan Parker

CHARLOTTE'S WEB *1979 85m/C*

Hanna-Barbera studios made this tender adaptation of the classic E. B. White story about the relationship between a friendly spider and a shy pig.

V: Debbie Reynolds, Henry Gibson, Paul Lynde D: Charles A. Nichols

CHITTY CHITTY BANG BANG *1968 142m/C (G)*

Wacky genuinely appealing pic with Dick Van Dyke playing a kooky inventor who dreams up a flying car and takes his two kids on a strange adventure filled journey.

C: Dick Van Dyke, Sally Ann Howes, Lionel Jeffries, Gert Frobe, Anna Quayle, Benny Hill D: Ken Hughes

CINDERELLA 1950 76m/C

Wonderfully animated re-telling of the young beauty who, with the help of some magical friends, goes to the ball and rises above her sinful step sisters. Great songs, great pumpkin chariot, great "singing mice."

D: Wilfred Jackson

DUMBO 1941 63m/C

Charming tale of a baby circus elephant cruelly tormented about his gigantic ears. He makes friends with Timothy the Mouse, learns his ears can make him fly, and becomes a star. Includes famous surreal dream sequence with dancing pink elephants and some lovely tunes like "I See An Elephant Fly."

D: Ben Sharpsteen

E.T.: THE EXTRA-TERRESTRIAL 1982 115m/C (PG)

See "Top 100"

FANTASIA 1940 83m/C

Sort of an avant-garde Disney feast with stunning animation behind sometimes furious, sometimes mellow classical music. A lack of narrative structure (there's no real plot), proved a critical dud, but over the years the film has gained an enormous following.

C: Mickey Mouse   D: Ben Sharpsteen

FLIPPER 1963 87m/C

A boy befriends a wounded dolphin and tries to teach his fisherman dad that dolphins should not be harmed. Famous '60s children's film that spawned the television series.

C: Chuck Connors, Luke Halprin, Kathleen Maguire, Connie Scott
D: James B. Clark

THE FOX AND THE HOUND 1981 83m/C (G)

A fox and a hound's friendship is tested when the hound is

trained by a hunter to track down the fox. An engaging story with Kurt Russell and Mickey Rooney taking part in the voice-overs.

D: Art Stevens, Ted Berman, Richard Rich

FREE WILLY 1993 112m/C (PG)

A young boy gets a job in an aquarium and becomes friends with an orca whale. When he learns of the owner's exploitative plans for his new companion, he decides to take action. A great story of friendship, suitable for the whole family.

C: Jason James Richter, Lori Petty, Jayne Atkinson, August Schellenberg, Michael Madsen   D: Simon Wincer

THE GREAT MOUSE DETECTIVE 1986 74m/C (G)

A mouse who is the Sherlock Holmes of the rodent world has a tough fight when he goes up against the devious Professor Ratigan. Horror guru Vincent Price provides the voice of the villain.

D: John Musker, Ron Clements, Dave Michener, Bunny Mattison

HEIDI 1965 95m/C

Famous, charming tale of the reluctant young girl who's taken by her aunt and put to work for a rich family. She longs for her mountain life to return and only her kind grandpa can help. Beautifully filmed on location in the Swiss Alps. A winner.

C: Eva Marie Singhammer, Gustav Knuth, Lotte Ledi   D: Werner Jacobs

HOME ALONE 1990 105m/C (PG)

An 8-year-old boy is left "home alone" when his family leaves for a Christmas vacation in Paris. If that's not enough trouble, two bumbling thieves have their eye on the place and he must fend them off with a variety of "Three Stooges" like skits. One of the highest grossing films of all time.

C: Macaulay Culkin, Catherine O'Hara, Joe Pesci, Daniel Stern, John Candy D: Chris Columbus

HOMEWARD BOUND: THE INCREDIBLE JOURNEY
1993 84m/C (G)

A trio of pets (two dogs and a cat) become separated from their masters and have the adventure of their lives as they try to track them down. Michael J. Fox, Sally Field, and Don Ameche provide the three voices. Remake of 1963 film *The Incredible Journey.*

C: Kevin Timothy Chevalia, Robert Hayes, Kim Greist, Jean Smart, Benj Thall, Veronica Lauren D: Dwayne Durham

HONEY, I SHRUNK THE KIDS *1989 101m/C (G)*

Rick Moranis plays a wacky scientist whose kids accidentally become involved in his shrinking experiment. Smaller than an ant, they're now miles from their house (actually they're in the backyard) and battle obstacle after obstacle to make it to their dad and find a cure. Fast paced with great special effects.

C: Rick Moranis, Matt Frewer, Marcia Strassman, Kristine Sutherland, Thomas Wilson Brown D: Joe Johnson, Rob Minkoff

THE INDIAN IN THE CUPBOARD *1995 98m/C (G)*

A young boy learns that a cupboard in his bedroom has magical powers that can give his toys life. He chooses a three inch Indian as his new friend, but trouble begins when his classmate gives life to a cowboy. Good story of friendship and respect.

C: Hal Scardino, Litefoot, Rishi Bhat, Lindsay Crouse, Richard Jenkins, David Keith D: Frank Oz

INTO THE WEST *1992 97m/C (PG)*

Adults as well as children will enjoy this tale of two young boys and their poor widowed father who are saved from the perils of life by a mystical white horse. A spiritual, sweeping picture, beautifully photographed and wonderfully acted.

C: Gabriel Byrne, Ellen Barkin, Ciaran Fitzgerald, Ruaidhri (Rory) Conroy, David Kelly   D: Mike Newell

THE JOURNEY OF NATTY GANN 1985 101m/C (PG)

A young, Depression era girl is helped by a friendly wolf and a hobo as she rides boxcars across the country in search of her father. Sentimental tender Disney picture was a favorite with the critics.

C: Meredith Salenger, John Cusack, Ray Wise, Scatman Crothers, Lainie Kazan   D: Jeremy Paul Kagan

THE JUNGLE BOOK 1967 78m/C

A jungle boy, raised by wolves, goes through a series of adventures as he must decide whether to stay in the jungle with his life-long friends or move on to the civilized world. Includes some great songs like "Bare Necessities" and "I Wanna Be Like You."

D: Wolfgang Reitherman

KARATE KID 1984 126m/C (PG)

A high school student is harassed by the class tough guys until the handyman who works in his apartment shares his gift of karate and teaches him to believe in himself. Effectively told with solid performances by the two leads.

C: Ralph Macchio, Noriyuki "Pat" Morita, Elisabeth Shue, Randee Heller, Martin Kove, Chad McQueen   D: John G. Avildsen

LADY AND THE TRAMP 1955 76m/C (G)

The age old story of a spoiled rich girl who falls in love with a wild, carefree boy is brought to the canine world in this sweet, much loved romantic tale.

D: Hamilton Luske

LILI *1953 81m/C*

Lovely musical about a 16-year-old French orphan girl who joins a carnival and slowly finds love with a crippled puppeteer. Introduced the hit song "Hi-Lili, Hi-Lo."

C: Leslie Caron, Jean-Pierre Aumont, Mel Ferrer, Kurt Kasznar, Zsa Zsa Gabor D: Charles Walters AA: '53 Nom: Best Actress (Caron), Director, Screenplay

LITTLE LORD FAUNTLEROY *1936 102m/B&W*

A young boy with no father learns he is actually royalty. He's taken to live with a mean-spirited Lord in England and, little by little, melts the old man's cold heart.

C: Freddie Bartholomew, C. Aubrey Smith, Mickey Rooney, Dolores Costello, Jessie Ralph D: John Cromwell

THE LITTLE MERMAID *1989 82m/C (G)*

Ariel is a love struck mermaid who longs to be with the human prince she adores. She's offered the chance by a conniving sea witch who promises to give her legs if Ariel gives her her wonderful voice. Great songs include "Under the Sea" and "Kiss the Girl." Based on a Hans Christian Andersen tale.

D: John Muskev, Ron Clements

LITTLE WOMEN *1933 107m/B&W*

The ups and downs of the lives and loves of four sisters during the civil war is masterfully told in this classic reworking of Louisa May Alcott's novel.

C: Katharine Hepburn, Joan Bennett, Paul Lukas, Edna May Oliver, Frances Dee D: George Cukor AA: '33 Best Adapted Screenplay, Nom: Best Director, Picture

THE LOONEY LOONEY LOONEY BUGS BUNNY MOVIE *1981 80m/C (G)*

A lively collection of Bugs Bunny cartoons that surface in the form of a movie. It's divided into three sections with

Yosemite trying to bring Bugs to the devil, Bugs helping Tweety escape from thugs, and a satire on Hollywood awards programs.

D: Friz Freleng, Chuck Jones, Bob Clampett

THE LOVE BUG *1968 110m/C (G)*

Disney made some great '60s live action films and this is one of the best. When Herbie, a white Volkswagen with human qualities, befriends a race car driver, wild wackiness soon follows. An audience favorite that begat several sequels.

C: Dean Jones, Michele Lee, Hope Lange, Robert Reed, Bert Convy
D: Robert Stevenson

MARY POPPINS *1964 139m/C*

An enchanting nanny (Julie Andrews) with magical powers arrives at the London home of a straight laced banker and teaches the family that with the right state of mind you can do anything. Dick Van Dyke, as her chimney-sweeping love interest, is a non-stop riot. Snappy songs include "Spoonful of Sugar" and "Chim Chim Cheree."

C: Ed Wynn, Hermione Baddeley, Julie Andrews, Dick Van Dyke, David Tomlinson   D: Robert Stevenson   AA: '64 Best Actress (Andrews), Nom: Best Director, Picture

THE MUPPET MOVIE *1979 94m/C (G)*

Kermit the Frog, Miss Piggy, and a few pals head out west in search of Hollywood gold. Kooky energy propels this pic. Filled with goofy songs and crammed with cameos including Steve Martin, James Coburn, Orson Welles, and Madeline Kahn.

D: James Frawley

MY BODYGUARD *1980 96m/C (PG)*

A new kid at a high school has a serious problem with a bunch of bullies who want a daily payoff for "protection." So the boy enlists the aid of a lumbering outcast whose rumored background has made him a cold, feared legend. What begins as a business relationship turns to true friendship. Far above the normal coming-of-age pic.

C: Chris Makepeace, Adam Baldwin, Martin Mull, Ruth Gordon, Matt Dillon, Joan Cusack   D: Tony Bill

NATIONAL VELVET *1944 124m/C*

Elizabeth Taylor and Mickey Rooney star in this lavishly produced pic about a young girl who wins a horse and their blossoming relationship as she trains it for the Grand National Steeplechase.

C: Elizabeth Taylor, Mickey Rooney, Arthur Treacher, Donald Crisp, Anne Revere, Angela Lansbury   D: Clarence Brown   AA: '44 Best Supporting Actress (Revere)

OLD YELLER *1957 84m/C (G)*

Another winner from Disney, this time centering on a boy who brings home a stray dog and the happy adventures he and his older brother have with him. Get out your handkerchief for the ending.

C: Dorothy McGuire, Fess Parker, Tommy Kirk, Kevin Corcoran, Jeff York, Chuck Connors   D: Robert Stevenson

101 DALMATIONS *1961 79m/C (G)*

Two dog owners are shocked when an evil villainess, Cruella de Vil, steals two of their puppies. She plans to make a spotted coat out of them and it's up to a bunch of kooky animals to save them. One of the most commercially successful animated films ever made, it has spawned a live action version released in 1996. Chock full of top-notch songs like "Cruella de Vil" and "Remember When."

D: Wolfgang Reitherman, Hamilton Luske

THE PARENT TRAP *1961 127m/C*

Famous Disney pic about two twins who meet for the first time at summer camp and lovingly plot to shoot a cupid's arrow at their divorced parents. Sweet, funny wackiness.

C: Hayley Mills, Maureen O'Hara, Brian Keith, Charlie Ruggles, Una Merkel   D: David Swift

PEE WEE'S BIG ADVENTURE *1985 92m/C (PG)*

Kooky cult figure Pee-Wee Herman goes on a roller coaster ride of adventure as he searches for his stolen bicycle. Brilliantly colorful sets and a truly cartoon-like style, as well as a few classic scenes (a bar room encounter, the Alamo) make it click.

C: Paul (Pee Wee Herman) Reubens, Elizabeth Daily, Mark Holton, Diane Salinger, Judd Omen   D: Tim Burton

PETER PAN *1953 76m/C (G)*

Enjoyable Disney version of the much loved story about a boy who doesn't want to grow up and his adventures with Wendy, Michael, and John Darling, as they battle Captain Hook in Never Never Land.

D: Hamilton Luske

PHANTOM TOLLBOOTH *1969 89m/C (G)*

Chuck Jones, the Warner Brothers animator and director responsible for a slew of the Bugs Bunny cartoons, directed this feature about a boy who steers into the Land of Wisdom and into the middle of a strange war between numbers and letters. Like the Bugs Bunny cartoons, kids will enjoy it and adults will get the many hidden meanings. Mel Blanc provides some of the voices.

D: Chuck Jones

PINOCCHIO *1940 87m/C (G)*

Disney classic with the famous small puppet brought to life by a magic fairy. Still a puppet, he wishes to be a boy and begins a series of adventures to make his dream come true. Includes some truly frightening scenes like "Pleasure Island" where bad boys become jackasses.

D: Ben Sharpsteen

PIPPI LONGSTOCKING *1973 99m/C (G)*

Children's film about a little girl who's left by herself after her father heads out to sea. She uses her pet monkey and horse to cause innocent mischief throughout the town.

C: Inger Nilsson   D: Ollie Hellbron

POLLYANNA *1960 134m/C*

Hayley Mills stars as the happy, enthusiastic little girl who brightens every life she comes in contact with and turns around a New England town.

C: Hayley Mills, Jane Wyman, Richard Egan, Karl Malden, Nancy Olson   D: David Swift

REBECCA OF SUNNYBROOK FARM *1938 80m/B&W*

Shirley Temple plays a young girl who, against the wishes of her aunt, becomes a huge starlet of the radio waves. A perky little musical which includes Temple's famous performance of "On the Good Ship Lollipop" and her tap dance with legend Bill "Bojangles" Robinson.

C: Shirley Temple, Randolph Scott, Jack Haley, Phyllis Brooks, Gloria Stuart   D: Allan Dwan

THE RESCUERS *1977 76m/C (G)*

Disney fare about two mice who are part of an All-Mouse Rescue Aid Team and their efforts to save a little girl who's been kidnapped by the nefarious Madame Medusa. They are helped by a cast of zany fun-loving characters including Evinrude the dragon fly and Orville the albatross. Your kids will love it.

D: Wolfgang Reitherman, John Lounsbery

RING OF BRIGHT WATER *1969 107m/C (G)*

A city man buys an otter at a pet shop and relocates to the country where he finds a simpler, more truthful meaning to life. Well done pic that's a treat for both children and adults.

C: Bill Travers, Virginia McKenna, Peter Jeffrey, Archie Duncan
D: Charles Lamont

ROOKIE OF THE YEAR *1993 103m/C (PG)*

Kids will enjoy this pic about a young boy who breaks his arm and, subsequently, becomes a pitching sensation for the Chicago Cubs. Light hearted fun that includes a funny cameo by the late, great John Candy as a sports announcer.

C: Thomas Ian Nicholas, Daniel Stern, Gary Busey, Dan Hedaya
D: Daniel Stern

SANDLOT *1993 101m/C (PG)*

A new kid comes to town and learns about baseball from a group of neighborhood boys who have a sandlot team. In the process an everlasting friendship is made. There's also an ongoing battle to get a Babe Ruth autographed baseball away from a junk yard dog.

C: Tom Guiry, Mike Vitar, Patrick Renna, Chauncey Leopardi, Marty York, James Earl Jones   D: David Mickey Evans

THE SECRET GARDEN *1993 102m/C (G)*

A young girl whose parents have just died is sent to England to live with her uncle. She finds a garden at his mansion and works diligently to restore it and its magic changes the lives of everyone around it.

C: Kate Maberly, Maggie Smith, Haydon Prowse, Andrew Knott, John Lynch   D: Agnieszka Holland

SECRET OF NIMH *1982 84m/C (G)*

A recently widowed mouse is in danger and discovers a secret organization of genius rats who help her protect her family. First film from Don Bluth Studios, a company formed by former Disney animators.

D: Don Bluth

SLEEPING BEAUTY *1959 75m/C (G)*
A beautiful princess is put to sleep by a fiendish, hideous queen who's got something up her sleeve. Fortunately, the power of good arrives in the form of a prince. Another model of excellence from Disney and his animators.

D: Clyde Geronomi, Eric Larson, Wolfgang Reitherman, Les Clark

SNOW WHITE AND THE SEVEN DWARFS *1937 83m/C*
See "Top 100"

SWISS FAMILY ROBINSON *1960 126m/C*
A family, shipwrecked on an island, turn it into their own little paradise. But a battle is soon to take place when bloodthirsty pirates pay them a visit. A swashbuckling good time.

C: John Mills, Dorothy McGuire, James MacArthur, Tommy Kirk, Janet Munro, Sessue Hayakawa   D: Ken Annakin

TOM THUMB *1958 92m/C*
The classic Brothers Grimm fairy tale about a spunky boy the size of a thumb whose heroics save an entire village. Great special effects and a terrific story make this a winner for the whole family.

C: Russ Tamblyn, Peter Sellers, Terry Thomas   D: George Pal

TOY STORY *1995 81m/C (G)*
A family is moving and a young boy's toys are worried that they'll be left behind. They need to band together but after the boy gets a spaceman for this birthday (voice of Tim Allen) a rivalry ensues between the astronaut and a cowboy (voice of

Tom Hanks) that may endanger them all. Animated completely by computer.

D: John Lasseter

TREASURE ISLAND *1934/50*

The Robert Louis Stevenson story about a young boy's quest for buried treasure and his battles with nemesis Long John Silver. Great action for the whole family.

1934 - 102m/B&W C: Wallace Berry, Jackie Cooper, Lionel Barrymore, Lewis Stone, Otto Kruger   D: Victor Fleming

1950 - 96m/C (PG) C: Bobby Driscoll, Robert Newton, Basil Sydney, Walter Fitzgerald, Dennis O'Dea   D: Byron Haskin

WEE WILLIE WINKLE *1937 99m/B&W*

Shirley Temple travels with her widowed mom to a new home, a British outpost in India. There she meets her hard-edged granddad and a sympathetic sergeant. Considered to be Miss Temple's best work.

C: Shirley Temple, Victor McLaglen, C. Aubrey Smith, June Lang, Michael Whalen, Cesar Romero   D: John Ford

WHITE FANG *1991 109m/C (PG)*

It's the 1850s and a young prospector in Alaska must brave the treacherous weather with a new friend, a wolf. From the Jack London story. Solid family fun.

C: Klaus Maria Brandauer, Ethan Hawke, Seymour Cassel, James Remar, Susan Hogen   D: Randal Kleiser

WHO FRAMED ROGER RABBIT *1988 104m/C (PG)*

Human detective Bob Hoskins takes on a routine infidelity case between two cartoon rabbits, but it turns explosive when he discovers something much more evil, which puts all the Hollywood "toons" in peril. Jaw dropping, Oscar winning visual effects that mix live-action and animation.

C: Bob Hoskins, Christopher Lloyd, Joanna Cassidy, Alan Tilvern
D: Robert Zemeckis

WILLIE WONKA AND THE CHOCOLATE FACTORY
1971 100m/C (G)

Charley, a nice boy from a dirt poor family, buys a chocolate bar with a golden ticket that allows him to be one of five special children invited to take a tour of the famous Willy Wonka Chocolate Factory. But it's not just any old tour, for owner Wonka has a special plan for one lucky child. One of the best children's films ever made, filled with great musical numbers.

C: Gene Wilder, Jack Albertson, Denise Nickerson, Peter Ostrum, Roy Kinnear   D: Mel Stuart

THE WIZARD OF OZ *1939 101m/B&W, C*
See "Top 100"

THE WORLD'S GREATEST ATHLETE *1973 89m/C (G)*

A down and out coach and his bumbling assistant travel to Africa to visit the coach's homeland. They come back with a tarzan-like man who can run, jump and throw like an olympic superman. Funny, fast moving script and great special effects add up to pleasure for the kids.

C: Jan-Michael Vincent, Tim Conway, John Amos, Roscoe Lee Browne, Dayle Haddon   D: Robert Scheerer

THE YEARLING *1946 128m/C*

A boy's love for a deer is confused by his father's understanding and his mother's anger. A classic coming-of-age story.

C: Gregory Peck, Jane Wyman, Claude Jarman, Jr., Chill Wills, Henry Travers   D: Clarence Brown   AA: '46 Nom: Best Actor (Peck), Actress (Wyman), Director, Picture

ABBOTT AND COSTELLO MEET FRANKENSTEIN
1948 83m/B&W

The wacky comedy duo deliver a crate containing the remains of Dracula and Frankenstein to a wax museum. The monsters wake up and madcap hijinx ensue as Dracula attempts to get Lou's brain into the Frankenstein monster.

C: Bud Abbott, Lou Costello, Lon Chaney, Jr., Bela Lugosi, Glenn Strange   D: Charles T. Barton

ADAM'S RIB *1950 101m/B&W*

Spencer Tracy and Katharine Hepburn team in this comedic classic about husband and wife lawyers who are on opposing sides of an attempted murder case. Judy Holliday plays the knockout blonde being tried for trying to kill her husband's lover.

C: Spencer Tracy, Katharine Hepburn, Judy Holliday, Tom Ewell, David Wayne   D: George Cukor

AIRPLANE *1980 88m/C (PG)*

A bumbling former pilot's attempt to save an airplane from disaster sets the stage for this hilarious lampooning of '70s disaster movies. Loaded with a very high joke-per-minute ratio and some classic scenes including a passenger who fortunately speaks "jive" and a pilot who likes gladiator movies.

C: Robert Hays, Julie Hagerty, Lloyd Bridges, Peter Graves, Robert Stack   D: Jerry Zucker, Jim Abrahams

ANNIE HALL *1977 94m/C (PG)*
See "Top 100"

THE APARTMENT *1960 125m/B&W*

A worker lets his boss use his apartment for secret affairs, hoping it will help his career. The arrangement is fine until he falls for his boss's girlfriend.

C: Jack Lemmon, Shirley MacLaine, Fred MacMurray, Ray Walston, Jack Kruschen D: Billy Wilder AA: '60 Best Director (Wilder), Picture, Screenplay, Nom: Best Actor (Lemmon), Actress (MacLaine), Supporting Actor (Kruschen)

ARSENIC AND OLD LACE 1944 158m/B&W

Two old ladies have a strange favorite pastime; they like to invite gentlemen over to their house, spike their wine with arsenic, and kill them. Then they bury their bodies in the cellar. Their nephew (Grant) finds out about the hobby and is less than pleased. Classic gallows humor.

C: Cary Grant, Josephine Hull, Jean Adair, Raymond Massey, Jack Carson, Priscillia Lane D: Frank Capra

ARTHUR 1981 97m/C (PG)

Dudley Moore plays a happy-go-lucky lush who is about to be financially cut from his father unless he drops the lady he loves (a kooky waitress) and agrees to a pre-arranged marriage. Moore shines as the wacky drunk.

C: Dudley Moore, Liza Minnelli, John Gielgud, Geraldine Fitzgerald, Stephen Elliott D: Steve Gordon AA: '81 Best Supporting Actor (Gielgud), Nom: Best Screenplay, Actor (Moore)

THE AWFUL TRUTH 1937 92m/B&W

Cary Grant and Irene Dunne star as an unhappily married couple who break up so they can find true love with another. They end up trying to spoil each other's new romances and realize their own romantic pairing was meant to be. Great screwball comedy.

C: Irene Dunne, Cary Grant, Ralph Bellamy, Alexander D'Arcy, Cecil Cunningham D: Leo McCarey AA: '37 Best Director, Nom: Best Picture, Screenplay, Actress (Dunne), Supporting Actor (Bellamy)

BACK TO SCHOOL 1986 96m/C (PG-13)

Rodney Dangerfield plays a self-made millionaire who decides to fulfill a life long dream of getting a college diploma. Hilarity begins when he enters the same school as his son. Great cameos by Sam Kinison and Kurt Vonnegut, Jr.

C: Rodney Dangerfield, Keith Gordon, Robert Downey, Jr., Sally Kellerman   D: Alan Metter

BANANAS 1971 82m/C (PG)

Woody Allen stars in this film about an invention tester who becomes a South American revolutionary after a pretty young woman arrives at his door with a petition for the cause. Classic scenes, including Woody the mercenary ordering a few thousand egg salad sandwiches to go for his troops and Howard Cosell doing a play by play sex commentary.

C: Woody Allen, Louise Lasser, Carlos Montalban, Howard Cosell, Charlotte Rae (and a bit part by Sylvester Stallone)   D: Woody Allen

THE BANK DICK 1940 73m/B&W

W. C. Fields plays an average citizen who bungles a robbery by accidentally tripping a thief and ends up an esteemed guard. One of his best.

C: W. C. Fields, Cora Witherspoon, Una Merkel, Mahatma Kane Jeeves, Jack Norton, Shemp Howard   D: Eddie Cline

BARTON FINK 1991 116m/C (R)

In 1940s a New York playwright is reluctantly lured to Hollywood by big money and the dream of turning out a masterpiece. He's quickly disillusioned by a bizarre studio head, a maniacal neighbor who gets him involved in a murder, and an eye opening meeting with his idol who turns out to be a drunk. Stylish, eerie scenes highlight this surreal black comedy.

C: John Turturro, John Goodman, Judy Davis, Michael Lerner, John Mahoney   D: Joel Coen   AA: '91 Best Supporting Actor (Lerner)

BEETLEJUICE 1988 92m/C (PG)

Davis and Baldwin play a married "ghost" couple "living" in a cozy, quaint home. When obnoxious real people move in, the spirits must call on "Beetlejuice" a poltergeist-for-hire who can scare any human out of any house. Keaton shines in the role of the hyper off-the-wall poltergeist, and Burton's stylish direction makes it interesting for the eyes.

C: Michael Keaton, Geena Davis, Alec Baldwin, Sylvia Sydney, Catherine O'Hara, Winona Ryder   D: Tim Burton

BEING THERE 1979 130m/C (PG)
A gardener who has not been off the estate in 40 years is forced to leave when the owner dies. He unwittingly becomes the hero of a nation, who mistake his feeble-mindedness for genius. Wrapped up perfectly with a surprise ending.

C: Peter Sellers, Shirley MacLaine, Melvyn Douglas, Jack Warden, Richard Dysart   D: Hal Ashby   AA: '79 Best Supporting Actor (Douglas), Nom: Best Actor (Sellers)

BLAZING SADDLES 1974 90m/C (R)
A convicted criminal is offered a deal of freedom if he agrees to become the sheriff of one of the meanest towns of the west. He does and every western movie cliche is lampooned to the limit in this much loved goofball comedy. Watch for ex-football star Alex Karras punching out a horse.

C: Cleavon Little, Harvey Korman, Madeline Kahn, Gene Wilder, Mel Brooks   D: Mel Brooks

THE BLUES BROTHERS 1980 132m/C (R)
Jake and Elwood go on a "mission from God" and try to put their blues band back together to save an orphanage, destroying the entire city of Chicago in the process.

C: John Belushi, Dan Aykroyd, Ray Charles, Aretha Franklin, James Brown, Carrie Fisher   D: John Landis

BORN YESTERDAY 1950 103m/B&W
A high-end junk dealer (Crawford) falls in love with a young,

pretty lady (Holliday) but believes she needs to be better educated. So he hires a professor (Holden) to teach her life's finer points, but when the two fall for each other, he learns a lesson himself. Far superior to the 1993 remake.

C: Judy Holliday, Broderick Crawford, William Holden   D: George Cukor   AA: '50 Best Actress (Holliday), Nom: Best Picture, Screenplay, Director

BRINGING UP BABY *1938 103m/B&W*

Grant and Hepburn team up in one of the best films ever made. The madcap hilarity never stops as Grant, playing a professor, is targeted for love by Hepburn and her pet, a baby leopard.

C: Katharine Hepburn, Cary Grant, May Robson, Charlie Ruggles, Walter Catlett   D: Howard Hawks

BROADWAY DANNY ROSE *1984 85m/B&W (PG)*

Allen plays Rose, a down and out good-hearted talent scout who strikes it big with a new singing sensation. But it's more trouble than it's worth when his star falls for a mobster's girl, and the mobster mistakes Rose for the love struck Romeo.

C: Woody Allen, Mia Farrow, Nick Apollo Forte, Sandy Baron, Milton Berle   D: Woody Allen

BULLETS OVER BROADWAY *1994 100m/C (R)*

Classic comedy has Cusack in the role of a Broadway writer/director whose play is backed by a mobster on the condition his girl (who happens to be a horrible actress) has a major role. The play has huge script problems until the girl's bodyguard/thug feeds a reluctant, but appreciative Cusack good rewrites on the sly. The question of who's the real artist is answered with flawless comic/tragic consequences.

C: John Cusack, Dianne Wiest, Chazz Palminteri, Jennifer Tilly   AA: '94 Best Supporting Actress (Wiest), Nom: Best Original Screenplay, Supporting Actress (Tilly), Supporting Actor (Palminteri)

CADDYSHACK *1980 99m/C (R)*

Michael O'Keefe plays a caddy who's gearing up for the course College Scholarship Tournament. He's surrounded by the course locals who include a deranged, psychotic groundskeeper (Murray - "it's in the hole"), a mellow playboy (Chase), the obnoxious Country Club president (Knight) and a loud mouth, but likeable, billionaire (Dangerfield). Classic scenes including Chase checking out Murray's living quarters and Murray eyeing some female golfers.

C: Chevy Chase, Rodney Dangerfield, Ted Knight, Michael O'Keefe, Bill Murray   D: Harold Ramis

THE CAMERAMAN *1928 78m/B&W*

Buster Keaton plays a photographer who believes he can win the heart of a secretary if he bags an impressive photo opportunity. He gets the shot, but an organ grinder's monkey makes off with the footage.

C: Buster Keaton, Marceline Day, Harold Goodwin, Harry Gribbon   D: Edward Sedgwick

CITY LIGHTS *1931 86m/B&W*

See "Top 100"

THE COURT JESTER *1956 101m/C*

A comedy classic with Danny Kaye as a former clown who impersonates a court jester so he can learn the evil king's secrets and, along with a band of outlaws, dethrone the fiendish tyrant. Loaded with songs, dances, and endless jokes. Kaye's shining moment.

C: Danny Kaye, Glynis Johns, Basil Rathbone, Angela Lansbury, Cecil Parker, John Carradine   D: Norman Panama, Melvin Frank

CROCODILE DUNDEE *1986 98m/C (PG-13)*

A female reporter brings an Australian "cowboy" to New York

City for a magazine story. His out-of-place-in-the-big-city charm causes comic mishaps and endears him to everyone he meets, including her. First rate romantic comedy.

C: Paul Hogan, Linda Kozlowski, John Meillon, David Gulpill, Mark Blum   D: Peter Faiman   AA: '86 Nom: Best Original Screenplay

DR. STRANGELOVE OR HOW I LEARNED TO STOP WORRYING AND LOVE THE BOMB *1964 93m/B&W*
See "Top 100"

DUCK SOUP *1933 70m/B&W*
See "Top 100"

EDUCATING RITA *1983 110m/C (PG)*
Critically acclaimed pic about an undereducated hairdresser who hires an alcoholic English professor to show her the literary light. What results is an equal exchange of inspiring lessons as she learns the classics and he learns to appreciate life.

C: Michael Caine, Julie Walters, Michael Williams, Maureen Lipman   D: Lewis Gilbert   AA: '83 Nom: Best Actor (Caine), Actress (Walters), Adapted Screenplay

FAST TIMES AT RIDGEMONT HIGH *1982 91m/C (R)*
A group of high school seniors undergo all of the nerve racking rituals associated with everyday teenage life. What could have been just another teen sex comedy is transformed into a hilarious coming-of-age pic by an excellent script and top notch performances by a half dozen future stars.

C: Sean Penn, Jennifer Jason Leigh, Judge Reinhold, Phoebe Cates, Eric Stoltz, Forest Whitaker, Anthony Edwards, Robert Romanus, Brian Backer, Ray Walston   D: Amy Heckerling

FATHER OF THE BRIDE *1950 94m/C*
Spencer Tracy stars as the on-edge father who must go through the exciting, but nerve wracking rigors of preparing

for his only daughter's wedding.

C: Spencer Tracy, Elizabeth Taylor, Joan Bennett, Billie Burke, Leo G. Carroll, Don Taylor   D: Vincente Minnelli

FERRIS BUELLER'S DAY OFF *1986 103m/C (PG-13)*
John Hughes directed this fast paced pic about a high school senior cutting a day of school and the graceful and hilarious way he enjoys his free time, while eluding his parents, his cut-throat sister, and the diabolical principal who's been trying to nab him at something for years.

C: Matthew Broderick, Mia Sara, Alan Ruck, Jeffrey Jones, Jennifer Grey, Charlie Sheen   D: John Hughes

THE FORTUNE COOKIE *1966 125m/B&W*
When a television cameraman is kicked over during a college football game his conniving brother-in-law lawyer convinces him to lie about his injury and file an expensive lawsuit. Lemmon and Matthau are perfect together and later re-teamed in several films, including *The Odd Couple* and *Grumpy Old Men*.

C: Jack Lemmon, Walter Matthau, Ron Rich, Cliff Osmond, Judi West   D: Billy Wilder   AA: '66 Best Supporting Actor (Matthau), Nom: Best Story and Screenplay

FOUL PLAY *1978 116m/C (PG)*
Detective/goofball Chase meets stranger Hawn and the two try to foil a plot to assassinate the Pope. A box office winner with great chemistry between the two leads.

C: Goldie Hawn, Chevy Chase, Dudley Moore, Burgess Meredith, Billy Barty   D: Colin Higgins

THE GENERAL *1927 78m/B&W*
See "Top 100"

GET SHORTY *1995 105m/C (R)*
Low level mobster Travolta is in L.A. looking for a crook who

---

ran out on a debt. He soon decides he has the charisma, style, and intelligence that would make him perfect for the producing side of tinseltown. He begins to hobnob with some big shots and is on his way to Hollywood gold. Filled with endless string of fast moving scenes.

C: John Travolta, Gene Hackman, Danny DeVito, Rene Russo D: Barry Levinson

GHOSTBUSTERS 1984 103m/C (PG)

Bill Murray, Harold Ramis, and Dan Aykroyd play a trio of paranormal researchers living off a government grant. When the well runs dry, they go into business for themselves, blasting demons out of buildings and apartments. Then something truly wicked comes along to give the boys the fight of their lives. Great special effects with some classic scenes.

C: Bill Murray, Dan Aykroyd, Harold Ramis, Rick Moranis, Sigourney Weaver, Ernie Hudson D: Ivan Reitman

THE GOLD RUSH 1925 85m/B&W
See "Top 100"

THE GRADUATE 1967 106m/C (PG)
See "Top 100"

THE GREAT DICTATOR 1940 126m/B&W

Charlie Chaplin's classic spoof of Nazis and the Third Reich has him playing two roles; his own "Little Tramp" and a Hitleresque barber, Adenoid Hynkel. Hitler banned any showings in Germany, and Chaplin was never again seen with his small Hitler-type mustache.

C: Charlie Chaplin, Paulette Goddard, Jack Oakie, Billy Gilbert, Reginald Gardiner D: Charlie Chaplin AA: '40 Nom: Best Picture, Actor (Chaplin), Supporting Actor (Oakie)

HAIL THE CONQUERING HERO *1944 101m/B&W*

A man (Bracken) is rejected from the military, but when he returns home, he's amazed to find a mistake has been made and he's thought of as a hero. One of director Preston Sturges' (*The Lady Eve*, *Sullivan's Travels*) best.

C: Eddie Bracken, Ella Raines, William Demarest, Franklin Pangborn, Raymond Walburn   D: Preston Sturges

HANNAH AND HER SISTERS *1986 103m/C (PG)*

Considered one of Allen's best, this picture explores the romantic lives of three sisters and is highlighted by Caine's hilarious obsession with Hershey and Allen's fear of death.

C: Mia Farrow, Barbara Hershey, Dianne Wiest, Michael Caine, Woody Allen   D: Woody Allen   AA: '86 Best Supporting Actor (Caine), Supporting Actress (Wiest), Original Screenplay, Nom: Best Picture, Director

HARVEY *1950 104m/B&W*

An amicable drunk (Stewart) has an imaginary friend in the form of a six foot rabbit named Harvey. His sister thinks he's lost his mind and wants him institutionalized. But a psychiatrist meets with Stewart and reaches a different conclusion. A touching warm hearted treat.

C: James Stewart, Josephine Hall, Victoria Horne, Peggy Dow, Cecil Kellaway   D: Henry Koster   AA: '56 Best Supporting Actress (Hall), Nom: Best Actor (Stewart)

THE HEARTBREAK KID *1972 106m/C (PG)*

Charles Grodin is excellent as a honeymooning husband who realizes he's made a terrible mistake after he meets a beautiful girl (Cybill Shepherd) on the beach. ("You're in my spot.") Thus begins his obsessive quest to win her heart.

C: Charles Grodin, Cybill Shepherd, Eddie Albert, Jeannie Berlin, Audra Lindley   D: Elaine May

HIS GIRL FRIDAY *1940 92m/B&W*

Classic Hollywood comedy has Cary Grant playing an editor and Rosalind Russell his ex-wife reporter. Together they help a convicted man flee the police and uncover some serious political corruption. Remake of the 1931 pic *The Front Page*, remade in 1974 (*The Front Page*) and again in 1988 (*Switching Channels*).

C: Cary Grant, Rosalind Russell, Ralph Bellamy, Gene Lockhart, John Qualen   D: Howard Hawks

THE IN-LAWS *1979 103m/C (PG)*

Hilarious pic has Falk playing a top secret agent looking to score a fortune in U.S. currency engravings. He picks an unwilling accomplice in straight-laced dentist Arkin, his son's future father-in-law, and the resulting madcap journey for the booty is filled with perfect comedic timing and flawless scenes of non-stop hilarity.

C: Peter Falk, Alan Arkin, Richard Libertini, Nancy Dussault
D: Arthur Hiller

IT HAPPENED ONE NIGHT *1934 104m/B&W*

See "Top 100"

IT'S A GIFT *1934 71m/B&W*

Fields plays the head of a family that seeks a better life way out west. This change results in a series of comic nightmares. Fields at his finest.

C: W.C. Fields, Baby LeRoy, Kathleen Howard   D: Norman Z. McLeod

KIND HEARTS AND CORONETS *1949 104m/B&W*

A young heir fiendishly plans to murder his eight living relatives, all of whom, coincidentally, are planned recipients in a hefty will. Excellent script with Guinness playing all eight of the intended victims. One of the best comedies ever made.

C: Alec Guinness, Dennis Price, Valerie Hobson, Joan Greenwood
D: Robert Hamer

THE LADY EVE 1941 93m/B&W
See "Top 100"

THE LADY KILLERS 1956 87m/C
Two masters of comedy, Sellers and Guinness, play a couple of thieves with plans for the perfect crime that will set them up for life. Unfortunately, a sweet little old lady gets in their way.

C: Alec Guinness, Cecil Parker, Katie Johnson, Herbert Lom, Peter Sellers   D: Alexander MacKendrick

THE LAVENDER HILL MOB 1951 78m/B&W
Guinness stars in this classic about a shy bank clerk who hooks up with a few friends to rob a shipment of gold. They plan to melt it down, turn it into miniatures of the Eiffel Tower, and sell them to tourists. They pull the heist off but a small problem arises.

C: Alec Guinness, Stanley Holloway, Sidney James, Alfie Bass, Marjorie Fielding   D: Charles Crichton   AA: '51 Best Story and Screenplay, Nom: Best Actor (Guinness)

LIBELED LADY 1936 98m/B&W
A newspaper is hit with a libel suit from a wealthy young lady. The editor engages the help of his fiancee and one of the paper's former reporters, and the trio wages a hilarious war. Classic pairing of Loy and Powell.

C: Myrna Loy, Spencer Tracy, Jean Harlow, William Powell, Walter Connolly   D: Jack Conway

THE LONGEST YARD 1974 121m/C (R)
Reynolds plays an ex-pro quarterback sent to prison for stealing his girlfriend's car. Once there, the hard edged warden

makes him put together a team of convicts to play his own semi-pro team made up of guards. Great stuff.

C: Burt Reynolds, Eddie Albert, Bernadette Peters, Ed Lauter, Richard Keil   D: Robert Aldrich

LOST IN AMERICA 1985 91m/C (R)

Everyone who's stuck in a 9–5 job dreams of throwing it all away and hitting the road in search of a non-materialistic "better life." That's why everyone should see this film about a fed up ad executive and his wife who sell all their belongings, buy a mobile home, and head out on the highway for a new life in which they're sure to find the truth. The results are hilarious.

C: Albert Brooks, Julie Hagerty, Michael Greene, Tom Tarpey, Garry Marshall   D: Albert Brooks

MANHATTAN 1979 96m/B&W (R)

See "Top 100"

M*A*S*H 1970 116m/C (R)

See "Top 100"

MIRACLE OF MORGAN'S CREEK 1944 98m/B&W

A free-wheelin' high speed farce that has a town party girl (Hutton) getting into a night of drinking, sleeping with a soldier on leave, becoming pregnant, not remembering any of the episode, and quickly marrying a respectable man to cover her impregnated tracks. In the meantime, the sextuplets are on the way. Very risque for the '40s. Great comment on American morals, considered Sturges' masterpiece.

C: Eddie Bracken, Betty Hutton, Diana Lynn, Brian Donlevy, Akim Tamiroff   D: Preston Sturges

MISTER ROBERTS 1955 120m/C

A navy crew is situated in war free waters during WWII. To fight off the relentless boredom, Lt. Roberts (Fonda) a man who'd rather be in the middle of combat, engages in endless practical jokes. The hard-edged captain (Cagney) has no sense of humor and plots revenge. Lemmon gives a classic performance as the cool con man, Ensign Pulver.

C: Henry Fonda, James Cagney, Jack Lemmon, William Powell, Betsy Palmer   D: John Ford, Mervyn LeRoy   AA: '55 Best Supporting Actor (Lemmon), Nom: Best Picture

MODERN TIMES *1936 87m/B&W*
See "Top 100"

MONTY PYTHON AND THE HOLY GRAIL *1975 90m/C*
The legend of King Arthur is outrageously ripped to shreds complete with a noble knight who guards his territory even after all his limbs have been cut off. Sick stuff, not for all tastes.

C: Graham Chapman, John Cleese, Terry Gilliam, Eric Idle, Terry Jones, Michael Palin, Patsy Kensit   D: Terry Gilliam

THE MOUSE THAT ROARED *1959 83m/C*
Peter Sellers stars as the leader of a tiny country on the verge of collapse. He concocts a scheme to go to war with the U.S. believing that after the inevitable defeat, America will shell out big money for the rebuilding process. The plan doesn't go as expected. Sellers is hysterical in all three roles he plays.

C: Peter Sellers, Jean Seberg, Leo McKern   D: Jack Arnold

MR. BLANDINGS BUILDS HIS DREAM HOUSE *1948 93m/B&W*
Cary Grant plays an ad executive who tires of the rat race and seeks the solitude of the country. So he re-roots his family to the simple life only to find out it's not so simple after all.

C: Cary Grant, Myrna Loy, Melvyn Douglas, Lex Barker, Reginald Denny   D: H. C. Potter

MR. DEEDS GOES TO TOWN *1936 118m/B&W*

Gary Cooper plays a simple man with a down to earth code of life. When he inherits $20 million and donates it to the needy, a reporter jumps on the story to uncover Cooper's true intentions. A classic.

C: Gary Cooper, Jean Arthur, Raymond Walburn, Walter Catlett, Lionel Stander   D: Frank Capra   AA: '36 Best Director, Nom: Best Actor (Cooper), Picture, Screenplay

MR. MOM *1983 92m/C (PG)*

Michael Keaton stars as an auto executive who finds himself without a job. He now must watch the kids while his wife moves up the corporate ladder. Keaton is hysterical as he goes to war against simple household chores, gets addicted to soap operas, and joins the "neighborhood mom gang."

C: Michael Keaton, Teri Garr, Christopher Lloyd, Martin Mull, Ann Jillian   D: Stan Dragoti

MY COUSIN VINNY *1992 120m/C (R)*

Cultures clash when a loud Italian New York lawyer goes to Wahzoo, Alabama, to defend his cousin who's accused of killing a store clerk. Pesci couldn't have been better cast as the brash attorney and Tomei is brilliant as his "big hair" girlfriend.

C: Joe Pesci, Marisa Tomei, Ralph Macchio, Fred Gwynne   D: Jonathan Lynn   AA: '92 Best Supporting Actress (Tomei)

MY FAVORITE BLONDE *1942 78m/B&W*

Good news comes for vaudevillian Bob Hope when his pet penguin snags a big time movie contract. Bad news comes when, on his way out west, he becomes involved with a beautiful British spy, non-stop danger, and foreign intrigue.

C: Bob Hope, Madeline Carroll, Gale Sondergaard, George Zucco, Lionel Royce   D: Sidney Lanfield

MY MAN GODFREY *1936 95m/B&W*

A classic story about a rich girl (Lombard) on a scavenger hunt who needs to find a "lost man" (Powell). She locates what seems to be a bum, takes him home, and later keeps him as a butler. But she's in store for a few life lessons.

C: William Powell, Carole Lombard, Gail Patrick, Alice Brady, Mischa Auer, Eugene Pallette   D: Gregory LaCava

NATIONAL LAMPOON'S ANIMAL HOUSE *1978 109m/C (R)*

The Delta House fraternity has racked up too many demerits and is being thrown out of school so it's up to John Belushi and company to make sure they at least go down in history. This is the film that launched food fights and toga parties and includes a wacky parade finale with a giant cake float that says "Eat Me."

C: John Belushi, Tim Matheson, John Vernon, Donald Sutherland, Tom Hulce, Peter Riegert   D: John Landis

NATIONAL LAMPOON'S VACATION *1983 98m/C (R)*

Chevy Chase is Clark "Sparky" Griswald, all-American dad who decides his family would love to drive cross-county to see the mother of amusement parks, "Wally World." Along the way they get lost in a St. Louis ghetto, pick up a very scary aunt, and engage in other hilarious escapades. ("Sparky" becomes obsessed with a Ferrari-driving Brinkley.) Very funny, quick moving flick.

C: Chevy Chase, Beverly D'Angelo, Imogene Coca, Randy Quaid, Christie Brinkley   D: Harold Ramis

A NIGHT AT THE OPERA *1935 92m/B&W*

The kooky brothers take their zaniness to the opera and come up with an endless parade of gags including the classic contract scene and a skit that has fifteen people in a tiny stateroom. One of their best.

C: Groucho Marx, Chico Marx, Harpo Marx, Allan Jones, Kitty Carlisle Hart   D: Sam Wood

NIGHT SHIFT 1982 106m/C (R)

The film that launched Michael Keaton has the former "Batman" playing a wacky guy who takes a job as an assistant to night time morgue manager Henry Winkler. Keaton, a self-proclaimed "idea man" decides they could make good money turning the morgue into a swinging brothel. Funny stuff.

C: Henry Winkler, Michael Keaton, Shelley Long, Kevin Costner, Pat Corley   D: Ron Howard

THE NUTTY PROFESSOR 1963 107m/C

The best of the Lewis comedies has him playing a shy reserved professor who discovers a potion that transforms him into a cool mannered ladies' man extraordinaire. Lewis, besides starring, also wrote and directed this slapstick fest.

C: Jerry Lewis, Stella Stevens, Howard Morris, Kathleen Freeman   D: Jerry Lewis

O'LUCKY MAN 1973 178m/C (R)

A British coffee salesman (McDowell) goes through one of the oddest, most surreal series of events ever put on film in this rise-and-fall-and-rise story of his success. The pic is set up in vignettes split by great songs by Alan Price. A classic black comedy.

C: Malcolm McDowell, Rachel Roberts, Alan Price, Helen Mirren, Arthur Lowe   D: Lindsay Anderson

PAPER MOON 1973 102m/B&W (PG)

Part drama, part comedy, about a Depression era con man (Ryan O'Neal) who reluctantly agrees to transport a 9-year-old orphan (Tatum O'Neal) across the midwest. She starts to take part in the schemes and becomes better at it than he is.

Ten-year-old Tatum O'Neil became the youngest person ever to win an Academy Award.

C: Ryan O'Neal, Tatum O'Neal, Madeline Kahn, John Hillerman, Randy Quaid D: Peter Bogdanovich AA: '73 Best Supporting Actress (O'Neal), Nom: Best Adapted Screenplay, Supporting Actress (Kahn)

THE PHILADELPHIA STORY *1940 112m/B&W*
See "Top 100"

PILLOW TALK *1959 102m/C*
Fans of the light hearted comedy style of Doris Day will have a great time with this story about a man's primal desire for a woman who can't stand the sight of him.

C: Rock Hudson, Doris Day, Tony Randall, Thelma Ritter, Nick Adams D: Michael Gordon AA: '59 Best Screenplay, Nom: Best Actress (Day)

PLANES, TRAINS, AND AUTOMOBILES *1987 93m/C (R)*
Steve Martin plays a businessman who's cursed by transportation problems as he attempts to make it home to his family for the holidays. John Candy is the happy-go-lucky stranger who tries to "help" him. Includes classic "going the wrong way" scene.

C: Steve Martin, John Candy, Edie McClurg, Kevin Bacon, Michael Mokian D: John Hughes

PLAY IT AGAIN, SAM *1972 85m/C (PG)*
Woody Allen stars in, but does not direct, this imaginative pic about a nerdish man's attempt to woo his best friend's wife. He's helped out by the ghost of "Bogie," who guides him on his romantic quest.

C: Woody Allen, Diane Keaton, Tony Roberts, Susan Anspach, Jerry Lacy D: Herbert Ross

THE PLAYER 1992 123m/C (R)

Dark comedy about a studio executive who receives threatening postcards from a frustrated screenwriter, and the resulting ironic twists that follow. Famous for endless real-life star cameos including Jack Lemmon, Burt Reynolds, Gary Busey, John Cusack, Cher, Bruce Willis, and Julia Roberts.

C: Tim Robbins, Greta Scacchi, Fred Ward, Peter Gallagher, Vincent D'Onofrio, Whoopi Goldberg   D: Robert Altman

PRIZZI'S HONOR 1985 130m/C (R)

Jack Nicholson plays a dimwitted mafia hitman who falls hard for a sophisticated lady who also happens to be a paid assassin. Dark humor.

C: Jack Nicholson, Kathleen Turner, Anjelica Huston, Robert Loggia D: John Huston   AA: '85 Best Supporting Actress (Huston), Nom: Best Picture, Director, Actor (Nicholson), Adapted Screenplay

THE PRODUCERS 1968 90m/C

Very funny story about a con man producer and his accountant who raise much more money than is needed to put on an awful play they're sure will fold, leaving them with a nice payday. The plan goes sour when the show becomes a huge hit, throwing them in a bundle of trouble. Brooks' directorial debut.

C: Zero Mostel, Gene Wilder, Dick Shawn, Kenneth Mars, Estelle Winwood   D: Mel Brooks   AA: '68 Best Story and Screenplay, Nom: Best Supporting Actor (Wilder)

RISKY BUSINESS 1983 99m/C (R)

Stylish comedy has Cruise playing a suburban teenager whose parents go away on vacation, leaving the house in his young curious hands. An innocent spin in his dad's Porsche sparks a series of events that have him falling in love with a call girl (DeMornay), turning his house into a brothel, and being in danger of a bullet from her pimp. Curtis Armstrong is hilarious as Cruise's fun loving "sometimes you just gotta say what the #@$%" friend. Contains Cruise's famous underwear dance scene.

C: Tom Cruise, Rebecca DeMornay, Curtis Armstrong, Bronson Pinchot, Joe Pantoliano   D: Paul Brickman

THE RUGGLES OF RED GAP *1935 90m/B&W*

A Washington rancher wins a butler from a wealthy Parisian, forcing the uptight servant to leave his sophisticated dwelling and re-root in the Washington state wilderness. Considered a classic.

C: Charles Laughton, Mary Boland, Charlie Ruggles, Zasu Pitts   D: Leo McCarey   AA: '35 Nom: Best Picture

A SHOT IN THE DARK *1964 101m/C*

For Pink Panther fans, this is the best. Peter Sellers plays the hilarious Inspector Clouseau, investigating a beautiful maid's involvement in a murder. Although all the evidence points to her, Closeau's lust makes him desperately want to avoid the clues.

C: Peter Sellers, Elke Sommer, Herbert Lom, George Sanders, Bryan Forbes   D: Blake Edwards

SILVER STREAK *1976 113m/C (PG)*

Gene Wilder plays an exhausted businessman who decides to take a leisurely trip by train, hoping to relax. Richard Pryor plays the passenger who involves Wilder in murder, chaos, and madcap hijinx.

C: Gene Wilder, Richard Pryor, Jill Clayburgh, Ned Beatty, Patrick McGoohan   D: Arthur Hiller

SLAP SHOT *1977 123m/C (R)*

Newman is the over-the-hill player/coach of a rag tag hockey team of losers. This suddenly changes when he instructs the players to win by any means necessary. Great stuff.

C: Paul Newman, Michael Ontkean, Jennifer Warren, Lindsay Crouse, Jerry Houser   D: George Roy Hill

SLEEPER *1973 88m/C (PG)*

Woody plays a health store owner who goes in for an operation and wakes up two hundred years later. He falls for a revolutionary (Keaton) and gets into endless mishaps including stealing giant vegetables and a plot to steal a nose.

C: Woody Allen, Diane Keaton, John Beck, Howard Cosell D: Woody Allen

SOME LIKE IT HOT *1959 120m/C*
See "Top 100"

THE STING *1973 129m/C (PG)*
See "Top 100"

SULLIVAN'S TRAVELS *1941 90m/B&W*
See "Top 100"

TAKE THE MONEY AND RUN *1969 85m/C*

Woody Allen's first true feature film (*What's Up Tiger Lily* was a dubbed Japanese spy flick) follows the career of criminal Virgil Starkwell from his humble beginnings to legendary bank robber. A feast of sight gags and slapstick humor that rarely misses. Classic scenes like a sloppily written hold-up note that a bank teller can't read, and a pet store heist foiled by an angry gorilla.

C: Woody Allen, Janet Margolin, Marcel Hillaire, Louise Lasser D: Woody Allen

THIS IS SPINAL TAP *1984 82m/C (R)*

In this hilarious "rockumentary/mockumentary" Reiner follows over-the-hill heavy metal "legends" Spinal Tap on their U.S. tour as they reach for one more hit while clinging to the glory of yesteryear. The critically acclaimed spoof includes the band singing tunes like "Sex Farm," and "Hell Hole" and a hilarious cameo by *Late Show* band leader Paul Shaffer.

C: Michael McKean, Christopher Guest, Harry Shearer, Tony Hendra, Bruno Kirby   D: Rob Reiner

TOM JONES *1963 121m/C*

The rowdy adventures and misadventures of a charismatic young 18th century Englishman working his way up in society while trying to win the affections of beautiful Sophie. Stylishly directed.

C: Albert Finney, Susannah York, Hugh Griffith, Edith Evans, Joan Greenwood, Diane Cilento, Joyce Redman   D: Tony Richardson
AA: '63 Best Director, Picture, Nom: Best Actor (Finney), Supporting Actor (Griffith), Supporting Actress (Evans, Cilento, Redman)

TOOTSIE *1982 100m/C (PG)*

Dustin Hoffman plays Michael Dorsey, an out of work actor who decides to disguise himself as a woman to land a job on a soap opera. Amazingly, he gets the job, and soon "she" is a cult hero, creating major problems for the real Mike Dorsey.

C: Dustin Hoffman, Jessica Lange, Teri Garr, Dabney Coleman, Bill Murray   D: Sidney Pollack   AA: '82 Best Supporting Actress (Lange), Nom: Best Picture, Director, Actor (Hoffman), Supporting Actress (Garr)

TOPPER *1937 97m/B&W*

A married couple die in a car accident and come back as ghosts who are determined to help a stuffy banker, Cosmo Topper, live the good life. Successful flick spawned two sequels (*Topper Takes a Trip* -1939, *Topper Returns* -1941), a TV series, and a 1979 TV movie.

C: Cary Grant, Roland Young, Constance Bennett, Billie Burke, Eugene Pallette   D: Norman Z. MacLeod

WAR OF THE ROSES 1989 116m/C (R)

Great black comedy about a seemingly perfect marriage disintegrating and the extreme lengths (running each over with cars, etc), the ex-lovers go to make each other's lives miserable while the never ending divorce drags on and on. Turner shows her strong comedic talents and Douglas is perfect as the overboard husband.

C: Michael Douglas, Kathleen Turner, Danny DeVito, Marianne Sagebrecht, Sean Astin   D: Danny DeVito

WHISKEY GALORE 1948 81m/B&W

Comedic masterpiece about a "dry" island that comes to life when a cargo of whiskey is shipwrecked off their coast. An obsessive quest to rescue the liquor follows.

C: Basil Radford, Joan Greenwood, Gordon Jackson, James Robertson Justice   D: Alexander MacKendrick

WOMAN OF THE YEAR 1942 114m/B&W

One of the all-time great comedies revolving around the ups and downs of the marriage between a high powered political journalist and a not so high-powered sportswriter. First pairing of Hepburn and Tracy proved to be magic.

C: Spencer Tracy, Katharine Hepburn, Fay Bainter, Dan Tobin, Reginald Owen   D: George Stevens   AA: '42 Best Original Screenplay

WORLD OF HENRY ORIENT 1964 106m/C

Peter Sellers stars as a concert pianist who's being followed all over New York City by two adoring 15-year-old groupies. A fun script with Sellers excellently cast.

C: Peter Sellers, Tippy Walker, Merrie Spaeth, Tom Bosley, Angela Lansbury   D: George Roy Hill

YOUNG FRANKENSTEIN 1974 108m/B&W

Inspired trashing/homage of the Frankenstein classic with Wilder the grandson of the famous doctor. He's left the castle and accompanying business and soon his only goal in life is to build another creature. Things go terribly wrong when assistant Feldman, who's told to bring an "A-B normal" brain goofs up and delivers an "ABnormal" organ.

C: Peter Boyle, Gene Wilder, Marty Feldman, Madeline Kahn, Cloris Leachman, Teri Garr   D: Mel Brooks

CULT

THE ADVENTURES OF BUCKAROO BANZAI ACROSS THE EIGHTH DIMENSION *1984 100m/C (PG)*

Peter Weller plays a surgeon/physicist who decides he needs a little more action in his life. So he travels through a few dimensions of space, becomes a seeker of truth and justice, and rages a war against the evil forces of Planet 10. A tongue-in-cheek pleaser with some great scenes.

C: Peter Weller, Ellen Barkin, Jeff Goldblum, Christopher Lloyd, John Lithgow   D: W. D. Richter

ALL YOU NEED IS CASH *1978 70m/C*

Spoof of the life and times of the Beatles beginning in a small pub and ending up with worldwide fame. Actually very funny with some inspired sequences and cameos from Mick Jagger, John Belushi, Paul Simon, and real life Beatle George Harrison.

C: Eric Idle, Neil Innes, Rikki Fataar, Dan Aykroyd, Gilda Radner, John Belushi, George Harrison, Paul Simon, Mick Jagger   D: Eric Idle

ATTACK OF THE 50 FT. WOMAN *1958 72m/B&W*

A housewife has an encounter with a very large, bald spaceman. Soon after, she begins to grow to enormous heights and has a bone to pick with abusive hubby. Cult classic with Allison Hayes dressed to kill in a very, very, very, large bikini.

C: Allison Hayes, William Hudson, Roy Gordon   D: Nathan Hertz

ATTACK OF THE KILLER TOMATOES *1977 87m/C*

Well-known wackiness that has your everyday tomatoes banding together and killing people. Contains some unforgettably absurd song and dance numbers. Spawned two sequels.

C: David Miller, Sharon Taylor   D: John DeBello

BAD TASTE *90m/C*

Some alien entrepreneurs have traveled to Earth to bring home a fresh batch of the new food sensation: human flesh. But a crackerjack squad of law enforcers known as the Alien Invasion Defense Service sets out to stop the madness. Over-the-top gore. A must for your cult library.

C: Peter Jackson, Pete O'Herne, Mike Minett, Terry Potter, Craig Smith   D: Peter Jackson

BARBARELLA *1968 98m/C (PG)*

Jane Fonda, in an acting stretch from her exercise workout tapes, plays a space vixen cruising the galaxy and acting goofy. Written by Terry Southern, who later penned *Easy Rider*.

C: Jane Fonda, John Phillip Law, David Hemmings, Marcel Marceau, Anita Pallenberg   D: Roger Vadim

BARFLY *1987 100m/C (R)*

Based on the life of late, great poet/writer Charles Bukowski, this pic follows the day to day adventures of the talented writer who would rather spend his time at a bar than in front of a typewriter. Rourke is well cast as the brawling poet and Dunaway, as his drunk sidekick, is on the mark.

C: Mickey Rourke, Faye Dunaway, Alice Krige, Frank Stallows,

J. C. Quinn   D: Barbet Schroeder

BASKET CASE *1982 89m/C*

A young man and his disconnected, disfigured Siamese twin brother (who he carries around in a picnic basket) spend their days and nights vengefully searching for the twisted surgeon who sloppily separated them at birth.

C: Kevin Van Hentenryck, Terri Susan Smith, Beverly Bonner
D: Frank Henenlotter

BLACULA *1972 92m/C (PG)*

An African prince who has been bitten by the infamous fanged monster is now looking for new blood on the streets of L.A. Spawned the sequel *Scream Blacula, Scream*.

C: William Marshall, Thalmus Rasulala, Denise Nichols, Vonetta McGee   D: William Crain

BORN LOSERS *1967 112m/C (PG)*

Tom Laughlin wrote, directed, and starred in this drive-in classic about a peace loving, free spirited Indian named Billy Jack who kicks the crap out of a bunch of bikers and creeps who are bothering his friends. Spawned the better known, but less interesting sequel, *Billy Jack*.

C: Tom Laughlin, Elizabeth James, Jeremy Slate, William Wellman, Jr., Robert Tessier   D: Tom Laughlin

A BOY AND HIS DOG *1975 87m/C (R)*

A young man and his canine roam a post apocalyptic landscape, then the boy is taken in by a village which needs a male to repopulate their dwindling race. He's head over heels about the idea until he learns about the brutal mechanical methods they plan on using. Ouch!

C: Don Johnson, Suzanne Benton, Jason Robards, Jr., Charles McGraw, Alvy Moore   D: L. Q. Jones

THE BRAIN THAT WOULDN'T DIE *1963 92m/B&W*

After his fiancee's head is cut off in a terrible car crash what does a distraught doctor do? He keeps it alive and searches for a voluptuous body to attach it to. A solid cult entry with funny scenes like the doc taping the talkative head's mouth shut.

C: Herb Evers, Virginia Leith, Adele Lamont   D: Joseph Green

BRAZIL *1985 131m/C (R)*

It's definitely not for all tastes, but if you like the bizarre style of Terry Gilliam, you'll enjoy this strange pic about an average clerk lost in the shuffle of a chaotic future society. He tries to survive, but even the world around him is on the verge of collapse. Visually striking with a cameo from Robert DeNiro.

C: Jonathan Pryce, Robert DeNiro, Michael Palin, Katherine Helmond, Kim Greist, Bob Hoskins   D: Terry Gilliam

BREWSTER MCCLOUD *1970 101m/C (R)*

A boy who lives in the Houston Astrodome is building wings and dreams of one day flying away. He's got a blood thirsty guardian angel who's making sure no one gets in his way and a cop hot on his tail. One of the best of the bizarre cult lot.

C: Bud Cort, Sally Kellerman, Shelley Duvall, Michael Murphy, William Windom, Stacy Keach   D: Robert Altman

BUCKET OF BLOOD *1959 66m/B&W*

Dick Miller plays a sculptor whose secret to his critically praised masterpieces is pouring wet clay over the dead bodies of people he's just killed. Great '60s beatnik mood.

C: Dick Miller, Barboura Morris, Antony Carbone, Julian Burton, Ed Nelson, Bert Convy   D: Roger Corman

CALIGULA *1980 143m/C*

Wacky bio of the Roman emperor who dated his sister and ruled with a sadistic streak, right up to his bloody end. Extremely popular video title, financed by Penthouse owner Bob Guccione.

C: Malcolm McDowell, John Gielgud, Peter O'Toole, Helen Mirren
D: Tinto Brass

CANNIBAL WOMEN IN THE AVOCADO JUNGLE OF DEATH *1989 90m/C (PG-13)*

Tweed stars as an uptight feminist anthropologist who travels to the jungle with a goofy female assistant and a male chauvinist guide in search of a famous tribe of cannibalistic woman who eat their male partners. Tweed has a definite gift for comedy and makes it all worthwhile.

C: Shannon Tweed, Adrienne Barbeau, Karen Mistal, Barry Primus, Bill Maher   D: J. D. Athens

CARNIVAL OF SOULS *1962 80m/B&W*

A girl driving in her car suddenly skids off a bridge and plunges into the depths of a river. Hours later she surfaces unharmed. She drifts into a church and gets a job playing the organ but has ghoulish, ghost-filled hallucinations. Very weird, effective cult favorite.

C: Candace Hillgoss, Sidney Berger, Frances Feist, Stan Levitt, Art Ellison   D: Herk Harvey

CHEECH AND CHONG'S UP IN SMOKE *1979 87m/C (R)*

The stoned, bungle brothers are on a hunt for the ultimate doobie. They are, of course, joined by madcap sex/rock and roll hijinx. Good, not-so-clean fun.

C: Richard "Cheech" Marin, Thomas Chong, Stacy Keach, Tom Skerritt, Edie Adams   D: Lou Adler

CLEOPATRA JONES *1973 89m/C (PG)*

Take the vengeful tough guy nature of Rambo and mix with Miss Black America. Shake well, watch, laugh.

C: Tamara Dobson, Shelley Winters, Bernie Casey, Brenda Sykes
D: Jack Starrett

CLERKS 1994 99m/B&W

A cashier at a convenience store goes through a series of escapades during his double shift behind the register. Looks and feels like it was shot on a broken camcorder with acting school dropouts, but the story behind the film (it was made for $25,000 in the store where the director worked) and a kooky script has created a curious cult following.

C: Brian O'Halloren, Jeff Anderson   D: Kevin Smith

THE DARK BACKWARD 1991 97m/C (R)

A comedian (Nelson) meets with unending failure until a third arm grows out of his back. Wacky premise is stretched to the limit by director Rifkin and boasts some great art direction and hilarious performances. Contains the only sex scene ever put on film between an average weight male and three 400 pound women.

C: Judd Nelson, Bill Paxton, Wayne Newton, Lara Flynn Boyle, James Caan, Rob Lowe   D: Adam Rifkin

DARK STAR 1974 95m/C (G)

John Carpenter's second film is a spoof on Stanley Kubrick's *2001: A Space Odyssey*. A few astronauts cruise the galaxy, get on each other's nerves, battle a beach ball, and try to talk their computer out of blowing up the space ship. A true cult classic.

C: Dan O'Bannon, Brian Narelle   D: John Carpenter

DEATH RACE 2000 1975 80m/C (R)

Famous cult flick about a car race where the drivers score points for killing pedestrians. Fast paced, violent, gory. One of Sly's first pics.

C: David Carradine, Simone Griffeth, Sylvester Stallone, Mary Woronov   D: Paul Bartel

DETOUR *1946 67m/B&W*

Ann Savage is a female devil-in-the-flesh in this low budget well-crafted suspense flick about a pianist who is on his way to meet his fiance and ends up getting seduced into a dangerous crime. Huge, well-deserved cult following.

C: Tom Neal, Ann Savage, Claudia Drake, Edmund MacDonald
D: Edgar G. Ulmer

ERASERHEAD *1978 90m/B&W*

One of the most bizarrely deadpan films ever made, centering around a weird guy who gets his girlfriend pregnant and becomes the father of a freakish mutant. Lynch style and sensibilities fill every frame. If you like him, you'll love it. If you don't like him, run.

C: Jack Nance, Charlotte Stewart, Jack Fisk, Jeanne Bates
D: David Lynch

FASTER PUSSYCAT! KILL! KILL! *1966 83m/B&W*

Aggressive go-go dancers hang out in the desert, drag racing and talking shop. It doesn't take long before they're in the middle of murder and mayhem with some lust thrown in. As always, Myer uses "big" girls. His best pic.

C: Tura Satana, Haji, Lori Williams, Susan Bernard, Stuart Lancaster
D: Russ Meyer

FRITZ THE CAT *1972 77m/C (X)*

An x-rated cartoon about a cool hip cat who goes through free love and all the other "groovy" fads of the '60s. Based on Robert Crumb's underground comic book character. (See Documentary, *Crumb* for Robert Crumb's hilarious opinion of Bakshi's film.)

D: Ralph Bakshi

GUN CRAZY *1949 87m/B&W*

There was a movie made with Drew Barrymore in 1992 entitled *Gun Crazy*. It's very bad. This is the original. It's very good. A pistol lovin' man meets a trigger happy girl at a wild west show. They get married but when the money runs out she pulls him into a "Bonnie and Clyde" lifestyle. Stylishly cool.

C: Peggy Cummins, John Dall, Berry Kroeger, Morris Carnovsky, Anabel Shaw   D: Joseph H. Lewis

HEAD *1968 86m/C (G)*

The only film the Monkees ever made has no real plot but enough energy and crazy ideas to make it fly. Jack Nicholson stars and co-wrote with director Bob Rafelson (*Five Easy Pieces*). The Monkees perform half a dozen songs, including the psychedelic "The Porpoise Song." Watch for Frank Zappa.

C: Peter Tork, Mickey Dolenz, Davy Jones, Michael Nesmith, Frank Zappa, Annette Funicello   D: Rafelson

HEATHERS *1989 102m/C (R)*

Snobbish clique of high school girls, all named Heather, bark up the wrong tree when they infuriate a non-Heather girl. Her loner boyfriend begins to kill them off, making it look like a rash of suicides. Dark pic with some great lines like "we better motor if we want to make that funeral" and "**** me gently with a chainsaw."

C: Winona Ryder, Christian Slater, Kim Walker, Shannen Doherty, Lisanne Falk   D: Michael Lehmann

THE HOUSE ON TOMBSTONE HILL *1990 85m/C*

Some new homeowners smash an old tombstone in the backyard and wake up the ghost of the old hag who use to own the place. The resulting mayhem includes a guy getting chopped in half in a window, an old lady beating the crap out of two young men, and a screwdriver entering one ear and coming out the other. Fun for the whole family.

C: Mark Zobian, Victor Verhaege, John Cerna, Doug Gibson, Naomi

Kooker, Eugene Sautner, Sarah Newhouse   D: Jim Riffel

JOHNNY GUITAR *1953 110m/C*

Riotous western has the girls brandishing the weapons and the men looking on. Saloon keeper Crawford and lynch-hungry McCambridge fight with fire in their eyes and the pain of love in their hearts. Cult Hall of Fame.

C: Joan Crawford, Ernest Borgnine, Sterling Hayden, Mercedes McCambridge, Scott Brady   D: Nicholas Ray

LITTLE SHOP OF HORRORS *1960 70m/B*

A wimpy florist shop worker crossbreeds seeds and stumbles onto a plant that turns the shop into a local tourist attraction. To keep the action alive, the young man must constantly feed the "flower," which poses a problem since it only dines on humans. Corman classic shot in three days and includes famous cameo by Jack Nicholson.

C: Jackie Joseph, Jonathan Haze, Mel Welles, Jack Nicholson, Dick Miller   D: Roger Corman

MAN OF FLOWERS *1984 91m/C*

Bizarre tale about a strange reclusive collector of art and flowers who pays women to undress but for some odd reason can't look at them completely naked.

C: Norman Kaye, Alyson Best, Chris Haywood, Sarah Walker, Julia Blake   D: Paul Cox

MEET THE FEEBLES *1990 90m/C*

A kind of grown up, burnt out, drug crazed *Sesame Street* with an all puppet cast, some having severe depression and alcohol problems. Crazy, inspired pic with a very beyond-the-limit ending. From the director of *Bad Taste* and *Heavenly Creatures*.

D: Peter Jackson

MONDO CANE *1963 105m/C (R)*

Bizarre behavior from around the world, including that much loved peculiarity cannibalism, is the centerpiece for this shockumentary. The first of its kind.

D: Gualtiero Jacopetti

MOTHRA *1962 101m/C*

An enormous caterpillar combs Tokyo in search of two insect-size princesses. Frustrated at its lack of success, it later metamorphoses into a giant evil moth. Weird, hilarious, of the "must-be-seen-to-be-believed" variety.

C: Yumi Ito, Frankie Sakai, Lee Kresel, Emi Ito   D: Inoshiro Honda

NAKED LUNCH *1991 117m/C (R)*

A drug induced locale called Interzone is the setting for this twisted story filled with bizarre visuals like a typewriter turning into huge insect and Judy Davis shooting up bug repellent. Based on William S. Burroughs' autobiographical novel and contains many characters resembling Beat Generation writers like Allen Ginsberg and Jack Kerouac.

C: Peter Weller, Judy Davis, Ian Holm, Julian Sands, Roy Scheider
D: David Cronenberg

NIGHT OF THE DAY OF THE DAWN OF THE SON OF THE BRIDE OF THE RETURN OF THE REVENGE OF THE TERROR OF THE ATTACK OF THE EVIL, MUTANT, HELLBOUND, ZOMOFIED, FLESH-EATING LIVING DEAD, PART II *1992 90m/B&W/C*

This is the perfect pic to take out during a party and pop into the VCR. You'll soon have a small crowd around the TV. Writer/director Mason took George Romero's classic horror pic, *Night Of The Living Dead*, wiped out the soundtrack, and redubbed it a comedy. Some classic scenes include a high energy argument about who's going to drive through the zombies to pick up a pizza and Duane Jones' rap-like sex plea to Judith O'Dea.

C: Judith O'Dea, Duane Jones, Karl Hardman, D. Adam Young, E. K. Sautner   D: Lowell Mason

OH DAD, POOR DAD (MOMMA'S HUNG YOU IN THE CLOSET AND I'M FEELING SO SAD) *1967 86m/C*

A woman takes her son on vacation to a tropical island and brings along her husband who's dead and in a coffin. More bodies soon follow.

C: Rosalind Russell, Robert Morse, Barbara Harris, Hugh Griffith, Lionel Jeffries, Jonathan Winters   D: Richard Quine

PERFORMANCE *1970 104m/C (R)*

Oddly appealing dark thriller about a criminal on the run who takes refuge in a house inhabited by a weird rock star (Jagger) and his two strange girlfriends.

C: James Fox, Mick Jagger, Anita Pallenberg   D: Donald Cammell, Nicholas Roeg

PINK FLAMINGOS *1973 85m/C*

Why would anyone want to eat dog excrement? Why would anyone else want to watch? Both these questions remain unsolved but play an important role in this sick pic. Divine, a three hundred pound transvestite, enters the "World's Filthiest Person" contest and performs the aforementioned act.

C: Divine, David Lochary, Mary Vivian Pearce, Danny Mills, Mink Stole   D: John Water

PLAN 9 FROM OUTER SPACE *1956 78m/B&W*

It was made over forty years ago and still no one can make sense out of it. Some aliens try to resurrect graveyard corpses to take over the world. The director's wife's doctor, who took over for a dead Lugosi, walks around with a cape covering his face to give the impression Lugosi starred in the whole film. Considered the worst picture ever made, complete with the paper plate flying saucers.

C: Bela Lugosi, Tor Johnson, Lyle Talbot, Vampira, Gregory Walcott
D: Edward D. Wood, Jr.

PRETTY POISON 1968 89m/C

"Psycho" star Perkins plays a whacked out arsonist who picks a sexy high school girl to help his vengeful plans of burning down a building. He soon finds out she's got a fire inside for something else. Weld, like Perkins, is great.

C: Anthony Perkins, Tuesday Weld, Beverly Garland, John Randolph, Dick O'Neill   D: Noel Black

ROCK 'N' ROLL HIGH SCHOOL 1979 94m/C (PG)

A new principal is trying to turn the high school into a boot camp but one of the students fights this by playing her Ramones tunes as loud as they go and rallying the students to rebel. High energy romp with lots of Ramones tunes like "Teenage Lobotomy" and "I Wanna Be Sedated."

C: The Ramones, P. J. Soles, Vincent Van Patten, Clint Howard, Mary Woronov, Paul Bartel   D: Allan Arkush

SANTA CLAUS CONQUERS THE MARTIANS 1964 80m/C

This Christmas classic, complete with child star Zadora, will add just the right touch to your cozy yuletide festivities. Old Kris Kringle and two kids have been kidnapped by martians who want him to bring his cheer to their planet. Ho-Ho-Ho.

C: John Call, Pia Zadora, Leonard Hicks, Vincent Beck, Victor Stiles
D: Nicholas Webster

THEY CALL ME TRINITY 1972 110m/C (G)

Western cult classic with two bumbling cowpokes who team up to protect a bunch of Mormons from ruthless outlaws.

Great fight scenes with lumbering giant Spencer doing in the villains with stiff swats to the head. Lampoons all the western cliches with hilarious success.

C: Terence Hill, Bud Spencer, Farley Granger, Steffen Zacharias
D: E. B. Clucher

WHAT'S UP, TIGER LILY? *1966 90m/C*

Woody Allen, in his directional debut, takes a Japanese spy flick, wipes out the soundtrack, and redubs it as a comedy. The results are hilarious. Instead of a serious "James Bond" plot, he has the spies killing each other over a top secret recipe for egg salad.

C: Woody Allen, Tatsuya Mihashi, Mie Hama, Akiko Wakabayashi
D: Woody Allen, Senkichi Taniguhi

WILLARD *1971 96m/C (PG)*

Willard is a teenager who has a deep love for rats. They love him too and so, when he needs them to kill neighborhood bullies and other annoying people, the army of rodents are more than happy to sharpen up their teeth and oblige. Creepy box-office smash spawned the sequel *Ben* whose theme song of the same title was a number one hit for Michael Jackson.

C: Bruce Davison, Ernest Borgnine, Elsa Lanchester, Sondra Locke
D: Daniel Mann

DOCUMENTARY

AMERICAN DREAM *1988 100m/C*

Barbara Kopple's powerful look at the strike of the Hormel Plant workers (makers of ham and other meat products) in Austin, Minnesota, and how it tore the city apart and, in some tragic cases, pitted brother against brother.

D: Barbara Kopple   AA: '88 Best Feature Documentary

ATOMIC CAFE *1982 92m/C*

Great tongue-in cheek study of America's obsession with the A-bomb using 1940s and 1950s government films and newsreels. A must see for anyone into political propaganda.

D: Kevin Rafferty

BASEBALL: A FILM BY KEN BURNS *1994*
18hrs/C/B&W

Engrossing history of American pastime from its birth in the mid 1800s to its present state. Includes amazing, never-before-seen footage and interviews. Divided into nine episodes.

D: Ken Burns

BEST BOY *1979 111m/C*

Three years in the life of Philly, a retarded man who, turning 52 years old, begins to make preparations to move out of his parent's home and live on his own.

D: Ira Wohl   AA: '79 Best Feature Documentary

BLAST 'EM *1992 100m/C*

Hilarious and sometimes frightening depiction of the world's fixation with fame and one paparazzi's obsession to get the first and very valuable picture of Michael J. Fox with his newborn baby. Look for "Queerdonna," the Material Girl's most loyal fan until she belittled his "ridiculous, pathetic worship." Now he dresses in drag and does a show lampooning her.

D: Joe Blaziolli

BROTHER'S KEEPER *1992 104m/C*

Involving story of five elderly brothers who had lived together in a small farmhouse all their lives. One morning one of them was found dead in bed and one of the brothers was brought to trial for a murder he claimed he didn't commit. Named to over

50 critics "top ten of the year" lists.

D: Bruce Sinofsky, Joe Berlinger

THE BURDEN OF DREAMS 1982 94m/C

Les Blank's chronicling of Werner Herzog's *Fitzcarraldo*, a movie filmed in the jungle with behind-the-scenes tragedies like hurricanes, angry tribes, horrific diseases, and endless other brutalities. This is the film where the maddening Herzog had his crew actually carry a ship up a mountain. Classic.

D: Les Blank

CHUCK BERRY: HAIL! HAIL! ROCK 'N' ROLL 1987 121m/C (PG)

An entertaining portrait of the granddaddy of rock and roll with performance clips and behind-the-scenes footage. Interviews include Eric Clapton, John Lennon, Linda Ronstadt, and Bruce Springsteen.

D: Taylor Hackford

THE CIVIL WAR 1990 680m/C/B&W

Incredibly in-depth history of America's bloodiest war, told almost exclusively through photos and voice-overs. Divided into nine episodes. Critically lauded.

D: Ken Burns

CRUMB 1994 115m/C

Mesmerizing and bizarre portrait of cartoon artist and American pop culture hater Robert Crumb who created, among other characters, Fritz the Cat and the "Keep on Truckin" logo of the early '70s. Insight into his highly controversial, valuable early work, his sexual preference and his dysfunctional family members leave the viewer with an experience not easily forgotten. One of the greatest documentaries ever made.

D: Terry Zweigoff

ENDLESS SUMMER 1966 90m/C

Beautifully made surfing documentary revolving around two "dudes" traveling to beaches all over the world looking for that perfect wave. Critically hailed.

D: Bruce Brown

GATES OF HEAVEN 1978 85m/C

Hilarious deadpan look at one man's emotional attempt to set up a pet cemetery and the other bizarre players in, what turned out for him, to be a nightmare. Includes interviews with many dog owners about proper burial procedures, and a startling talk with a businessman whose attitude on the dead animals is extremely frank and a little less than polite.

D: Errol Morris

GIMME SHELTER 1970 91m/C

The Rolling Stones perform some of their classic tunes ("Gimme Shelter," "Under My Thumb") at the 1969 free concert at the Altamont Speedway outside San Francisco. This is the one that ended up causing a riot and the murder of a civilian by a Hell's Angel.

D: David Maysles

HARLAN COUNTY U.S.A. 1976 103m/C (PG)

This chronicling of a mining strike in Kentucky in which families are ultimately torn apart is disturbing, tragic, and powerful.

D: Barbara Kopple   AA: '76 Best Feature Documentary

HEARTS AND MINDS 1974 110m/C

Strong, thought-provoking look at the Vietnam War using no narration, simply cutting from shots of war torn ravaged Vietnam to interviews with military officers.

D: Peter Davis   AA: '74 Best Feature Documentary

HEARTS OF DARKNESS *1992 96m/C (R)*

A behind-the-scenes masterpiece that chronicles the making of *Apocalypse Now, Hearts of Darkness* is considered by some critics to be better than the actual movie. Francis Ford Coppola's dealings with devastating hurricanes, Martin Sheen's heart attack, Dennis Hopper's drug problem and Marlon Brando's bizarre eccentricities are all captured here in 96 minutes of mind-boggling movie making. If you've never seen *Apocalypse Now*, watch it, and then watch *Hearts of Darkness*. You'll never look at the movies the same way again.

D: Fax Bahr, George Hickenlooper

THE HECK WITH HOLLYWOOD *1972 70m/C*

Riveting, often hilarious look at the world of independent filmmakers and what it takes not only to get a film made but to get it sold and seen. Follows three directors on their road to success or failure. Not to be missed by high school graduates heading off to film school.

D: Doug Block

THE HELLSTROM CHRONICLE *1971 90m/C (G)*

Using amazing close-up photography of insects and narration by "Dr. Hellstrom," director Walen Green examines the theory of insects taking over human life.

D: Walon Green   AA: '71 Best Feature Documentary

HOOP DREAMS *1994 171m/C (PG-13)*

Engrossing, expertly made pic chronicles the struggles of two inner-city high school students as they go through four years of basketball with dreams of college scholarships and the NBA. Film includes in-depth look at both student's families and surrounding characters which include an imprisoned father, a pregnant high school girlfriend, a hardcore win-or-die coach, and an older brother who was an all-state basketball player but lost his chance for the NBA and now works as a security guard. Named to over 100 critics "ten best of year" lists.

C: Arthur Agee, William Gates   D: Steve James

HOTEL TERMINUS: THE LIFE AND TIMES OF KLAUS BARBIE *1988 267m/C*

Brutally disturbing look at Klaus Barbie, the notorious SS captain known as the "Butcher of Lyon" who tortured and killed thousands of innocent Jews. He escaped to Bolivia but, decades later, was brought to France to stand trial.

D: Marcel Ophuls   AA: '88 Best Feature Documentary

IMAGINE: JOHN LENNON *1988 105m/C*

A combination of interviews, his life with the Beatles, and never before seen home movies combined to give an insightful, thoroughly interesting look at musician John Lennon, from his upbringing to his tragic murder.

D: Andrew Solt

INCIDENT AT OGLALA: THE LEONARD PELTIER STORY *1992 90m/C (PG)*

During a 1975 "incident" at the Pine Ridge Indian Reservation in South Dakota, two FBI men were allegedly shot by Leonard Peltier, an American Indian Movement leader. Apted makes a very worthy case for a retrial of Peltier, who many believe was framed and is serving two consecutive life prison terms.

D: Michael Apted

KOYAANISQATSI *1987 83m/C*

The only movie to tell the story of man, from prehistoric times to modern life, without using one word of dialogue. It even makes a brutal comment on man's misuse of progress using absolutely stunning visuals (it's one of the most beautifully photographed films every produced) of natural and man-made scenery. The title comes from a Hopi Indian word meaning "Life out of balance, life out of control."

D: Godfrey Reggio

LET IT BE *1970 80m/C*

The final months of the Beatles are chronicled as they record an album and, though not scripted, realize they've grown too far apart to ever come back together. Excellent soundtrack (it won the Academy Award) makes it work. Includes famous rooftop performance.

D: Mark Lindsay-Hogg

LET'S GET LOST *1988 125m/B&W*

The life and times of jazz trumpet great Chet Baker are examined as filmmaker Bruce Weber follows the drug dependent musician through self-absorbed recording sessions and ego-ridden meetings with family and fans. Baker died a year later. Beautifully filmed in black and white with great Baker music.

D: Bruce Weber

THE LIFE AND TIMES OF ROSIE THE RIVETER
1980 60m/B&W/C

Engaging pic about the women who worked in the factories during WWII. Newsreel footage and interviews are mixed with five actual "riveters" and the result is both heartwarming and insightful.

D: Connie Field

LOUISIANA STORY *1948 77m/B&W*

Engrossing chronicle of an oil company in the Louisiana Bayou and the effect it has on a young boy, his family, and his pet raccoon.

D: Robert Flaherty   AA: Nom: '48 Best Story

MARJOE 1972 88m/C (PG)

Fascinating look at the life of Marjoe Gortner, a preacher who spent the first part of his life spreading the word of God all over the country and later shifted gears to become an actor.

D: Howard Smith, Sarah Kernochan

MEETING THE BEAUTIFUL PEOPLE 1994 85m/C

This fast moving look at fame contains interviews with people who have met or worked with famous figures including a physicist who worked with Albert Einstein, a woman who collects celebrity hair, and a man who has attended over 150 of the "big celebrity funerals." Also contains engrossing footage of Walter Gollender, a talent scout/promoter who's been seeking fame for over 30 years and discusses his "long, hard, torturous climb to this level of obscurity."

D: Jim Riffel

MICROCOSMOS 1996 75m/C (G)

This is a look at the world of insects but it is a look like none you've seen before. Incredible close-ups make butterflies look like angels and beetles look like martians. The cinematography of the insects is so beautiful and technologically advanced that at times it seems like the film was made in a Steven Spielberg special effects lab. An amazing achievement.

D: Claude Nuridsany, Marie Perennou

MOTHER TERESA 1987 81m/C

One of the most loved individuals in the history of the world is poignantly portrayed in this beautiful look into the life of Nobel Peace Prize winner, Saint Mother Teresa. Spiritually uplifting.

D: Ann and Jeannette Petrie

NANOOK OF THE NORTH 1922 55m/B&W

The life of the eskimo is captured in brilliant detail in this picture that became the blueprint for documentaries to come. Includes famous "walrus hunt" scene. One of the best documentary films ever made.

D: Robert Flaherty

THE PANAMA DECEPTION *1992 91m/C*

This burning look at the events leading up to the invasion of Panama show how the Reagan and Bush administration fed a steady diet of misinformation to the mainstream media who, in turn, poured it out to the American public. Filled with disturbing facts and haunting images of war.

D: Barbara Trent   AA: '92 Best Feature Documentary

PARIS IS BURNING *1992 71m/C (R)*

Jennie Livingston's brilliant portrait of a yearly New York City transvestite ball where men dress as women and compete for a grand prize. The pic shows the behind-the-scenes lives of many of the contestants, who are mainly black and Hispanic and documents their dreams, frustrations, and day to day existence.

D: Jennie Livingston

THE PLOW THAT BROKE THE PLAINS *1934–36 78m/B&W*

Pare Lorentz's powerful pic about man's destruction of the Great Plains, namely the farmers who abused the land and created the "Dust Bowl" and the "Oklahoma-Kansas-Nebraska" exodus.

D: Pare Lorentz

PUMPING IRON *1976 90m/C (PG)*

An engrossing behind-the-scenes look at the competition surrounding the 1975 Mr. Olympia competition. Pre-Hollywood icon Arnold Schwarzenegger trains for the contest against Lou Ferrigno, Franco Colombo, and Mike Katz, and is seen as an insanely obsessed competitor who missed his father's funeral because it conflicted with his training. The pic is also famous because it shows Arnold smoking what appears to be a joint. Schwarzenegger recently purchased the rights to the film.

D: George Butler

ROGER AND ME *1989 91m/C (R)*

Michael Moore's potent pic which documents his attempt to question General Motors' Chairman Roger Smith about the unfair closing of three major plants in Flint, Michigan. Though much is tongue-in-cheek, Moore also tackles the serious repercussions of the shutdowns (loss of jobs and homes) with a heartfelt sincerity that makes this film an entertaining wake-up call. Critically hailed.

D: Michael Moore

SALESMAN *1968 90m/B&W*

The American door-to-door salesman is shown on the roller coaster ride of success and failure as a few bible salesman are followed through Florida and New York in the 1960s as they sell their wares. A straight forward, deadpan classic.

D: Albert Maysles, David Maysles

SHERMAN'S MARCH *1986 155m/C*

Director Ross McElwee received a grant from an arts foundation to make a documentary film on General Sherman's historical Civil War march through the south. Around this time, McElwee's girlfriend dumped him so he used the money to document his attempt to find a new love. He kept the historical title intact.

D: Ross McElwee

THE SORROW AND THE PITY *1971 265m/B&W*

A long powerful look at a small French town's resistance

against the Nazis. Though it's over four hours in length, it's always compelling.

D: Marcel Ophuls

STREETWISE 1985 92m/C

A gripping look into the lives of homeless children as they survive by prostitution, pimping, drug dealing, and any other way imaginable. Filmed in the streets of Seattle, Washington.

D: Martin Bell   AA: '85 Nom: Best Feature Documentary

SUPERSTAR: THE LIFE AND TIMES OF ANDY WARHOL 1990 87m/C

Andy Warhol established himself as a force in the art world by bringing commercial art into the world of fine art. The pic reviews his life from beginning to end including the assassination attempt on his life by a deranged female. Interviews with Dennis Hopper, Roy Lichtenstein, and others.

D: Chuck Workman

THE THIN BLUE LINE 1988 96m/C

Errol Morris's incredible examination of the 1977 murder of a Texas lawman and the subsequent conviction of a drifter, Randall Adams, who claimed he was innocent. After recreating the crime, interviewing countless authorities and civilians, and gathering and regathering facts, Morris put together this pic which ultimately freed Adams.

D: Errol Morris

THE TIMES OF HARVEY MILK 1983 90m/C

Powerful look at gay activist, Harvey Milk, and elected San Francisco Mayor George Moscone, and their assassination by Milk's political partner, Dan White. Critically lauded.

D: Robert Epstein   AA: '83 Best Feature Documentary

TWENTY-EIGHT UP *1984 133m/C/B&W*

A group of Englanders have been filmed every seven years since they turned seven and this pic follows their lives and loves as some of their dreams come true and others don't. One, who at 28 became homeless and was living in a bus, talked openly, honestly and insightfully about his life and philosophies, subsequently becoming a cult hero in England.

D: Michael Apted

VINCENT: THE LIFE AND DEATH OF VINCENT VAN GOGH *1987 99mi/C*

The struggles and tribulations which produced some of the greatest artwork known to man comes to light in this exquisite pic. Director Cox mixes Van Gogh's letters to his brother Theo (voiced over by John Hurt) with his paintings and lush photography of natural wonders to achieve a beautifully insightful result.

D: Paul Cox

VISIONS OF LIGHT: THE ART OF CINEMATOGRAPHERS *1993 95m/B&W/C*

Stunning clips from more than 125 of the most famous films in the history of cinema are joined with the directors of photography who discuss how these "visions of light" were achieved. Cinematographers include Michael Ballhaus, Vilmos Zsigmond, and Ernest Dickerson. A feast for the eyes.

D: Arnold Glassman, Todd McCarthy, Stuart Samuels

THE WAR ROOM *1993 93m/C (PG)*

Bill Clinton's 1992 presidential campaign is documented in this behind-the-scenes look at the mechanics of what goes into, essentially, a low down dirty political dog fight. Effective and insightful.

D: D.A. Pennebaker, Chris Hegedus

WHO ARE THE DEBOLTS AND WHERE DID THEY GET 19 KIDS? *1978 90m/C*

Examines the touching story of Dorothy and Bob Debolt, a saintly, married couple who have adopted many children with physical and mental disabilities. The movie shows how this amazing arrangement is handled and the positive power and love of life that these amazing people possess. Truly inspiring.

D: John Korty   AA: '78 Best Feature Documentary

WILD WHEELS *1992 70m/C*

Harrod Blank's bizarre look at a sub-culture of America: people obsessed with turning their cars into strangely beautiful show pieces. Includes a gentlemen whose auto is completely covered with real, growing grass and a man who's plastered thousands of silver dollars to his van. Visually intoxicating.

D: Harrod Blank

WOODSTOCK *1970 180m/C (R)*

The true feeling of the free-spirit, free-love '60s has never been better captured then in this "groovy" showpiece of the famous Woodstock festival in the Summer of '69. Contains concert footage of Hendrix, Joan Baez, Jefferson Airplane, Joe Cocker, and others.

D: Michael Wadleigh   AA: '70 Best Feature Documentary

DRAMA

THE AFRICAN QUEEN *1951 105m/C*
See "Top 100"

ALL ABOUT EVE *1950 138m/B&W*
See "Top 100"

AMERICAN GRAFFITI *1973 112m/C (PG)*

One night in the life of a group of early '60s teenagers as they cruise the strip, listen to rock and roll, and have a burger and fries at the drive-in. But this is a special night since the next day one of them is flying across the U.S. to start college. Great soundtrack.

C: Richard Dreyfuss, Ron Howard, Cindy Williams, Mackenzie Phillips, Paul LeMat, Candy Clark   D: George Lucas   AA: '73 Nom: Best Picture, Director, Supporting Actress (Clark)

AND JUSTICE FOR ALL *1979 120m/C (R)*

The American justice system is brought to its knees in this blistering look at a judge who's on trial for rape and the prosecuting attorney who's pressured to "make a deal." Pacino's "you're all out of order" rant at the end is classic.

C: Al Pacino, Jack Warden, Christine Lahti, Thomas G. Waites, Craig T. Nelson   D: Norman Jewison   AA: '79 Nom: Best Actor (Pacino)

ATLANTIC CITY *1981 104m/C (R)*

A down and out waitress becomes involved with an aging, unsuccessful criminal and the two step into the middle of a stash of cash and all the trouble it brings with it. A gritty realistic portrayal of chasing a dream.

C: Burt Lancaster, Susan Sarandon, Kate Reid, Michael Piccoli, Hollis McLaren   D: Louis Malle   AA: '81 Nom: Best Picture, Director, Actor (Lancaster), Actress (Sarandon)

BAD DAY AT BLACK ROCK *1954 81m/C*

See "Top 100"

BANG THE DRUM SLOWLY *1973 97m/C (PG)*

Touching story about the friendship between two ballplayers, one a star pitcher and the other a catcher who learns he is terminally ill.

C: Robert DeNiro, Michael Moriarty, Vincent Gardenia, Phil Foster,

Danny Aiello   D: John Hancock   AA: '73 Nom: Best Supporting Actor (Gardenia)

BLACK NARCISSUS *1947 101m/C*

Strange story about a group of nuns who are trying to set up a school in the Himalayas, and the conflict they must deal with from natives, physical elements, and their longing for a male who works there. Visually stunning.

C: Deborah Kerr, David Farrar, Sabu, Jean Simmons, Kathleen Byron D: Michael Powell

THE BLACKBOARD JUNGLE *1955 101m/B&W*

Classic story of a caring teacher who comes to a inner-city school and tires to break through to his wild abusive students. The pic opens with the song, "Rock Around The Clock," marking the first time rock was used in a Hollywood picture.

C: Glenn Ford, Anne Francis, Sidney Poitier, Louis Calhern, Vic Morrow   D: Richard Brooks

BODY AND SOUL *1947 104m/B&W*

A young fighter claws his way to the top of the boxing profession, disregarding his self-respect and honesty for win after win. Then he finds out if it was all worth it. One of the best boxing movies ever made.

C: John Garfield, Lili Palmer, Hazel Brooks, Anne Revere, William Conrad   D: Robert Rossen   AA: '47 Nom: Best Actor (Garfield), Screenplay

BOYZ N THE HOOD *1991 112m/C (R)*

First-time director Singleton became the youngest person ever to be nominated for a Best Director Oscar with this amazingly effective coming-of-age film about four black high school students trying to cope with the pressures of an inner-city upbringing.

C: Laurence (Larry) Fishburne, Ice Cube, Cuba Gooding, Jr., Nia Long, Morris Chestnut   D: John Singleton   AA: '91 Nom: Best Director, Original Screenplay

BREAKFAST AT TIFFANY'S 1961 114m/C

Truman Capote's masterful story about the kooky relationship between a young New York City writer (Peppard) and an eccentric ex-country girl turned playgirl. Hepburn is classic as Holly Golightly.

C: Audrey Hepburn, George Peppard, Patricia Neal, Buddy Ebsen, Mickey Rooney   D: Blake Edwards   AA: '61 Nom: Best Actress (Hepburn)

BREAKING AWAY 1979 100m/C (PG)

Uplifting coming-of-age story centers around four friends, all out of college, all without promising futures. Their one hope at filling themselves with confidence for the years ahead lies in a bicycle race they've entered against Indiana University's finest athletes.

C: Dennis Christopher, Dennis Quaid, Daniel Stern, Jackie Earle Haley, Barbara Barrie   D: Peter Yates   AA: '79 Best Original Screenplay, Nom: Best Picture, Director, Supporting Actress (Barrie)

THE CAINE MUTINY 1954 125m/C

See "Top 100"

CASABLANCA 1942 102m/B&W (PG)

See "Top 100"

CITIZEN KANE 1941 119m/B&W

See "Top 100"

THE COLOR PURPLE 1985 154m/C (PG-13)

Alice Walker's Pulitzer Prize winning play is brought to the screen by Steven Spielberg in this tender story of a young

---

black girl who is separated from her sister and forced to marry a man she doesn't love. She relies on strength she didn't know she had to ultimately put her life back together.

C: Whoopi Goldberg, Danny Glover, Oprah Winfrey, Margaret Avery, Adolph Caesar D: Steven Spielberg AA: '85 Nom: Best Picture, Actress (Goldberg), Supporting Actress (Winfrey, Avery), Adapted Screenplay

COME BACK, LITTLE SHEBA 1952 99m/B&W
Shirley Booth is brilliant as a lonely housewife whose spirit is beaten further down by her alcoholic husband and a young pretty boarder. "Intoxicating" performance by Lancaster.

C: Burt Lancaster, Shirley Booth, Terry Moore, Richard Jaeckel D: Daniel Mann AA: '52 Best Actress (Booth), Nom: Best Supporting Actress (Moore)

COOL HAND LUKE 1967 126m/C
See "Top 100"

CRIMES AND MISDEMEANORS 1989 104m/C (PG-13)
See "Top 100"

DAVID COPPERFIELD 1935 123m/B&W
Excellent adaptation of the Dickens novel about an English orphan's adventures as he goes from boy to man during the 1800s. Lavishly produced with excellent performances all around.

C: Lionel Barrymore, W. C. Fields, Freddie Bartholomew, Maureen O'Sullivan, Basil Rathbone D: George Cukor AA: '35 Nom: Best Picture

DELIVERANCE 1972 109m/C (R)
See "Top 100"

DINER 1982 110m/C (R)

A group of friends have frequent "life" discussions at a local diner as they go through the rites of passage into manhood. Touching, realistic, character studies.

C: Steve Guttenberg, Daniel Stern, Mickey Rourke, Kevin Bacon, Ellen Barkin, Paul Reiser   D: Barry Levinson

DO THE RIGHT THING 1989 120m/C (R)

A Brooklyn pizza parlor owner (Aiello) and a black youth with a loud "boombox" are the ongoing, feuding centerpiece that leads to a race riot in Lee's expertly told pic that has both sides believing they're "doing the right thing." One of his best.

C: Spike Lee, Danny Aiello, Richard Edson, Ruby Dee, Ossie Davis, John Turturro   D: Spike Lee

DODSWORTH 1936 101m/B&W

A self-made mogul and his wife take a vacation in Europe which causes a period of reflection in which they question their marriage and their lives. Adapted from the Sinclair Lewis novel.

C: Walter Huston, David Niven, Paul Lukas, John Payne, Mary Astor, Maria Ouspenskaya   D: William Wyler   AA: '36 Nom: Best Picture, Director, Adapted Screenplay, Actor (Huston), Supporting Actress (Ouspenskaya)

DOG DAY AFTERNOON 1975 124m/C (R)

See "Top 100"

DRIVING MISS DAISY 1989 99m/C (PG)

The relationship between an elderly Jewish woman and her black chauffeur is explored against the backdrop of the deep south. Their business arrangement begins a little rough but, after years and years of service, she realizes he's the only real friend she's got.

C: Jessica Tandy, Morgan Freeman, Dan Aykroyd, Esther Rolle, Patti LuPone   D: Bruce Beresford   AA: '89 Best Actress (Tandy), Picture, Adapted Screenplay, Nom: Best Actor (Freeman), Supporting Actor (Aykroyd)

EAST OF EDEN *1954 115m/C*
See "Top 100"

EASY RIDER *1969 94m/C (R)*
What is basically a plotless film has become the definitive picture of the free-spirit attitude of the '60s. Hopper and Fonda play two bikers who head out on the highway in search of themselves. They come across an odd assortment of characters including a jailed Nicholson who ends up joining them in their quest. The ending of this film is absolutely shocking. A box-office smash, Hopper was given carte-blanche by the Hollywood bigwigs. He set out into the jungle to make "The Last Movie," but ran into so many problems that he didn't direct another film for eight years.

C: Peter Fonda, Dennis Hopper, Jack Nicholson, Karen Black, Toni Basil, Robert Walker, Jr.   D: Dennis Hopper

EIGHT MEN OUT *1988 121m/C (PG)*
John Sayles does an incredibly effective job of restaging the events that surrounded one of the most famous controversies in the history of baseball, the 1919 Black Sox scandal, in which eight Chicago White Sox players were accused of throwing the World Series. Sayles portrays writer Ring Lardner. Expertly written with great performances all around.

C: John Cusack, D. B. Sweeney, Perry Lang, Jane Alexander, Michael Rooker, Charlie Sheen   D: John Sayles

THE FISHER KING *1991 138m/C (R)*
A loudmouth deejay who feels responsible for a caller's suicide wanders the streets and meets a crazy homeless man

whose wife's death has destroyed his life. A bizarre, magical journey begins as they both pull each other out of their bottomless pits.

C: Robin Williams, Jeff Bridges, Mercedes Ruehl, Amanda Plummer D: Terry Gilliam   AA: '91 Best Supporting Actress (Ruehl), Nom: Best Actor (Williams), Original Screenplay

FIVE EASY PIECES *1970 98m/C (R)*
See "Top 100"

FORREST GUMP *1994 142m/C (PG)*
A simple minded man comes in contact with a long list of characters who learn that his innocent way of thinking holds the secret to a peaceful life. Great special effects. Swept the 1994 Academy Awards.

C: Tom Hanks, Robin Wright, Sally Field, Gary Sinise, Mykelti Williamson D: Robert Zemeckis AA: Best Picture, Director, Adapted Screenplay, Actor (Hanks), Nom: Best Supporting Actor (Sinise)

GLENGARRY GLEN ROSS *1992 100m/C (R)*
Masterpiece of character study about a group of real estate salesman, all working out of the same office, who are pitted against each other in a 48 hour deadline for job security. Four star script.

C: Al Pacino, Jack Lemmon, Ed Harris, Alan Arkin, Alec Baldwin, Kevin Spacey D: James Foley   AA: '92 Nom: Best Supporting Actor (Pacino)

THE GODFATHER *1972 171m/C (R)*
See "Top 100"

THE GODFATHER II *1974 200m/C (R)*
See "Top 100"

GONE WITH THE WIND *1939 231m/C*

See "Top 100"

GOODBYE MR. CHIPS *1939 115m/B&W*

Heartwarming, uplifting tale about a Latin professor at an all boys school in England. He's shy and his first days are awkward, but as the years go by, he becomes a much loved legend who has the ability to change the students' lives forever.

C: Robert Donat, Greer Garson, Paul Henried, John Wills   D: Sam Wood   AA: '39 Best Actor (Donat), Nom: Best Picture, Director, Actress (Garson), Screenplay

GOODFELLAS *1990 146m/C (R)*

Violent, expertly told story of Henry Hill (Ray Liotta), a mobster who started out parking cars for high caliber gang members, rose to a "successful" level in organized crime, and turned informant when faced with a lengthy prison sentence. Pesci's Oscar winning performance ("am I a clown?") is unbelievable.

C: Ray Liotta, Robert DeNiro, Joe Pesci, Paul Sorvino, Lorraine Bracco   D: Martin Scorsese   AA: '90 Best Supporting Actor (Pesci), Nom: Best Picture, Director, Supporting Actress (Bracco)

THE GRAPES OF WRATH *1940 129m/B&W*

See "Top 100"

THE GREAT SANTINI *1980 118m/C (PG)*

Duvall is the overbearing, hardcore marine officer whose inability to deal with his unrealized dreams makes him take his "commander" attitude home with him and "share" it with his family. Michael O'Keefe is the son who battles his father and tries to make sense of his strange ways.

C: Robert Duvall, Blythe Danner, Michael O'Keefe, Julie Ann Haddock, Lisa Jane Persky   D: Lewis John Carlino   AA: '80 Nom: Best Actor (Duvall), Supporting Actor (O'Keefe)

GREED *1924 140m/B&W*

A dentist tragically loses his business and, with no money or hope (but a manipulating and fiendish wife), falls into a pit of despair, corruption, murder, and greed. Erich Von Stroheim makes a simple plot go a long way, giving us one of the all-time great films, even though a silent film.

C: Dale Fuller, Gibson Gowland, ZaSu Pitts, Jean Hersholt, Chester Conklin   D: Erich von Stroheim

HAMLET *1948 153m/B&W*

Olivier stars in the title role as the Danish prince who seeks to avenge his father's murder. Critically lauded.

C: Laurence Olivier, Basil Sydney, Felix Aylmer, Jean Simmons, Stanley Holloway   D: Laurence Olivier   AA: '48 Best Actor (Olivier), Picture, Nom: Best Director, Supporting Actress (Simmons)

HAROLD AND MAUDE *1971 92m/C (PG)*

See "Top 100"

HENRY V *1989 138m/C*

Kenneth Branagh remakes Olivier's 1944 remake of Shakespeare's play and comes up with a highly praised result. The difference between the two is Branagh decided to give his a strong anti-war message, delving into the psychology of war with all its egos and mind playing madness.

C: Kenneth Branagh, Derek Jacobi, Brian Blessed, Alec McCowen, Ian Holm   D: Kenneth Branagh   AA: '89 Nom: Best Director, Actor (Branagh)

HOW GREEN WAS MY VALLEY *1941 118m/C*

See "Top 100"

HOWARDS END *1992 143m/C (PG)*

Greed, deception, passionate love, and honor, play equal parts in this intelligent and engrossing story of a woman who leaves a home to a friend only to have her family secretly go against her will. Lushly produced and beautifully photographed.

C: Anthony Hopkins, Emma Thompson, Helena Bonham Carter, Vanessa Redgrave, James Wilby D: James Ivory AA: '92 Best Actress (Thompson), Adapted Screenplay, Nom: Best Picture, Director, Supporting Actress (Redgrave)

HUD *1963 112m/B&W*

Newman gives a stunning performance as a rebellious son who would rather drunkenly chase the housekeeper than help his father save the ranch. An emotionally raw, gritty classic.

C: Paul Newman, Melvyn Douglas, Patricia Neal, Brandon de Wilde, John Ashley D: Martin Ritt AA: '63 Best Actress (Neal), Supporting Actor (Douglas), Nom: Best Director, Actor (Newman)

HUNCHBACK OF NOTRE DAME *1939 117m/B&W*

Members of the church accuse a young pretty gypsy woman of practicing witchcraft. The girl flees and a physically deformed church bell operator lets her hide in his bell tower. Beautifully told Victor Hugo novel contains the famous scene when the townspeople charge the church. Charles Laughton's performance as the hunchback is unforgettable.

C: Charles Laughton, Maureen O'Hara, Edmond O'Brien, Cedric Hardwicke, Thomas Mitchell D: William Dieterle

I AM A FUGITIVE FROM A CHAIN GANG *1932 93m/B&W*

Classic story of a WWI soldier who returns home to start a new life, unwittingly becomes involved in the robbery of a hamburger joint, and is sentenced to time on a Georgia chain gang. Beaten and degraded, he plans his escape.

C: Paul Muni, Glenda Farrell, Helen Vinson, Preston Foster, Edward Ellis D: Mervyn LeRoy AA: '33 Nom: Best Picture, Actor (Muni)

JFK *1991 189m/C (R)*

Fascinating, in-depth analysis of the assassination of John F. Kennedy and the resulting conspiracy-opening investigation by New Orleans D.A., Jim Garrison.

C: Kevin Costner, Sissy Spacek, Tommy Lee Jones, Laurie Metcalf, Kevin Bacon D: Oliver Stone AA: '91 Nom: Best Picture, Director, Supporting Actor (Jones)

JUDGEMENT AT NUREMBERG *1961 178m/B&W*

Powerful pic details a trial against high ranking Nazi officers who committed war crimes. All-star cast, four star script.

C: Spencer Tracy, Burt Lancaster, Maximilian Schell, Richard Widmark, Judy Garland D: Stanley Kramer AA: '61 Best Actor (Schell), Nom: Best Picture, Director, Actor (Tracy), Supporting Actor (Montgomery Clift), Supporting Actress (Garland)

KING OF COMEDY *1982 101m/C (PG)*

Great story of wannabe comedian Rupert Pupkin (DeNiro) who, after painstakingly trying to get his material heard, kidnaps late-night talk show host Jerry Langford (Jerry Lewis) in order to appear on his show. Classic performances by Lewis and DeNiro help rank this among Scorsese's best and the best of the '80s.

C: Robert DeNiro, Jerry Lewis, Sandra Bernhard, Tony Randall, Diahnne Abbott D: Martin Scorsese

THE LAST DETAIL *1973 104m/C (R)*

Jack Nicholson and Otis Young play Navy guards who are assigned to transport a 19-year-old sailor to a new prison. The "convict" has received a stiff sentence, eight years, for stealing $40, and the guards, out of kindness, decide to show him a good time. They soon find out this may not have been a good idea.

C: Jack Nicholson, Otis Young, Randy Quaid, Clifton James, Michael Moriarty D: Hal Ashby AA: '73 Nom: Best Actor

(Nicholson), Supporting Actor (Quaid)

THE LAST PICTURE SHOW 1971 118m/B&W (R)

The closing of a small Texas town's movie theater is the back-drop for intertwining stories of romance, longing, broken dreams, and back door affairs. Bridges and Shepherd lead a strong cast and the film was shot in a beautifully textured black and white.

C: Jeff Bridges, Timothy Bottoms, Ben Johnson, Cloris Leachman, Cybill Shepherd, Ellen Burstyn D: Peter Bogdanovich AA: '71 Best Supporting Actor (Johnson), Supporting Actress (Leachman), Nom: Best Picture, Director, Adapted Screenplay, Supporting Actor (Bridges), Supporting Actress (Burstyn)

THE LION IN THE WINTER 1968 134m/C (PG)

Peter O'Toole is Henry II, and Katharine Hepburn his wife Eleanor of Aquitaine, in this striking pic about the power struggle inside the monarchy and Henry and his wife's battle for who will be the next ruler.

C: Peter O'Toole, Katharine Hepburn, Jane Merrow, Nigel Terry, Timothy Dalton, Anthony Hopkins D: Anthony Harvey AA: '68 Best Actress (Hepburn), Adapted Screenplay, Nom: Best Picture, Director, Actor (O'Toole)

LOCAL HERO 1983 112m/C (PG)

A materialistic oil company executive is sent to a small coastal village to convince the people to sell their land to his conglomerate. As he waits weeks for an answer, he becomes intoxicated with the beautiful simplicity of their lives and has a change of heart.

C: Peter Riegert, Denis Lawson, Burt Lancaster, Fulton Mckay, Jenny Seagrove D: Bill Forsyth

LONG DAY'S JOURNEY INTO NIGHT 1962 174m/B&W

Eugene O'Neill's heartwrenching study of one day in the life of a self-destructing family. The wife is an alcoholic, the husband a selfish actor, one son is a drug addict, and the other is dying of leukemia. Sad, but incredibly powerful.

C: Ralph Richardson, Katharine Hepburn, Dean Stockwell, Jeanne Barr, Jason Robards, Jr. D: Sidney Lumet AA: '62 Nom: Best Actress (Hepburn)

LOST WEEKEND 1945 100m/B&W

One of the greatest pics ever made shows one weekend in the life a a writer who fails to recognize he's an alcoholic. Ray Milland is amazing in the lead, giving a must-see performance.

C: Ray Milland, Jane Wyman, Phillip Terry, Howard da Silva, Doris Dowling D: Billy Wilder AA: '45 Best Actor (Milland), Director (Wilder), Picture, Screenplay

THE MAGNIFICENT AMBERSONS 1942 88m/B&W

See "Top 100"

A MAN FOR ALL SEASONS 1966 120m/C (G)

Critically acclaimed telling of the scandalous events involving Sir Thomas Moore, King Henry VIII, Henry's wife and mistress, and the King's angry decision to leave the Catholic Church and become head of the Church of England.

C: Paul Scofield, Robert Shaw, Orson Welles, Wendy Hiller, Susannah York D: Fred Zinneman AA: '66 Best Picture, Director, Adapted Screenplay, Actor (Scofield), Nom: Best Supporting Actor (Shaw), Supporting Actress (Hiller)

MARTY 1955 91m/B&W

An introverted young man (Borgnine) feels trapped in a meaningless life of petty events, until he finds love, which in turn, gives him the strength to turn his world around.

C: Ernest Borgnine, Betsy Blair, Joe Mantell, Joe DeSantis, Ester Minciotti, Jerry Paris D: Delbert Mann AA: '55 Best Actor (Borgnine), Director, Picture, Nom: Best Supporting Actor (Mantell), Supporting Actress (Blair)

MATEWAN *1987 130m/C (PG-13)*

The events surrounding the famous coal miner rebellion in 1920s West Virginia is masterfully brought to the screen in this excellently acted and realistically told pic. Beautiful cinematography.

C: Chris Cooper, James Earl Jones, Mary McDonnell, William Oldham, Kevin Tighe D: John Sayles

MEAN STREETS *1973 112m/C (R)*

Scorsese's gritty street life pic revolves around a punk (DeNiro) who borrows some money and adapts an "I'll pay it back when I'm good and ready" attitude, spending any cash he has on drinks and girls. Keitel plays his friend who tries to help him, and Romanus is the loan shark who's had enough.

C: Harvey Keitel, Robert DeNiro, David Proval, Amy Robinson, Richard Romanus D: Martin Scorsese

MICHAEL COLLINS *1996 132m/C (R)*

Michael Collins began his "career" as a rough Irish guerilla soldier, stepped up to an elite statesman, was a major figure in the Irish Civil War, and was ultimately executed by his former friends. Neeson stars as Collins and Rickman plays Eamon de Valera, Collins' comrade turned enemy.

C: Liam Neeson, Alan Rickman, Aidan Quinn, Julia Roberts D: Neil Jordan

MIDNIGHT COWBOY *1969 113m/C (R)*

See "Top 100"

MIDNIGHT EXPRESS *1978 120m/C (R)*

Powerful, true story about an American caught smuggling

drugs out of Turkey and his nightmarish ordeal with the insane Turkish justice system, and its harrowing "once you're in you never get out" prison process. Brad Davis portrays Billy Hayes, the prisoner whose dreams of escape barely keep his spirit alive. Oliver Stone wrote the screenplay.

C: John Hurt, Randy Quaid, Brad Davis, Paul Smith, Bo Hopkins D: Alan Parker AA: '78 Best Adapted Screenplay, Nom: Best Picture, Director, Supporting Actor (Hurt)

MISSING 1982 122m/C

During a political uprising, a young American journalist disappears. His wife and father begin the frustrating and difficult task of finding him and are led down a trail of lies, deceit, and heartbreak. Based on the true story of Charles Horman.

C: Jack Lemmon, Sissy Spacek, John Shea, Melanie Mayron, David Clennon D: Constantin Costa-Gavras AA: '82 Best Adapted Screenplay, Nom: Best Picture, Actor (Lemmon), Actress (Spacek)

MR. SMITH GOES TO WASHINGTON 1939 130m/B&W

See "Top 100"

NETWORK 1976 121m/C (R)

Scathing comment on television's immorality in the name of ratings and cash has Peter Finch playing a newscaster slipping into mental madness "on air," complete with philosophical, "I'm mad as hell and I'm not going to take it anymore" rants. The station keeps him on as a ratings grabbing inspirational freak show, leading to a twisted, sick conclusion.

C: Faye Dunaway, Peter Finch, William Holden, Beatrice Straight, Ned Beatty, Robert Duvall D: Sidney Lumet AA: '76 Best Actor (Finch), Actress (Dunaway), Supporting Actress (Straight), Original Screenplay, Nom: Best Picture, Director, Actor (Holden), Supporting Actor (Beatty)

NORTH DALLAS FORTY 1979 119m/C (R)

Nolte stars in this blistering account of pro football's many moral penalties, on and off the field. He's an aging ballplayer who loves to play for the sport and goes up against the team owners who play for the business. It never turns corny or cliched, and is one of the best sports films ever made.

C: Nick Nolte, Mac Davis, Charles Durning, Bo Svenson, Brian Dennehy, Dayle Haddon   D: Ted Kotcheff

OF MICE AND MEN 1939 107m/C

Classic Steinbeck story of two poor Depression era drifters who take jobs on a ranch and fall into tragedy when one of them accidentally kills a woman.

C: Lon Chaney, Jr., Burgess Meredith, Betty Field, Bob Steele, Noah Berry, Jr.   D: Lewis Milestone   AA: '39 Nom: Best Picture

ON THE WATERFRONT 1954 108m/B&W

See "Top 100"

ONE FLEW OVER THE CUCKOO'S NEST 1975 129m/C (R)

See "Top 100"

ORDINARY PEOPLE 1980 124m/C (R)

See "Top 100"

THE PAWNBROKER 1965 120m/B&W

A Jewish pawnbroker with haunting memories of the Holocaust is brought out of his hell by a young man he hires to work in his store. Poignant, heartfelt, and powerful.

C: Rod Steiger, Brock Peters, Geraldine Fitzgerald, Jaime Sanchez
D: Sidney Lumet   AA: 65 Nom: Best Actor (Steiger)

PETULIA 1968 105m/C (R)

Much loved pic has George C. Scott playing a recently divorced surgeon who has an affair with a flaky socialite who's out to make her husband jealous. The Grateful Dead perform on screen.

C: George C. Scott, Richard Chamberlain, Julie Christie, Shirley Knight, Arthur Hill   D: Richard Lester

PULP FICTION *1994 151m/C (R)*

Quentin Tarantino's wild, high energy interweaving of strange characters and strange stories include a hit man's problem watching his boss' girlfriend, a boxer throwing a mob-set fight, and a philosophical thug who decides, after witnessing an act of God, he should get out of the business. Film swings from normal mainstream moments to demented scenes of the underbelly of society. Fast moving and highly captivating, with a flashback/flash forward technique Stanley Kurbrick used in the 1957 classic *The Killing*.

C: Bruce Willis, Samuel L. Jackson, John Travolta, Uma Thurman, Harvey Keitel   D: Quentin Tarantino   AA: '94 Best Original Screenplay, Nom: Best Picture, Director, Actor (Travolta), Actress (Thurman), Supporting Actor (Jackson)

RAIN MAN *1988 128m/C (R)*

Cruise plays a greed infested wheeler dealer whose wealthy father just died and left the fortune to his other son, a brother Cruise never knew he had. When he finds his brother (Hoffman) is autistic and he could challenge him for the money, he gets him out of the mental institution and they begin a cross-country road trip that makes him re-evaluate his motivations and his life.

C: Dustin Hoffman, Tom Cruise, Valeria Golino, Jerry Molen, Jack Murdock   D: Barry Levinson   AA: '88 Best Picture, Director, Original Screenplay, Actor (Hoffman)

REBEL WITHOUT A CAUSE *1955 111m/C*

Nicholas Ray directed a slew of movies that have large, loyal followings and this is his most famous one. James Dean plays

Jim Stark, a troubled youth who finds no solace in his family or friends. He meets a couple of teenagers in a police station and the three form an ill-fated alliance.

C: James Dean, Natalie Wood, Sal Mineo, Jim Backus, Nick Adams D: Nicholas Ray   AA: '55 Nom: Best Supporting Actor (Mineo), Supporting Actress (Wood)

REVERSAL OF FORTUNE 1990 112m/C (R)

The true story of the highly publicized criminal case in which Klaus Von Bulow was charged with giving his wife Sunny a high dose of insulin which sent her into a coma she's never come out of. Gripping pic is told through a series of flashbacks giving both side's accounts. Irons is brilliant.

C: Jeremy Irons, Glenn Close, Ron Silver, Annabella Sciorra, Uta Hagen, Fisher Stevens   D: Barbet Schroeder   AA: '90 Best Actor (Irons), Nom: Best Director

THE RIGHT STUFF 1983 193m/C (PG)

Strong involving story of the space program, from its birth to the Mercury Missions. All star cast and some fantastic scenes.

C: Ed Harris, Dennis Quaid, Sam Shepard, Scott Glenn, Fred Ward D: Philip Kaufman   AA: '83 Nom: Best Picture, Supporting Actor (Shepard)

ROCKY 1976 125m/C (PG)

The film which made Sylvester Stallone a household name centers around a third-rate "bum" who's given a shot at the heavyweight championship of the world. Part love story, part human-spirit story, the film warms the heart of anyone who sees it. "Yo, Adrian."

C: Sylvester Stallone, Talia Shire, Burgess Meredith, Burt Young, Carl Weathers   D: John G. Avildsen   AA: '76 Best Director, Picture, Nom: Best Actor (Stallone), Actress (Shire), Supporting Actor (Young, Meredith)

ROOM AT THE TOP *1959 118m/B&W*

A tale of the warnings of not following your heart has Harvey abandoning the woman he loves for a marriage with the wealthy boss's daughter.

C: Laurence Harvey, Simone Signoret, Heather Sears, Hermione Baddeley, Anthony Elgar D: Jack Clayton AA: '59 Best Actress (Signoret), Adapted Screenplay, Nom: Best Picture, Director, Actor (Harvey), Supporting Actress (Baddeley)

ROOM WITH A VIEW *1986 117m/C*

See "Top 100"

SHAWSHANK REDEMPTION *1994 112m/C (PG)*

When a man is imprisoned for a murder he didn't commit, he undergoes an intense physical and spiritual battle that eventually leads him to make a moral decision against a corrupt warden. An uplifting, engrossing pic, one of the best of the '90s.

C: Tim Robbins, Morgan Freeman, William Sadler, Clancy Brown D: Frank Darabont AA: '94 Nom: Best Picture, Actor (Freeman)

SPLENDOR IN THE GRASS *1961 124m/C*

Warren Beatty and Natalie Wood play young lovers whose romance is ill-fated by family pressures. After the break up, Wood is institutionalized while Beatty's family believes the break-up is for the best and their boy is destined for greatness. A year later, Wood's recovered and finds Beatty's parents were wrong. A classic, beautifully told story.

C: Natalie Wood, Warren Beatty, Audrey Christie, Barbara Loder, Zohra Lampert D: Elia Kazan AA: '61 Best Screenplay, Nom: Best Actress (Wood)

A STREETCAR NAMED DESIRE *1951 122m/B&W (PG)*

Blanche DuBois (Leigh), an aging Southerner, moves in with her sister and brother-in-law. Brando plays the brother-in-law whose hard edged, brutish personality causes Blanche to have a mental meltdown. Intense, psychological drama.

C: Vivien Leigh, Marlon Brando, Kim Hunter, Karl Malden   D: Elia Kazan   AA: '51 Best Actress (Leigh), Supporting Actor (Malden), Supporting Actress (Hunter), Nom: Best Picture, Director, Actor (Brando)

SUNSET BOULEVARD *1950 100m/B&W*

Comedy-laced drama abut a fading star (Swanson) who can't cope with the lack of attention and hires a young scriptwriter to refuel her career. But the scriptwriter takes the job thinking she can help him. Tragic irony played to the limit. A classic.

C: Gloria Swanson, William Holden, Erich von Stroheim, Nancy Olson, Buster Keaton   D: Billy Wilder   AA: '50 Best Story and Screenplay, Nom: Best Picture, Director, Actor (Holden), Actress (Swanson), Supporting Actor (von Stroheim), Supporting Actress (Olson)

TALK RADIO *1988 110m/C (R)*

Great film with Bogosian as an acid-tongued deejay who spews venom at anyone who calls and, subsequently, becomes a sensation. Much of the film takes place in his radio booth, dealing with strange calls, weird guests, and repeated death threats he refuses to take seriously. Loosely based on the life of Alan Berg, a Denver radio host killed by skinheads.

C: Eric Bogosian, Ellen Greene, Alec Baldwin, John Pankow   D: Oliver Stone

TAXI DRIVER *1976 112m/C (R)*
See "Top 100"

TEN COMMANDMENTS *1956 220m/C (G)*
Lavish epic about the life of Moses, from birth through slav-

ery, to leading his people out of Egypt. Beautifully filmed with the famous parting of the Red Sea. A classic.

C: Charlton Heston, Yul Brynner, Anne Baxter, Edward G. Robinson, Yvonne DeCarlo   D: Cecil B. DeMille   AA: '56 Nom: Best Picture

TERMS OF ENDEARMENT *1983 132m/C (PG)*
See "Top 100"

TO KILL A MOCKINGBIRD *1962 129m/B&W*
A white girl is raped in a small town and the angry people want someone to pay, guilty or not. An innocent black man is scheduled for trial, and a white lawyer (Peck) is picked to defend him. Movingly told from the point of view of the white lawyer's daughter.

C: Gregory Peck, Brock Peters, Philip Alford, Mary Badham, Robert Duvall   D: Robert Mulligan   AA: '62 Best Actor (Peck), Adapted Screenplay, Nom: Best Picture, Director, Supporting Actress (Badham)

TO SIR, WITH LOVE *1967 105m/C*
Poignant and powerful story of a black teacher who takes a job at an all white school in '60s London. The students antagonize him until they begin to realize he may be the best teacher they have.

C: Sidney Poitier, Lulu, Judy Geeson, Christian Roberts, Suzy Kendall   D: James Clavell

TWELVE ANGRY MEN *1957 95m/B&W*
See "Top 100"

THE UNBEARABLE LIGHTNESS OF BEING *1988 172m/C (R)*
An esteemed doctor leads an emotionally and sexually carefree life until he meets a beautiful and innocent young woman. A complicated problem forces him to choose be-

tween the love for the girl or the love of his work. Set in the late 1960s in Czechoslovakia and produced with a grand, sweeping style.

C: Daniel Day-Lewis, Juliette Binoche, Lena Olin, Derek DeLint, Erland Josephson, Pavel Landovsky   D: Phillip Kaufman

THE VERDICT *1982 122m/C (R)*

Paul Newman plays a down-and-out attorney. (He crashes a funeral to hand out his business card to the widow.) His true character shows when he gets a case where he can take some easy cash or fight for the truth against a corrupt church organization.

C: Paul Newman, James Mason, Charlotte Rampling, Jack Warden, Milo O'Shea   D: Sidney Lumet   AA: '82 Nom: Best Picture, Director, Actor (Newman), Supporting Actor (Mason)

WHO'S AFRAID OF VIRGINIA WOOLF? *1966 127m/B&W*

Burton is an aging college professor who's sick of the grind. Taylor is his angry wife. They invite a young teacher (Segal) and his wife (Dennis) over for a nice friendly dinner. It doesn't take long before Burton and Taylor loudly and ruthlessly air their dirty laundry in front of their guests. A brutal study in human character.

C: Richard Burton, Elizabeth Taylor, George Segal, Sandy Dennis D: Mike Nichols   AA: '66 Best Actress (Taylor), Supporting Actress (Dennis), Nom: Best Picture, Director, Actor (Burton), Supporting Actor (Segal)

WUTHERING HEIGHTS *1939 104m/B&W*

See "Top 100"

ZORBA THE GREEK *1964 142m/B&W*

A young writer retreats from the busy world of England to a

simpler life, taking a job in a mine on the island of Crete. There he meets co-worker Zorba, a man with an unending zest for life, who changes the writer's life forever.

C: Anthony Quinn, Alan Bates, Irene Papas, Lila Kedrova
D: Michael Cacoyannis   AA: '64 Best Supporting Actress (Kedrova), Nom: Best Picture, Director, Actor (Quinn)

FOREIGN

AGUIRRE, THE WRATH OF GOD *1972 94m/C GE*

A jungle expedition for El Dorado is split when a group of men, led by power-monger Aguirre, are sent ahead to find information on their destination. They soon fall prey to the vicious problems that surround them, including the torrid river and dangerous natives. But Aguirre, hungry for victory and a place in the history books, refuses to give up. Shot on location in the Amazon Jungle by 29-year-old Werner Herzog.

C: Klaus Kinski, Ruy Guerra, Del Negro, Helena Rojo, Cecilia Rivera
D: Werner Herzog

ANDREI RUBLEV *1966 185m/C RU*

Masterfully told story of the 15th century painter who must decide whether to physically take part in a war or sit back and record it on canvas. The first part of the film, where he decides to fight, is in black and white. After taking a life in battle, he struggles through depression, moves forward (the B&W changes to color), and paints his masterpieces.

C: Anatoli Solonitzin, Ivan Lapikov, Nikolai Grinko, Nikolai Sergueiev
D: Andrei Tarkovsky

THE ASSAULT *1986 149m/C (PG) NL*

A family's murder by the Nazis is witnessed by the son. As he grows older the brutal vision haunts him. Later, he meets people related to the killings and tries to come to terms with the tragedy. Engrossing.

C: Derek DeLint, Marc Van Uchelen, Monique Van DeVen   D: Fons Rademakers   AA: '86 Best Foreign Language Film

AU REVOIR LES ENFANTS *1987 104m/C (PG) FR*

A headmaster at a Nazi occupied French Catholic School hides three Jewish boys among his students. One of the youngsters becomes friends with a French student and later their bond is put in jeopardy when the Nazi soldiers learn of the teacher's "crime." Considered Malle's best film.

C: Gaspard Manesse, Raphael Fejto, Francine Racette, Stanislas Carre de Malberg, Philippe Morrier-Genoud   D: Louis Malle   AA: '87 Nom: Best Foreign Language Film, Original Screenplay

BABETTE'S FEAST *1987 102m/C DK FR*

A woman who works as a housekeeper for two sisters cooks a luxurious meal for their dinner party and reveals a life-changing secret. A beautiful pic.

C: Stephane Audran, Bibi Anderson, Bodil Kjer, Brigette Federspiel, Jean-Philippe LaFont   D: Gabriel Axel   AA: '87 Best Foreign Language Film

BATTLE OF ALGIERS *1966 123m/B&W AL IT*

A docu-style film, using many non-professional actors and raw camera work, detailing the 1954 violent political uprising against the French Colonial rule of Algiers. Critically lauded.

C: Yasef Saadi, Jean Martin, Brahim Haggiag, Tommaso Neri, Samia Kerbash   D: Gillo Pontecorvo

BATTLESHIP POTEMKIN *1925 71m/B&W RU*

Eisenstein's masterpiece concerns the 1905 mutiny on the Russian ship Potemkin that resulted in political upheaval against the Czar. Includes pioneering techniques like the "montage" and the famous "Odessa Steps" sequence.

C: Alexander Antonov, Vladimir Barsky, Grigori Alexandrov, Mikhail Gomorov   D: Sergei Eisenstein

BEAUTY AND THE BEAST *1946 90m/B&W FR*

Jean Cocteau, already a well known painter, brought his amazing sense of visual style to this stunning, beautiful rendition of the famous fairy tale. Surreal and wonderfully moody, it has to be seen to be appreciated and is considered by many to be the best interpretation of the children's classic.

C: Jean Marais, Josette Day, Marcel Andre, Mila Parley, Nane Germon   D: Jean Cocteau

THE BICYCLE THIEF *1949 90m/B&W IT*

A working class man with a wife and children finally lands a much needed job as a delivery person. On his first day, the bike he needs for work is stolen. Together with his son they desperately try to relocate it. It's a simple story that seems to hold endless secrets to life.

C: Lamberto Maggiorani, Lianella Carell, Enzo Staiola, Elena Altieri, Vittorio Antonucci   D: Vittorio DeSica   AA: '49 Best Foreign Language Film

BLACK ORPHEUS *1958 103m/C BR FR PT*

Thrilling, updated version of the Orpheus and Eurydice legend with a black streetcar conductor falling in love with a country girl on the run from a killer. Expertly directed and acted and set against the Rio de Janeiro carnival with moody elements of black magic thrown in.

C: Breno Mello, Marpessa Dawn, Lea Garcia, Fausto Guerzoni, Lourdes DeOliveria   D: Marcel Camus   AA: '59 Best Foreign Language Film

THE BLUE ANGEL *1930 90/B&W GE*

Classic story of a professor who, hoping to nab some of his deviant students, visits a seedy nightclub. Once there he becomes enamored with LoLa, the sexy singer. They spend the night together and he becomes obsessed, losing his job and marrying her. It gets worse. A must see.

C: Marlene Dietrich, Emil Jannings, Kurt Gerron, Rosa Valetti, Hans Albers   D: Josef Von Sternberg

BREATHLESS *1959 90m/B&W FR*

A low life thief falls hard for a pretty American girl, puts the pedal to the metal, and speeds down a road toward doom. Godard, with this stylish influential first feature, was thrust to the front of French cinema.

C: Jean-Paul Belmondo, Jean Seberg, Daniel Boulanger, Jean-Pierre Melville, Lillane Robin   D: Jean-Luc Godard

BURNT BY THE SUN *1994 100m/C (R)*

A married woman's ex-lover, who she hasn't seen in ten years, mysteriously arrives at a large party she's throwing. He's now a member of the Secret Police and he's not exactly there to have a good time. Beautifully made.

C: Nikita Mikhalkov, Ingeborga Dapkounaite, Oleg Menchikov   D: Nikita Mikhalkov   AA: '94 Best Foreign Language Film

THE CABINET OF DR. CALIGARI *1919 52m/B&W GE*

A visual masterpiece with pioneering use of lighting and set design, this pic tells the twisted tale of a carnival hypnotist who puts a man under his spell and uses him to do his evil bidding of snatching women. An incredibly eerie, stunning film that the Nazi party said was "degenerate art."

C: Conrad Veidt, Werner Krauss, Lil Dagover   D: Robert Wiene

CHILDREN OF PARADISE 1944 188m/B&W FR

In 1800's Paris, a mime falls in love with a beautiful, seemingly out of reach actress and the love never dies, even as he achieves incredible stage success. Jealously, deceit and other dark emotions play roles in this film considered one of the greatest and most beautiful of all time.

C: Jean-Louis Barrault, Arletty, Pierre Brasseur, Maria Casares, Albert Remy   D: Marcel Carne

CHRIST STOPPED AT EBOLI 1979 118m/C IT FR

Story chronicling the exile of writer Carlo Levi to a remote primitive town in Southern Italy for his anti-fascist beliefs. Considered director Francesco Rosi's best work.

C: Gian Marie Volonte, Irene Papas, Paolo Bonacelli, Francois Simon, Alain Cuny   D: Francesco Rosi

CINEMA PARADISO 1988 123m/C IT

A sweet, charming story about a young boy's love for movies and his friendship with the projectionist at the town's cinema. First rate.

C: Phillipe Noiret, Jacques Perrin, Salvatore Cascio, Mario Leonard, Agnes Nano   D: Giueseppe Tomatore   AA: '89 Best Foreign Language Film

CLARIE'S KNEE 1971 105m/C FR

A man about to be married takes a trip and meets his friend's roommate's daughter. He soon becomes obsessed with her knee. Her right knee. A strange sensuous folly, the best of Rohmer's six "Moral Tales."

C: Jean-Claude Brialy, Aurora Coma, Beatrice Romand   D: Eric Rohmer

CLOSELY WATCHED TRAINS 1966 89m/B&W CZ

When a shy young man who works at a train station becomes

involved with the Czech underground he uses the opportunity to try to advance his sexual experiences. Amusing, engaging winner.

C: Vaclar Neckar, Jitka Bendova, Vladimir Valenta, Josef Somr
D: Jiri Menzel   AA: '67 Best Foreign Language Film

COME AND SEE 1985 142m/C RU

A Russian teenage soldier walks through the countryside and observes the Nazi army turning his homeland into a living hell. As the horrors of war scream through his mind he does his best to remain sane. Noted for its brutally realistic scenes of war which both disturb and amaze.

C: Alexei Kravchenko, Olga Mironova, Lubomiras Lauciavicus
D: Elem Kimor

THE CONFORMIST 1971 108m/C IT FR

A young man in the Italian fascist secret service tries to quell his homosexual urges and live a "normal" life but all his dreams are shattered when an odd set of circumstances force him to kill his old, anti-fascist professor.

C: Jean-Louis Trintignant, Stefania Sandrelli, Dominque Sanda, Pierre Clementi, Gastone Moschin   D: Bernardo Bertolucci   AA: '87 Nom: Best Adapted Screenplay

CYRANO DE BERGERAC 1990 135m/C (PG) FR

Gerard Depardieu lends his stylish brilliance to the role of the large nosed poet/swordsman who is in love with the beautiful Roxanne but does not have the courage to confront her. He does, however, help his friend win her heart by ghostwriting love letters and speeches until finally he can't take it anymore. Great.

C: Gerard Depardieu, Jacques Weber, Anne Brochet, Vincent Perez, Roland Bertin   D: Jean-Paul Rappeneau   AA: '90 Nom: Best Actor (Depardieu), Foreign Language Film

DARK EYES 1987 118m/C IT

A man who has dreamed of becoming an important architect gives it up and settles into a comfortable marriage with the daughter of a wealthy banker. He then has a chance meeting with a beautiful woman in a health spa and, later, embarks on a journey to find her and himself. Mastroianni shines.

C: Marcello Mastroianni, Silvana Mangano, Elena Sofonorva, Marthe Keller   D: Nikita Mikhalkov   AA: '87 Nom: Best Actor (Mastroianni)

DAS BOOT 1981 150m/C GE

Truly suspenseful, nerve chilling account of a German U-boat mission during WWII. Tensely directed with an incredible feel for wartime submarine conditions. German director Peterson went on to direct *In The Line Of Fire*.

C: Juergen Prochnow, Herbert Gronemeyer, Klaus Wennemann, Hubertus Begsch, Martin Semmelrogge   D: Wolfgang Petersen

DAY OF WRATH 1943 110m/B&W DK

Using actual witch trial records from the 1600's, Dreyer has concocted a chilling story of a woman, burned at the stake, who puts a curse on her killers.

C: Thorkild Roose, Sigrid Neiiendam, Lisbeth Movin, Preben Lerdorff, Anna Srierker   D: Carl Theodor Dreyer

DEATH IN VENICE 1971 124m/C (PG) IT

An acclaimed, world famous composer, elderly and cynical, tries to control his building passion for a beautiful young boy. Lavishly produced.

C: Dirk Bogarde, Mark Burns, Bjorn Andersen, Marisa Berenson, Silvano Mangano   D: Luchino Visconti

DIABOLIQUE 1955 107m/B&W FR

Signoret and Clouzot play the wife and mistress of a cruel schoolmaster. Fed up, they kill him and ditch the body but

---

soon grow increasingly (and rightfully) paranoid that they've left clues. Film builds masterfully and last half will have you glued to your seat.

C: Simone Signoret, Vera Clouzot, Paul Meurisse, Charles Venel, Michel Serrault   D: Henri-Georges Clouzot

THE DISCREET CHARM OF THE BOURGEOISIE
1972 100m/C (R) FR

Bunuel's plotless style over substance pic about a group of people who have a continuous dinner party but are never able to eat. First it's the wrong night, then a death ruins their appetite, then the police come, then they sit down only to realize they're on a stage in front of an audience. Surreal satire on modern society.

C: Fernando Rey, Delphine Seyrig, Jean-Pierre Cassel, Bulle Ogier, Michel Piccoli   D: Luis Bunuel   AA: '72 Best Foreign Language Film, Nom: Best Story and Screenplay

DIVA *1982 123m/C (R) FR*

A motorcycle driving mailman tapes an opera of his favorite diva, who does not let anyone record her performances. The bootleg tape ends up throwing him into the dangerous center of thieves and crooked cops. Stylish direction with a wicked motorcycle chase in the subway.

C: Frederic Andrei, Roland Berlin, Richard Bohringer, Gerard Damon, Jacques Fabbri   D: Jean-Jacques Beineix

DRIFTING WEEDS *1959 128m/B&W JP*

A traveling troupe of actors lands on an island and one of its members visits with an old girlfriend and his illegitimate son. A simple story that successfully builds its characters and leads us on an emotionally powerful journey.

C: Ganjiro Nakamura, Machiko Kyo, Haruko Sugimura, Ayako Wakao D: Yasujro Ozu

THE EARRINGS OF MADAME DE... *1954 105m/C FR*

A sophisticated social butterfly is given a pair of diamond earrings by her loving husband. She secretly sells them but the earrings keep coming back to haunt her. Considered one of the all-time greats.

C: Charles Boyer, Danielle Darrieux, Victoria DeSica, Lea di Lea, Jean Debucourt   D: Max Ophuls

8 1/2 *1963 135m/B&W IT*

Much studied Fellini self portrait about a director plagued by fear, depression and anxiety as he tries to put together a work of art. Filled with some of the most bizarre, surreal, hallucinatory images ever caught on celluloid.

C: Marcello Mastroianni, Claudia Cardinale, Anouk Aimee, Sandra Milo, Barbara Steele   D: Federico Fellini   AA: '63 Best Foreign Language Film, Nom: Best Director

EL NORTE *1983 139m/C (R) SP*

A brother and sister, living in their homeland of Guatemala, find themselves ostracized and so, seeking a better life, they head north to America ("el norte"). But the U.S. brings a new difficult struggle as they continue to look for their dream. An emotional, moving drama.

C: David Villalpando, Zaide Silvia Gutierrez, Emesto Cruz, Eracio Zepeda   D: Greogry Nava

EUROPA, EUROPA *1991 115m/C (R) GE*

The incredible true story of a young Jewish boy who passed himself off as a German to escape the holocaust only to be drafted into Hitler's Army. Tragic moments are masterfully mixed with segments of dark, eerie humor.

C: Marco Hofschenider, Klaus Abramowsky, Michele Gieizer, Rene Hofscheneider, Natalie Schmidt   D: Agnieszka Holland   AA: '91 Nom: Best Adapted Screenplay

EVERY MAN FOR HIMSELF AND GOD AGAINST ALL *1975 110m/C GE*

Intense true story of Kaspar Hauser, a young man who mysteriously appears in the Nuremburg town square, unable to speak or walk upright. It becomes known that he was kept in a basement for over 18 years and the townspeople find him an interesting curiosity as he tries to adjust to this "new" world. Powerful, moving picture.

C: Bruno S, Brigette Mira, Water Ladengast, Hans Masaus, Willy Semmeirogge D: Werner Herzog

FANNY AND ALEXANDER *1983 197m/C (R) SW*

One year in the life of a Swedish family as told through the eyes and hearts of the two young children, Fanny and Alexander. The gamut of emotions, from brutal pain to sheer joy, are all captured in this moving classic. Stunning cinematography.

C: Pernilla Allwin, Bertil Guve, Gunn Walgren, Allan Edwall, Eva Groling D: Ingmar Bergman AA: '83 Best Foreign Language Film, Nom: Best Director, Original Screenplay

FITZCARRALDO *1982 157m/C (PG) GE*

Herzog's amazing film about the incredible Irishman, Fitzcarraldo, who, at the turn of the century, ventured into the Amazon Jungle to build an opera house where he planned to have Enrico Caruso sing. Special effects were nonexistent in this film and the scene where an army of men carry a huge boat up the side of a mountain actually happened exactly as you see it. Watch this film with *Burden of Dreams*, the documentary detailing Herzog's making of the pic.

C: Klaus Kinski, Claudia Cardinale, Jose Lewgoy, Miguel Angel Fuentes, Paul Hittscher D: Werner Herzog

FORBIDDEN GAMES *1952 90m/B&W FR*

Engrossing story of war as seen through children's eyes. After a young girl's parents are killed by Nazis she is taken in by the family of a boy she meets. The two battle the horrors of war by retreating into a strange world of burying dead animals they find, stealing crosses from cemeteries for their own graveyard. A tragic, unforgettable anti-war statement.

C: Brigette Fossey, Georges Poujouly, Amedee, Louis Herbert D: Rene Clement   AA: '52 Best Foreign Language Film, Nom: Best Story

THE 400 BLOWS *1959 97m/B&W FR*

Truffaut's highly acclaimed pic about a twelve-year-old French schoolboy who feels he doesn't fit anywhere and the inner and outer rebellion which results.

C: Jean-Pierre Leaud, Claire Maurier, Albert Remy, Guy Decombie, Georges Flament   D: Francois Truffaut   AA: '59 Nom: Best Story and Screenplay

GET OUT YOUR HANDKERCHIEFS *1978 109m/C (R) FR*

A husband, distraught over his wife's depression, feels it has arisen from a sexual need he can't fill, and so he drags a man out of a restaurant to sleep with her. She's uninterested in both of them and doesn't snap out of it until she meets a 13-year-old genius. A comedic masterpiece with brilliant performances by Depardieu and Dewaere.

C: Gerard Depardieu, Patrick Dewaere, Carole Laure   D: Betrand Blier   AA: '78 Best Foreign Language Film

GRAND ILLUSION *1937 111m/B&W FR*

A group of French prisoners, whose backgrounds range from rich to poor, attempt to escape from a German POW Camp in WWI. A beautifully told anti-war classic.

C: Jean Gabin, Erich Von Stroheim, Pierre Fresnay, Marcel Dalio, Julien Carette   D: Jean Renoir   AA: '38 Nom: Best Picture

HIGH & LOW *1962 143m/B&W (R) JP*

Classic tale of a business tycoon whose son is abducted by kidnappers demanding a huge ransom. When it's discovered the kidnappers made a terrible mistake and have the chauffeur's son the tycoon must make a moral choice. Kurosawa at his best.

C: Toshiro Mifune, Tatsuya Mihashi, Tatsuya Nakodai   D: Akira Kurosawa

HIROSHIMA, MON AMOUR *1960 88m/B&W JP*

A young French girl who's had her head shaved for sleeping with a German soldier and a Japanese architect who feels a sense of guilt for escaping his city's annihilation, have an affair in which they share their personal anguish. Powerfully tender.

C: Emmanuelle Riva, Eigi Okada, Bernard Fresson, Stella Dassas, Pierre Barbaud   D: Alain Resnais

THE HORROR CHAMBER OF DR. FAUSTUS *1959 84m/B&W FR*

A doctor's daughter is in a terrible accident that leaves her face hideously scarred. The doctor slips into madness and begins slaughtering innocent young girls so he can graft their skin onto his daughter's face.

C: Alida Valli, Pierre Brasseur, Edith Scob, Francois Guerin   D: Georges Franju

IKIRU *1952 134m/B&W JP*

When a working class man discovers he is terminally ill and has a short time to live he questions the meaning of his life and decides he must do something good for the world. Emotionally heartwarming.

C: Takashi Shimura, Nobou Kaneko, Kyoko Seki, Mikl Odagari, Yunosulse Ito   D: Akira Kurosawa

IVAN THE TERRIBLE, PARTS 1 & 2
(PART 1) *1944 96m/B&W;* **(PART 2)** *1946 84m/B&W RU*

Joseph Stalin commissioned Sergei Eisenstein to make a biography of the first Czar of Russia, hoping people would appreciate their similar methods and learn to love the Czar. Instead, Eisenstein made a "power corrupts and absolute power absolutely corrupts" view of the Russian leader from his induction to his downfall to his 2nd rise. Part 2 was banned by Stalin but the two sagas are considered lush, epic-like masterpieces.

C: Nikolai Cherkassov, Ludmila Tselikovskaya, Serafina Birman, Piotr Kadochnikev D: Sergei Eisenstein

JEAN DE FLORETTE *1987 122m/C (PG) FR*

Two deceitful farmers block a spring that is feeding water to a neighboring farm, knowing it will drive the man and his family to ruin and they will be able to buy it for themselves. A sweeping, incredibly made masterpiece with beautiful cinematography and an awe-inspiring performance by Gerard Depardieu as the victimized landowner. Followed by an excellent sequel, *Manon Of The Spring*.

C: Gerard Depardieu, Yves Montand, Daniel Auteuil, Emmanuelle Beart D: Claude Berri

JESUS OF MONTREAL *1989 119m/C (R) FR CA*

A priest hires a drifter/actor to put on the Easter play at his church, not realizing that the man who will be playing Jesus may actually be "The Holy One" himself.

C: Gilles Pelletier, Lothaire Bluteau, Catherine Wilkening, Robert Lepage, Johanne-Marie Tremblay D: Denys Arcand AA: '89 Nom: Best Foreign Language Film

JU DOU *1990 98m/C (PG-13) CH*

An elderly mill owner is looking for a heir to his fortune and finds it in a young peasant girl he "decides" to wed. Her heart isn't into him or his abusive ways but she does find love with his nephew. Stunning cinematography adds to an already awesome viewing experience.

C: Gong Li, Li Bao-Tian, Li Wei, Zhang Yi   D: Zhang Yimou   AA: '90 Nom: Best Foreign Language Film

JULES AND JIM *1962 104m/B&W FR*

Two men share a love for the same woman. She marries one but after World War II, when all three meet again, she has an affair with the other which results in tragedy.

C: Jeanne Moreau, Oskar Werner, Henri Serre, Marie DuBois, Vanna Urbino D: Francois Truffaut

KNIFE IN THE WATER *1962 94m/B&W PL*

On their way to a day of boating a journalist and his wife pick up a hitchhiker and invite him on their sailboat. They later realize, in a twisted violent way, that this was a very bad idea. Polanski's flair for the thriller is at its best here.

C: Leon Niemczyk, Jolanta Umecka, Zygmunt Malandowicz D: Roman Polanski

LA CHIENNE *1931 93m/B&W FR*

A henpecked husband who works in a bank escapes the drudgery of his wife by becoming obsessed with a sultry prostitute. Soon the prostitute and her pimp use hubby as a pawn in their diabolical game of power.

C: Michel Simon, Janie Mareze, Georges Flament, Madeleine Berubet D: Jean Renoir

L'AGE D'OR *1930 65m/B&W FR*

A film with images like a cow walking into a bedroom, a bishop being pushed out a window and a blind man being kicked sounds like it was co-scripted by Salvador Dali. It was, and it must be seen to be believed. The "story" revolves around a man's fruitless mission to reach the girl of his dreams.

C: Gaston Modot, Max Ernst, Lya Lys, Pierre Prevert   D: Luis Bunuel

LA RONDE *1951 97m/B&W FR*

A wickedly funny farce in which a group of people make the rounds with each other's lovers until finally they all end up exactly where they started.

C: Simone Signoret, Anton Walbrook, Simone Simon, Serge Reggiani, Daniel Gelin   D: Max Ophuls

LA STRADA *1954 107m/B&W IT*

Fellini's spiritual journey beginning with the sale of young pretty girl to a circus strong man. Despite his coarse, abusive demeanor she loves him until the two meet a pure-hearted acrobat who unwittingly throws the strongman onto a strange, tragic road to redemption.

C: Giuletta Masina, Anthony Quinn, Richard Basehant, Aldo Silvani
D: Federico Fellini   AA: '56 Best Foreign Language Film

LATE SPRING *1949 108m/B&W JP*

An elderly man fears that his daughter, who still lives with him, will wind up an old maid so he tells her he is remarrying in hopes that she will finally start a life of her own.

C: Setsuko Hara, Chishu Ryu, Jun Usami, Haruko Sugimura
D: Yasujro Ozu

LIKE WATER FOR CHOCOLATE *1993 113m/C (R) SP*

A widow brings up her three daughters and the youngest becomes increasingly drawn to the power, enjoyment, and emotional comfort she receives from cooking. Her joy is shared with all who eat her beautiful dishes. A sensuous, charming film.

C: Lumi Cavazos, Marco Leonardi, Regina Tome, Mario Ivan Martinez, Ada Carrasco   D: Alfonso Arau

LOLA MONTES *1955 140m/C FR*

The true story of the prostitute and circus performer who became the mistress of famed pianist Franz Liszt and the King of Bavaria. Also available in a 110 minute version.

C: Martine Carol, Peter Ustinov, Anton Walbrook, Ivan Desny, Oskar Werner   D: Max Ophuls

M *1931 99m/B&W GE*

Fritz Lang's masterpiece about the tense final days of a child killer who's being hunted by the police and by other criminals who would like to treat him to their own brand of lone justice. Peter Lorre plays the killer with a twisted, frightened conviction. The real life "Vampire of Dusseldorf" was the alleged inspiration for the film.

C: Peter Lorre, Ellen Widmann, Inge Langut, Gustav Grundgens   D: Fritz Lang

MAN FACING SOUTHEAST *1986 105m/C AR*

A man in an asylum claims to be an extraterrestrial. A sax playing psychologist tries to uncover the man's true identity but is shocked when the patient seems to possess strange powers. Movingly told.

C: Lorenzo Quinteros, Hugo Soto, Ines Vernengo   D: Eliseo Subiela

MANON OF THE SPRING *1987 113m/C FR (PG)*

In this stunning sequel to *Jean de Florette*, Manon, the daughter of the dead, victimized farmer, learns who blocked the spring and destroyed her father. She plans a wicked revenge against the two schemers, one of which has fallen in love with her. Beautifully photographed, expertly acted.

C: Yves Montand, Daniel Auteuil, Emmanuelle Beart, Hippolyte Girardot   D: Calude Berri

MEDITERRANEO *1991 90m/C (R) IT*

With World War II exploding around them, eight Italian soldiers become stranded on a Greek island. They soon dive into the easygoing, love-of-life atmosphere and end up staying for years.

C: Diego Abatantuono, Giuseppe Cederna, Claudio Bigagli, Vanna Barba, Claudio Bisio   D: Gabriele Salvatores   AA: '91 Best Foreign Language Film

MEPHISTO *1981 144m/C HU*

A power hungry thespian sacrifices his ideals and joins with the wicked ways of the Nazi party, all to achieve acting glory. The end result is tragic. Based on the novel by Klaus Mann, who killed himself because he could not find a publisher for his work.

C: Klaus Maria Brandauer, Krystyne Janda, Ildiko Bansagi, Karin Boyd, Rolf Hoppe   D: Istran Szabo   AA: '81 Best Foreign Language Film

METROPOLIS *1926 115m/B&W GE*

A wealthy young man living in a high tech future society gives up his life of luxury to join the economically oppressed in a revolt against the rich. The story almost plays second fiddle to an absolutely mesmerizing "look" achieved by Fritz Lang and his team of experts.

C: Brigitte Helm, Alfred Abel, Gustav Froehlich, Rudolf Klein-Rogge, Fritz Rasp   D: Fritz Lang

MURIEL *1963 115m/C FR IT*

An involved drama about a widow and her lover trying to come to terms with episodes of their past and her stepson who, having haunting memories of his own, cannot forgive himself for taking part in the torture and death of Muriel, a young girl in the war. Highly acclaimed.

C: Delphine Seyrig, Jean-Pierre Kerien, Nita Klein, Jean-Baptiste Thierree   D: Alain Resnais

MY LIFE AS A DOG *1985 101m/C SW*

A 12-year-old boy's mother becomes bedridden and, to stop the fighting between he and his brother, she ships him off to an aunt and uncle in a small Swedish village. Once there he comes in contact with all the town's eccentric characters, begins to experience life's young rituals, and falls in love with a tomboy, all the while praying for his mom's recovery. One of the sweetest, most effective films about growing up ever made.

C: Anton Gianzelius, Tomas Van Bromssen, Anki Liden, Melinda Kinnaman, Kicki Rundgrew   D: Lasse Hallstrom   AA: '87 Nom: Best Director, Adapted Screenplay

NAPOLEON *1927 235m/B&W FR*

Abel Grance's silent epic of the French Emperor, from his youthful beginning to his violent, successful Italian Campaign. Incredible imagery and techniques, including the powerful, famous, three screen finale.

C: Albert Dieudonne, Antonin Artaud, Pierre Batcheff, Gina Manes, Armand Bernard   D: Abel Gance

NIGHT OF THE SHOOTING STARS *1982 106m/C (R) IT*

An Italian village during World War II is divided into two emotionally wrought groups: one, supporting the Germans, the other supporting their American allies. Their tension builds and leads up to a final showdown.

C: Omero Antonutti, Margarita Lozano, Claudio Bigagli, Massimo Bonetti, Norma Martel   D: Paolo Tariani, Vittorio Tariani

NIGHTS OF CABIRIA *1957 111m/B&W IT*

Giuletta Masina gives a rich, inspired performance as a "working girl" who walks the streets dreaming of a rich, better life. Unfortunately, reality relentlessly interferes with her wishes. Highly acclaimed.

C: Giuletta Masina, Amadeo Nazzari   D: Federico Fellini   AA: '57 Best Foreign Language Film

NOSFERATU *1922 63m/B&W GE*

The first and quite possibly the best dracula film ever made. Bloodsucker Max Schreck brings a terrifyingly creepy mood to the role with a bony frame, rodent like face, sharp ears, and long razor like fingernails. The film also went under another title, *Symphony of Horror*, which is an apt description for the beautiful terror it unleashes.

C: Max Schreck, Alexander Grannach, Gustav von Wangenheim, Greta Schroeder   D: F. W. Murnau

THE OFFICIAL STORY *1985 112m/C (R) AR*

The breakdown of an Argentinian family starts when a mother begins to feel that her adopted daughter may be a child of one of the ruthless government's political prisoners. A great story that never gets lost in the strong political message.

C: Norma Aleandro, Hector Alterio, Chunchuna Villafane, Patricio Conteras   D: Luis Puenzo   AA: '85 Best Foreign Language Film, Nom: Best Original Screenplay

ORDET *1955 126m/C DK*

Two families are caught in a feud over their religious beliefs but are brought together by a man who claims to be Jesus and, amazingly, begins to perform miracles. Expertly directed by the religious Dreyer, whose films all deal with spiritual beliefs and faith.

C: Emil Haas Christensen, Henrik Malberg   D: Carl Theodor Dreyer

PASSION OF JOAN OF ARC *1928 114m/B&W FR*

Silent film classic restages the inquisition and trial of St. Joan of Arc, ending with her death sentence of being burned at the stake. An excellent portrayal by Falconetti in her only film role.

C: Maria Falconetti, Eugena Sylvane, Maurice Schultz, Antonin

Artaud   D: Carl Theodor Dreyer

PELLE THE CONQUEROR *1988 160m/C SW, DK*

A father and a young boy leave their home in Sweden and move to Denmark. Their relationship becomes stronger as they must keep up what simple life they have in a cruel world. Critically hailed.

C: Max von Sydow, Pelle Hvenegaard, Erik Paaske, Bjorn Granath, Axel Strobye   D: Billie August   AA: '88 Best Foreign Language Film, Nom: Best Actor (von Sydow)

PIXOTE *1981 127m/C BR*

Graphic, amazing pic about an abandoned 10-year-old boy who hits the streets of Rio de Janiero and chisels out a living as a glue sniffing pimp. Life on the streets gets tougher and tougher, leading to murder. A disturbing film with scenes that stay with you for days.

C: Fernando Ramos DaSilva, Marila Pera, Jorge Juliano, Gilberta Moura, Jose Nilson dos Santos   D: Hector Babenco

THE RIVER *1951 100m/C FR*

Renoir's masterpiece about three young English girls in Bengal, India, and the infatuation and desire they all share for a crippled American soldier. A must see.

C: Patricia Walters, Adrienne Corri, Nora Swinburne, Radha, Arthur Shields, Thomas E. Breen   D: Jean Renoir

SEVEN BEAUTIES *1976 115m/C IT*

A ladies man, who works as a petty crook to support his seven unattractive sisters, is locked up in a German prison camp during WWII. He does anything and everything to survive, including sleeping with his repulsive commander. A classic black comedy.

C: Giancarlo Giannini, Fernando Rey, Shirley Stoler, Elena Fiore, Enzo Vitale   D: Lina Wertmuller

SEVEN SAMURAI *1954 204m/B&W JP*

Awesome, powerful picture about a village that is at the mercy of a gang of bandits until they hire seven professional warriors to do away with the thieves. One of the all-time great films, considered flawless. Remade in America as *The Magnificent Seven*.

C: Toshiro Mifune, Takashi Shimura, Yoshio Inaba, Kuninori Kodo, Ko Kimira D: Akira Kurosawa

THE SEVENTH SEAL *1956 96m/B&W SW*

The plague is wiping out Europe and a knight challenges "Death" to a game of chess. If the knight wins, he and his wife live. The duel sparks a deep discussion of life, death, and God.

C: Gunnar Bjornstrand, Max von Sydow, Bibi Andersson, Bengt Ekerot D: Ingmar Bergman

SHOESHINE *1947 90m/B&W IT*

Two best friends become involved in criminal activities and are sent to prison where their friendship is tested and ultimately destroyed. A classic tragedy of human feeling from the director of *The Bicycle Thief*.

C: Franco Interlenghi, Rinaldo Smordoni, Anniclo Mele, Bruno Ortensi, Pacifico Astrologo D: Vittorio DeSica AA: '47 Best Foreign Language Film

SHOOT THE PIANO PLAYER *1962 92m/B&W FR*

A former concert pianist is now playing in a small Paris cafe. His girlfriend wants him to try for the spotlight again, but a series of events gets him tied up with gangsters and murder. Tense, moody pic, one of Truffaut's best.

C: Charles Aznavour, Marie DuBois, Nicole Berger, Michele Mercier, Albert Remy D: Francois Truffaut

THE SHOP ON MAIN STREET *1965 111m/B&W CZ*

It's World War II in Czechoslovakia and an elderly Jewish

woman gives a man a job in her button shop. A strong friendship begins to blossom and when the Nazi army comes to town and demand all the Jews be deported, she puts her trust in her friend to hide and protect her.

C: Ida Kaminska, Josef Kroner, Hana Slivkova   D: Jan Kadar, Elmar Klos   AA: '65 Best Foreign Language Film

THE SPIRIT OF THE BEEHIVE *1973 95m/C SP*

A young girl in a small desolate Spanish town sees the movie, "Frankenstein" at a local theater. She becomes infatuated with the monster, sympathizing with his plight, and believes he's still alive. So she begins roaming the countryside searching for him, entering a dangerous world. Hauntingly poetic.

C: Fernando Gomez, Teresa Gimpera, Ana Torrent   D: Victor Erice

THE TIN DRUM *1979 141m/C GR, FR (R)*

A twelve-year-old boy in the 1920s is surrounded by the torment and chaos of the Nazis increasing rise to power. So he wills himself to stop growing and takes out his aggression by beating on a tin drum. An unforgettable mix of fantasy and reality.

C: David Bennent, Mario Adorf, Angela Winkler, Daniel Olbrychski, Katharina Thalbach   D: Rainer Werner Fassbinder, Volker Schlondorff   AA: '79 Best Foreign Language Film

TORMENT *1944 90m/B&W SW*

A young girl and a boy are in love but their world is destroyed when one becomes friends with their sadistic, psychotic school teacher. Written by Ingmar Bergman.

C: Mai Zetterling, Stig Jarrel, Alf Kjellin, Olaf Winnerstrand   D: Alf Sjoberg

THE TREE OF WOODEN CLOGS *1978 185m/B&W IT*

An engaging tale of peasant life in turn of the century Northern Italy and what happens when a father chops down one of the landowner's trees to make a pair of clogs for his shoeless son. Beautiful and endearing.

C: Luigi Ornaghi, Francesca Moriggi, Omar Brignoll D: Ermanno Olmi

TRIUMPH OF THE WILL *1934 115m/B&W GE*

An incredible documentary on the Hitler rallies at Nuremberg in 1934. Disturbing and engrossing. Considered the greatest propaganda film ever made.

D: Leni Riefenstahl

UGETSU *1953 95m/B&W JP*

A ghost tale of sorts about two peasants, wanting much more out of life, who leave their families in search of power. One wants wealth in the city, the other success as a samurai warrior. They both get much more than they bargained for.

C: Machiko Kyo, Masayuki Mori, Kinuyo Tanaka, Sakae Ozawa D: Kenji Mizoguchi

UMBERTO D *1955 89m/B&W IT*

An aging, retired working class man tires to keep up his self respect as he and his dog live off his meager pension. DeSica's personal favorite.

C: Carlo Battista, Maria Ria Casillio, Lina Gennari D: Vittorio DeSica

VAMPYR *1931 75m/B&W GE*

Moody surreal-like story of a man at a strange inn who finds an unconscious woman he believes has been attacked by a vampire. He soon realizes he's walked into a nightmare. Filled with hallucinatory scenes that will make you want to turn out the lights.

C: Julien West, Sybile Schmitz, Harnet Gerard, Maurice Schutz D: Carl Theodor Dreyer

THE VANISHING *1988 107m/C NL, FR*

When a man's girlfriend disappears at a gas station he's forced onto a terrifying path of chaos and mayhem trying to track her down.

C: Barnard Pierre Donnadieu, Johanna Ter Stoege   D: George Sluizer

VIRIDIANA *1961 90m/B&W ME, SP*

Complex compelling story about an innocent girl who wishes to be a nun but is physically and mentally dissuaded by her twisted, perverted uncle. After he dies, she and his illegitimate son inherit his estate and she turns it into a lodging house for beggars and the poor, who exploit her.

C: Silvia Pinal, Francesco Rabal, Fernando Rey   D: Luis Bunuel

WAGES OF FEAR *1955 138m/B&W FR*

An oil conglomerate which controls an economically depressed town offers four men a chance to get out by taking on a suicide mission of driving nitroglycerine 300 miles to a well-fire that needs to be extinguished. The pay is $2,000 a man, enough to leave their dreary lives behind. Intense, multi-layer character study.

C: Yves Montand, Charles Vanel, Peter Van Eyck, Vera Clouzot, Folco Lulli   D: Henri-Georges Clouzot

THE WANNSEE CONFERENCE *1984 87m/C GE*

The actual notes taken by a secretary at this famous meeting are used to recreate the evil conversation that took place between 14 powerful Nazi officers on January 20, 1942, as they casually discussed the ultimate resolution of the Jewish "problem." Realistic nightmare.

C: Dietrich Mattausch, Gerd Brockmann, Friedrich Beckhaus D: Heinz Schirk

WILD STRAWBERRIES *1957 90m/B&W SW*

While on his way to receive a honorary degree, an elderly professor looks back at his life and begins to come to terms with his regrets and disappointments. A heartfelt masterpiece filled with dream imagery like the professor seeing his own coffin being taken to the grave.

C: Victor Sjostrom, Bibi Andersson, Max von Sydow, Ingrid Thulin, Gunnar Bjornstrand   D: Ingmar Bergman

WINGS OF DESIRE *1988 130m/C (PG-13) GE*

A pair of angels watch over and wander through modern Berlin, slowly building a burning desire to see what life as a mortal would be like. A spiritual, visual feast. Considered Wenders' best film.

C: Bruno Ganz, Peter Falk, Solveig Dommartin, Otto Sander, Curt Bois   D: Wim Wenders

WOMAN IN THE DUNES *1964 122m/B&W JP*

Taut pic about an entomologist studying and collecting insects in the sand dunes. He misses his ride back to town and some locals take him to a woman who lives in a hut at the bottom of a deep pit. She offers him food and lodging but after he climbs down the ladder, the locals pull it up, trapping him.

C: Eiji Okada, Kyoko Kishida, Koji Mitsoi, Hiroko Ito, Sen Yano D: Hiroshi Teshigahara

WORLD OF APU *1959 103m/B&W IN*

The last of acclaimed director Satyajit Ray's trilogy (*Aparajito, Pather Panchali*). Apu, now grown, quits college and moves in with a friend. He marries his roommate's cousin and she dies giving birth to a boy. Disillusioned, Apu drifts for years until his friend finds him and helps him. Great, triumphant character study.

C: Soumitra Chatterjee, Sharmila Tagore, Alek Charkraverty, Swapan Makerji   D: Satyajit Ray

YOJIMBO *1963 110m/B JP*

Two feuding families unwittingly hire the same samurai warrior to spread destruction. Disaster follows.

C: Toshiro Mifune, Eijiro Tono, Suuzu Yamda, Seizaburo Kawazu
D: Akira Kurosawa

Z *1969 128m/C FR, AL*

A true incident is turned into a political thriller in Costa-Gavras' picture about the assassination of a Greek politician and the impending questions and chaos it causes.

C: Yves Montand, Jean-Louis Trintignant, Charles Denner, Irene Papas, Georges Geret   D: Constantin Costa-Gavras   AA: '69 Best Foreign Language Film

HOLIDAY

THE BISHOP'S WIFE *1947 109m/B&W*

Warm, engaging tale of a dapper angel (Grant) who arrives on Earth to help a struggling bishop (Niven) and his wife trumpet up funds for a new church. A treat for the whole family. Remade in 1996 as *The Preacher's Wife*.

C: David Niven, Loretta Young, Cary Grant   D: Henry Koster
AA: '47 Nom: Best Picture, Director

A CHRISTMAS CAROL *1951 86m/B&W*

Atmospheric, effective adaptation of Dickens' classic about a bitter old man who can't see through his greed until a fateful Christmas Eve wherein he's visited by three prophetic ghosts who show him the true meaning of Christmas and turn his life around.

C: Alastair Sim, Kathleen Harrison, Jack Warner   D: Brian Desmond-Hurst

CHRISTMAS IN CONNECTICUT 1945 101m/B&W

A "sophisticated" woman who writes a housekeeping column for a big magazine is forced to open her home to a war veteran, as a publicity gimmick, for the holidays. Unfortunately, her column expertise and her private housekeeping habits are not one and the same leading to lighthearted holiday hijinx. Remade in 1992 by Arnold Schwarzenegger.

C: Barbara Stanwyck, Reginald Gardiner, Sydney Greenstreet, Dennis Morgan D: Peter Godfrey

A CHRISTMAS STORY 1983 95m/C (PG)

Excellent 1950s yuletide pic about a young boy's Christmas wish of getting a Red Ryder BB-gun and the hilarious complications it brings him and his family. A perfect slice of life mix of Norman Rockwell and Woody Allen with an outstanding performance by Peter Billingsley as the rifle infatuated youth.

C: Peter Billingsley, Darren McGavin, Melinda Dillon, Ian `Petrilla D: Bob Clark

EASTER PARADE 1948 103m/C

Astaire plays half of a song and dance duo who breaks off with his other half (Miller), hooks up with new talent (Garland), and tries to climb to the top. Songs by Irving Berlin include "Happy Easter" and "Everybody's Doin' It."

C: Fred Astaire, Judy Garland, Peter Lawford, Ann Miller, Jules Munshin D: Charles Walters

HOLIDAY INN 1942 101m/B&W

A couple of feuding entertainers decide to drop their differences and team up so they can make a "Holiday Inn" out of an old Connecticut farm. Songs include "Be Careful, It's My Heart," and Bing Crosby's famous rendition of "White Christmas."

C: Bing Crosby, Fred Astaire, Marjorie Reynolds, Walter Abel, Virginia Dale D: Mark Sandrich

IT'S A WONDERFUL LIFE *1946 125m/B&W*
See "Top 100"

MARCH OF THE WOODEN SOLDIERS *1934 73m/B*
In this timeless classic, Laurel and Hardy are framed by the diabolical Barnaby and banished to Boogie Land. They escape their exile but unwittingly unleash an army of boogie men who attack the town. Down, but not out, Laurel and Hardy come up with one last hope to save everyone: the wooden soldiers.

C: Stan Laurel, Oliver Hardy, Charlotte Henry, Henry Kleinbach, Felix Knight   D: Charles "Buddy" Rogers, Gus Meins

MIRACLE ON 34TH STREET *1947 97m/B&W*
See "Top 100"

MRS. WIGGS OF THE CABBAGE PATCH *1934 80m/B&W*
Sentimental story of a woman who's forced to raise her children alone after her husband leaves her. A special Thanksgiving restores her faith in life. W.C. Fields gives the pic a dose of humor.

C: Pauline Lord, ZaSu Pitts, W. C. Fields   D: Norman Taurag

NATIONAL LAMPOON'S CHRISTMAS VACATION *1989 93m/C (PG-13)*
Clark Griswold (Chase) and his All-American family plan an old fashioned Christmas celebration, but the non-stop parade of wacky relatives and ridiculous mishaps (like a burning Christmas tree that fries the family cat) dampen the holiday cheer. To add insult to injury, the huge Christmas bonus he was planning on turns out to be a lovely membership to the Jelly-Of-The-Month Club. Loads of yuletide yuks, laced with a warm fireplace feel.

C: Chevy Chase, Beverly D'Angelo, Randy Quaid, Diane Ladd, Julia

Louis-Dreyfus D: Jeremiah S. Chechik

THE RAILWAY CHILDREN *1970 104m/C*

An English family is torn apart during Christmas when the father is wrongfully imprisoned. The mother and her three children, barely surviving on a dying farm near the railroad, are befriended by a kind stranger who helps them get their father out of jail. Sweet, tender story.

C: Jenny Agutter, William Mervyn, Bernard Cribbins, Dinah Sheridan, Ian Cuthbertson D: Lionel Jeffries

SCROOGE *1935 61m/B&W*

Moody re-telling of Dickens' classic about a cynical miser who can't understand people's happiness and love for Christmas until a few ghosts visit him on Christmas Eve and rattle his cage.

C: Seymour Hicks, Maurice Evans, Robert Cochran, Mary Glynne, Donald Cathrup D: Henry Edwards

SCROOGE *1970 86m/C (G)*

A rollicking energetic musical version of the classic yuletide tale about a cynical miser who despises Christmas and all its trimmings. Then, on Christmas Eve, he's visited by three ghosts who show him the light. Great musical numbers include "The Beautiful Day" and "Thank You Very Much."

C: Albert Finney, Alec Guinness, Edith Evans D: Ronald Neame

WHITE CHRISTMAS *1954 120m/C*

Danny Kaye and Bing Crosby team up in this delightful story about two entertainers who put on a Christmas charity show to save a Vermont inn. Includes fifteen musical numbers.

C: Danny Kaye, Bing Crosby, Rosemary Clooney, Vera-Ellen, Dean Jagger D: Mike Curtiz

HORROR

THE ABOMINABLE DR. PHIBES *1971 90m/C (PG)*

A car accident disfigures a man and his wife dies on the operating table. The tragedy propels him into a mode of madness and, believing his beloved could have been saved with proper medical care, he begins hunting down the "inept surgeons" saving a special torture for each one. Ghoulishly good.

C: Vincent Price, Joseph Cotten, Hugh Griffith, Terry Thomas, Virginia North   D: Robert Fuest

AN AMERICAN WEREWOLF IN LONDON *1981 97m/C (R)*

Two American youths backpacking through England are attacked by a werewolf. One is ripped to shreds while the other escapes, but not without taking along "full moon" problems. A frightening flick with some classic comic overtones, including the famous human-to-werewolf transformation (great f/x) behind Creedence Clearwater Revival's "Bad Moon Rising."

C: David Naughton, Griffin Dunne, Jenny Agutter, Frank Oz, Brian Glover   D: John Landis

THE BIRDS *1963 120m/C*

Dark story of apocalyptic proportions about birds forming an evil universal alliance to wipe out man. Film focuses on one town's battle. A horrifying stunner.

C: Rod Taylor, Tippi Hedren, Jessica Tandy, Veronica Cartwright, Suzanne Pleshette   D: Alfred Hitchcock

THE BLACK CAT *1934 65m/B&W*

The first pairing of Bela Lugosi and Boris Karloff resulted in what many critics believe is a classic of the genre. The twisted story revolves around the problems a straight laced architect has when he becomes involved with a passionate satanist.

C: Boris Karloff, Bela Lugosi, David Manners, Jacqueline Wells, Lucille Lund   D: Edgar G. Ulmer

BLACK SUNDAY *1960 83m/B&W*

A spooky tale revolving around the belief that one day out of each century Satan unleashes unspeakable horror on the planet. Well, that day is here and a witch and her assistant have returned from the grave to torture and slaughter those who killed her one hundred years ago. A favorite of horror buffs the world over.

C: Barbara Steele, John Richardson, Ivo Garrani, Andrea Cheechi, Arturo Dominici   D: Mario Bava

THE BODY SNATCHER *1945 77m/B&W*

One of Borlis Karloff's most famous roles has him playing a psychotic grave robber who provides a ghoulish doctor dead bodies to experiment on. Directed by *West Side Story* helmer Robert Wise.

C: Edith Atwater, Russell Wade, Rita Corday, Boris Karloff, Bela Lugosi   D: Robert Wise

THE BRIDE OF FRANKENSTEIN *1935 75m/B&W*

A first rate sequel to a first rate original. Frankenstein is persuaded by an oddball doctor to build a female companion for his male monster. A new world of horror follows. Contains the classic blind hermit sequence and a great over-the-top bride.

C: Boris Karloff, Elsa Lanchester, Ernest Thesiger, Colin Clive, Una O'Connor   D: James Whale

CARRIE *1976 98m/C (R)*

A shy, introverted teenager turns into the All-American girl from hell when she uses her telekinetic powers to avenge her mean-spirited, mocking classmates. Tension builds beautifully to the blood party on prom night.

C: Sissy Spacek, Piper Laurie, John Travolta, William Katt, Amy Irving
D: Brian DePalma

CAT PEOPLE 1942 73m/B&W

A woman is afflicted with an ancient curse that turns her into a creeping, crawling, bloodthirsty panther. If that's not bad enough, she needs human blood to survive. Look out! Eerie, atmospheric classic.

C: Jane Randolph, Elizabeth Russell, Jack Holt, Alan Napier, Simone Simon   D: Jacques Tourneur

THE CONQUEROR WORM 1968 95m/C

Moody Price vehicle about the infamous work of Dr. Matthew Hopkins, the real life ruthless witch hunter who did his evil deeds in the 17th century.

C: Vincent Price, Ian Ogilvy, Rupert Davies, Hillary Dwyer, Robert Russell   D: Michael Reeves

CREATURE FROM THE BLACK LAGOON 1954 79m/B&W

While researching in the Amazon, the crew of a scientific expedition discover a prehistoric half-man half-fish monster. It falls for one of the female scientists and a deadly battle begins. Great pic with a renowned score.

C: Richard Carlson, Julie Adams, Richard Denning, Antonio Moreno, Whit Bissell   D: Jack Arnold

THE CRIMES OF DR. MABUSE 1932 120m/B&W

A mad doctor who has been institutionalized does not let his confinement stop him from spreading his evil throughout the world. Truly ghoulish.

C: Rudolf Klein-Rogge, Otto Werwicke, Gustav Diesi, Karl Meixner
D: Fritz Lang

CURSE OF THE DEMON *1957 81m/B&W*

A famous American psychologist is sent to London to expose an evil cult of satanic worshippers. After prying a bit too long the cult's leader calls on a demon from hell to do away with the doctor. Spine-tingling horror.

C: Dana Andrews, Peggy Cummins, Niall MacGinnis, Maurice Denham D: Jacques Tourneau

DAWN OF THE DEAD *1978 126m/C*

Flesh-eating zombies are terrorizing the Earth so a group of humans take refuge in a shopping mall. A bloody battle with the monsters soon follows. Typical plot is transformed into tense, graphic pic that works as both a horror pic and social satire.

C: David Enge, Ken Foree, Gaylen Ross D: George A. Romero

DEAD OF NIGHT *1945 102m/B&W*

If you are a true horror enthusiast, this film is not be missed. Five nightmarish stories (revolving around five guests at a remote country home) culminate with the most famous one: a blood thirsty dummy going after its "master."

C: Michael Redgrave, Sally Ann Howes, Basil Radford, Naunton Wayne D: Alberto Cavalcanti, Charles Crichton, Basil Dearden, Robert Hamer

DRACULA *1931 75m/B&W*

Bela Lugosi's most famous role cast him as one of horror's most infamous figures, the blood sucking Dracula, constantly searching for his next victim so he can stay alive.

C: Bela Lugosi, David Manners, Dwight Frye, Helen Chandler, Edward Van Sloan D: Tod Browning

DR. JEKYLL AND MR. HYDE *1932 96m/B&W*

The bizarre, surreal-like classic about a well-minded doctor who, after drinking a secret potion, slips into his double life of a raving, maniacal lunatic. Brutal psychological overtones with brilliant performances.

C: Fredric March, Miriam Hopkins, Hallwell Hobbes, Rose Hobart, Holmes Herbert   D: Rouben Mamoulian   AA: '31–32 Best Actor (March)

EVIL DEAD 1983 126m/C

A gritty, raw, low budget shocker about five college friends who rent a creepy cabin in the woods. They unwittingly release a curse that turns the trees into bloodthirsty vicious killers and the woods into a brutal slayground. A gore lover's dream.

C: Bruce Campbell, Ellen Sandweiss, Betsy Baker, Hal Delrich   D: Sam Raimi

THE EXORCIST 1973 120m/C (R)

See "Top 100"

FALL OF THE HOUSE OF USHER 1960 85m/C

A man arrives at the house of Usher to propose to the beautiful young woman who lives there. He soon finds out that this was a very, very bad idea.

C: Vincent Price, Mark Damon, Myrna Fahey   D: Roger Corman

FRANKENSTEIN 1931 71m/B&W

See "Top 100":

GHOST STORY 1981 110m/C (R)

Creepy picture about four old-timers who have a monthly gathering where they tell ghost stories. The most horrifying tale, which is also true, is one they never share. They all were involved in the murder of a college girl more than fifty years ago. Soon they'll have to face facts because she's come back to even the score.

C: Fred Astaire, Melvyn Douglas, Douglas Fairbanks, Jr., John

Houseman, Craig Wasson   D: John Irvin

HALLOWEEN *1978 90m/C (R)*

A young man, institutionalized since he was 10 for a bizarre killing spree, escapes from the asylum and returns to his hometown for more bloodletting. Suspenseful, intelligent direction with a "you-know-he's-behind-you-but-when-you-turn-around-he's-gone" style, that keeps you on the edge of your seat.

C: Jamie Lee Curtis, Donald Pleasence, Nancy Loomis, P. J. Soles
D: John Carpenter

THE HAUNTING *1963 113m/B&W*

Masterfully told chiller about a parapsychologist, two mediums, and the owner of a haunted mansion who spend a weekend trying to rid the place of an evil spirit. Great final showdown. Very scary film is still as effective as when it was first released.

C: Julie Harris, Claire Bloom, Russ Tamblyn, Richard Johnson
D: Robert Wise

HELLRAISER *1987 94m/C (R)*

A woman is controlled by the ghost of her husband's brother. She can bring him back to life if she supplies an endless parade of flesh for his ghastly appetite.

C: Andrew Robinson, Clare Higgins, Ashley Laurence   D: Clive Barker

HENRY: PORTRAIT OF A SERIAL KILLER *1990 90m/C (X)*

Stark, brutal pic based loosely on the exploits of notorious mass murderer Henry Lee Lucas and his partner in mayhem, Otis Toole. Graphic in its depiction of the mindless killings and the mindless killers. Contains one of the most disturbingly realistic scenes ever filmed in which Henry and Otis enter a house and video tape their sickness in action. Critically acclaimed.

C: Michael Rooker, Tom Towles, Tracy Arnold   D: John McNaughton

THE HIDDEN *1987 98m/C (R)*

Highly regarded shocker about an alien life form that enters a human through his mouth and turns him into a killing machine. If the human dies, the alien moves into the next available body which means it can go from a 90-year-old woman to a ten-year-old boy to a dog. Two FBI agents, one with a secret, try to catch the hideous beast.

C: Kyle MacLachlan, Michael Nouri, Clu Gulager, Ed O'Ross, Claudia Christian   D: Jack Sholder

HORROR OF DRACULA *1958 82m/C*

The Hammer Studios released a string of horror films through the late '40s and '50s and this may be their best. Dracula is the same blood sucking menace but is now a bit more sophisticated and cunning as he duels his hated enemy, Professor Van Helsing. This pic pumped blood back into the horror genre.

C: Peter Cushing, Christopher Lee, Michael Gough, Melissa Stribling, Carol Marsh   D: Terrence Fisher

ISLAND OF LOST SOULS *1933 71m/B&W*

They just don't make them like this anymore. An evil scientist sets up shop on an uncharted island and performs fiendish experiments which turn jungle animals into strange men and women. When a shipwreck victim stumbles onto the doctor's compound, the maniacal medic toys with the idea of mating him with Lola, the "panther woman," to see what the word's first animal baby would look like.

C: Charles Laughton, Bela Lugosi, Richard Arlen, Leila Hyams, Kathleen Burke   D: Erle C. Kenton

I WALKED WITH A ZOMBIE *1943 69m/B&W*

Dark eerie picture about a nurse who travels to the island of Haiti to care for an ill woman. The two visit a local voodoo ceremony designed to cure the sick and strange things begin to happen. A horror fan favorite.

C: Frances Dee, Tom Conway, James Ellison, Christine Gordon, Edith Barrett D: Jacque Tourneur

LEGEND OF HELL HOUSE *1973 94m/C (PG)*

A group of spirit experts are hired to spend some time in a house which has a history of murder and poltergeists. Routine theme is supercharged with suspense and numerous shocks.

C: Roddy McDowall, Pamela Franklin, Clive Revill, Gayle Hunnicutt D: John Hough

THE MUMMY *1932 73m/B&W*

Archeologists dig up a 4,000-year-old mummified Egyptian priest (Karloff) and the holy one soon comes to life. The plot thickens when the mummy believes that his long lost love has been reincarnated in the form of a pretty young woman.

C: Boris Karloff, Zita Johann, Edward Van Sloan, David Manners D: Karl Freund

NIGHT OF THE LIVING DEAD *1968 90m/B&W*

A radiation fall-out causes recently deceased corpses to rise up from the dead and viciously seek "life" sustaining human flesh. A group of strangers take refuge in an old house and must fight off their attackers in what ends up a brutally graphic bloody battle. One of the most famous horror films ever made, complete with a classic ending.

C: Judith O'Dea, Duane Jones, Russell Streiner, Karl Hardman D: George A. Romero

A NIGHTMARE ON ELM STREET *1984 92m/C (R)*

A group of high school friends are all having creepy dreams and slowly realize the same blood thirsty lunatic is starring in all of them. Each time they go to sleep, they have the dreadful possibility of waking up dead. This leads to a horrific confrontation between one of the girls and the infamous killer, Mr. Freddy Krueger. Intelligently made.

C: John Saxon, Johnny Depp, Heather Langenkamp, Ronee Blakley, Robert Englund, Amanda Wyss   D: Wes Craven

THE OMEN *1976 111m/C (R)*

After a series of "accidental" deaths, a wealthy family comes to the horrifying realization that their son is also the son of Lucifer. Film is told in a completely believable manner that makes you constantly cringe with fear. Great score.

C: Gregory Peck, Lee Remick, Billie Whitelaw, David Warner, Holly Palance   D: Richard Donner

PHANTOM OF THE OPERA *1925 79m/B&W*

Horror classic about a disfigured composer whose mind has slipped over the edge. He makes an opera house his haunt and terrorizes its visitors, all for a very personal and twisted reason.

C: Lon Chaney, Sr., Norman Kerry, Mary Philbin, Gibson Gowland
D: Rupert Julian

POLTERGEIST *1982 114m/C (PG)*

A scarefest funded by Steven Spielberg and directed by the man who brought us *The Texas Chainsaw Massacre*. Freakish tale centers around a family whose child is stolen away by a fiendish supernatural force. How, you may ask? The evil being pulls her into a bizarre dimension inside the TV. (I think I used to go there when I watched *Gilligan's Island*). The family hires a spooky medium to get her out and the confrontation (and special effects) are mind-bending.

C: JoBeth Williams, Craig T. Nelson, Beatrice Straight, Heather O'Rourke, Zelda Rubinstein   D: Tobe Hooper

PSYCHO *1960 109m/B&W*

See "Top 100"

RE-ANIMATOR *1985 86m/C*

Graphically witty reworking of H.P. Lovecraft's *Herbert West, Re-Animator* about a med student who is conducting demented experiments to bring the dead back to life. (Hilarious scene where it works too well on a cat). The experiments get out of hand and before long West is in way over his head.

C: Jeffrey Combs, Bruce Abbott, Barbara Crampton, David Gale, Robert Sampson   D: Stuart Gordon

ROSEMARY'S BABY *1968 134m/C (R)*

A pregnant woman begins to get nervous when her husband becomes too friendly with the odd neighbors. She slowly suspects something is wrong and she's right. He's a member of their satanic cult and the newborn is satan's child. Truly horrifying.

C: Mia Farrow, John Cassavetes, Ruth Gordon, Maurice Evans, Patsy Kelly   D: Roman Polanski   AA: '68 Best Supporting Actress (Gordon)

THE SHINING *1980 143m/C (R)*

Kubrick's atmospheric telling of the Stephen King novel about a writer who, with his wife and son, takes on the winter caretaking duties of a remote mountaintop summer resort. Little by little, cabin fever eats away at the writer's brain ("all work and no play makes Jack a dull boy") and, during a blizzard that snow bounds them, he goes berserk. Visually stunning, perfect Nicholson, filled with classic scenes.

C: Jack Nicholson, Shelley Duvall, Scatman Crothers, Danny Lloyd, Joe Turkel   D: Stanley Kubrick

THE STEPFATHER *1987 89m/C (R)*

A seemingly normal dad hacks up his family, washes up in the bathroom, and leaves town. A few months later he meets a lovely single mom, marries again, and silently plans another blood party. Taut direction with classic O'Quinn performance as psycho dad. Based loosely on the real life murders of New Jerseyite John List.

C: Terry O'Quinn, Shelley Hack, Jill Schoelen, Stephen Shellan, Charles Lanyer D: Joseph Ruben

SUSPIRA *1977 92m/C (R)*

A young ballerina enters a European dance school hoping to sharpen her skills. Unknown to her, the school is run by satanic witches who make regular "changes" in the enrollment. From horror guru Argento.

C: Jessica Harper, Joan Bennett, Alida Valli, Udo Kier D: Dario Argento

THE TEXAS CHAINSAW MASSACRE *1974 86m/C (R)*

While visiting the abandoned house of their dead grandfather, a group of teenagers wander deep into the woods and come across a house owned by a sicko who puts humans on a meat hook and uses their skin as a face mask. Though gory at times, most of the terror of this film comes from what you think you see. Based loosely on the exploits of serial killer Ed Gaines. One for the most famous and financially successful horror films ever made.

C: Marilyn Burns, Allen Danzinger, Paul A. Partain, Gunnar Hansen D: Tobe Hooper

THEATER OF BLOOD *1973 104m/C (R)*

A Shakespearean actor who is ruthlessly trashed by the critics decides to do some trashing of his own. He stalks and kills the know-it-alls using death scenes from Shakespeare plays for inspiration. Much of the horror is played for laughs.

C: Vincent Price, Diana Rigg, Ian Hendry, Robert Morley, Dennis Price   D: Douglas Hickox

THE THING 1982 127m/C (R)

Remake of the '51 sci-fi classic has a stronger horror/gore edge with some great "F/X" scenes. Same story about a group of scientists in the Arctic who unearth an unfriendly alien beast. Masterfully made.

C: Kurt Russell, Wilford Brimley, T. K Carter, Richard Masur, Keith David   D: John Carpenter

TREMORS 1989 96m/C (PG-13)

This rollicking throwback to the monster films of the '50s is a perfectly paced, just-enough-gore winner. A couple of cowpokes in a small desert town discover a gruesomely dismembered sheep rancher and his bloody ripped-up herd. But that's not the bad news. The bad news is the giant worm like creature that did this is hungry and wants more. Run!

C: Kevin Bacon, Fred Ward, Finn Carter, Michael Gross, Reba McIntire   D: Ron Underwood

THE UNINVITED 1944 99m/B&W

A brother and sister move into a house on the coast of England and immediately witness strange, unexplainable occurrences. Soon, a woman from a nearby village is hypnotically drawn to the place, though she hasn't lived there since she was a child. Before long, they realize the terror behind the haunting.

C: Ray Milland, Ruth Hussey, Donald Crisp, Cornelia Otis Skinner, Gail Russell   D: Lewis Allen

THE WICKER MAN 1975 103m/C

An anonymous tip about a mysterious disappearance of a young girl leads a Scottish policeman to an island off the coast of England. He's soon inside the wicked twisted world of a pagan cult that practices bizarre sex rituals. A first rate achievement in eeriness and terror.

C: Edward Woodward, Christopher Lee, Britt Ekland, Diane Cilento, Ingrid Pitt   D: Robin Hardy

THE WOLF MAN *1941 70m/B&W*

Chaney plays Lawrence Talbot, a fellow who tries to save a woman from a wolf attack. Lugosi plays the wolf who bites him. Talbot soon realizes that this bite is forcing odd changes in his behavior and for him a full moon means big trouble.

C: Lon Chaney, Jr., Claude Rains, Maria Ouspenskaya, Ralph Bellamy, Bela Lugosi   D: George Waggner

MUSICALS

ALEXANDER'S RAGTIME BAND *1938 104m/B&W*

High energy pic that revolves around a musical trio (two men, one woman) and the two men's 20 year fight for the woman's affections. As the love triangle roars, their showbiz lives are filled with ups and downs and ups. Songs include the title tune, "Now It Can Be Told," and "Easter Parade."

C: Tyrone Power, Alice Faye, Don Ameche, Ethel Merman, Jack Haley   D: Henry King

AN AMERICAN IN PARIS *1951 113m/C*

See "Top 100"

ANNIE GET YOUR GUN *1950 105m/C*

Adaptation of the stage play based on the life of legendary gunslinger Annie Oakley. Strong cast of characters like Buffalo Bill Cody, Sitting Bull, and Frank Butler along with an Oscar winning score ("There's No Business Like Show Business," "Anything You Can Do," "Can't Get A Man With A Gun").

C: Betty Hutton, Howard Keel, Louis Calhern, J. Carrol Naish, Keenan Wynn   D: George Sidney

BELLS OF ST. MARY 1945 126m/B&W

A sequel to *Going My Way* in which Crosby once again plays a progressive priest who goes up against the traditional values of the strong willed Mother Superior regarding how the children should be taught. Songs include "Aren't You Glad You're You."

C: Bing Crosby, Ingrid Bergman, Henry Travers   D: Leo McCarey
AA: '45 Nom: Best Actress (Bergman), Actor (Crosby), Director, Picture

CABARET 1972 119m/C (PG)

Musicals don't get much better than this, one that combines drama, excitement, and a great score. It's 1931 in Germany and Hitler is on the way up. To escape from the pressures of society everyone comes to where the action is, the cabaret. Love, violence, and entertainment are all on stage. Songs include the title track and "Money, Money."

C: Liza Minnelli, Joel Grey, Michael York, Marisa Berenson   D: Bob Fosse   AA: '72 Best Actress (Minnelli), Director, Supporting Actor (Grey), Nom: Best Picture

CARMEN JONES 1954 105m/C

A rollicking updated version of the famous opera in which a soldier falls in love with a Southern Belle, murders his commanding officer, and goes permanent AWOL to be with her. Her eyes begin to wander, causing our hero to slip even deeper into madness. Songs include "Dat's Love."

C: Dorothy Dandridge, Harry Belafonte, Pearl Bailey, Roy Glenn, Diahann Carroll   D: Otto Preminger   AA: '54 Nom: Best Actress (Dandridge)

CAROUSEL 1956 128m/C

A carnival worker vows to change his irresponsible ways after meeting a beautiful woman but is killed trying to stop a crime. Once in heaven he begs to be let down to Earth for a short time to reconcile with his daughter. A box-office disaster when first released this pic has gained enormous acclaim over the years. Rodgers and Hammerstein songs include "If I Loved You," "You'll Never Walk Alone," and "Soliloquy."

C: Gordon MacRae, Shirley Jones, Cameron Mitchell, Gene Lockhart, Barbara Ruick   D: Henry King

THE COMMITMENTS 1991 116m/C (R)

Realistic look at a group of working class youths in Dublin who form a soul band and try to hit it big. Mostly cast with unknowns. The lead vocalist, Strong, was so good he got a record deal. Fast paced, well-written, engrossing, with a Grammy nominated soundtrack that includes music from Otis Redding and Aretha Franklin.

C: Andrew Strong, Bronagh Gallagher, Glen Hansard, Michael Aberne, Dick Massey   D: Alan Parker

THE COTTON CLUB 1984 121m/C (R)

Two dangerous love affairs, one between a musician and a gangster's sweetheart, the other between a tap dancer and a chorus girl, round out this slick stylish story of romance, violence and music. Songs included "Minnie The Moocher" and "Cotton Club Story."

C: Diane Lane, Richard Gere, Gregory Hines, Lonette McKee, Bob Hoskins   D: Francis Ford Coppola

COUNTRY GIRL 1954 104m/B&W

Kelly, in a break from her "pretty" roles, plays the wife of an alcoholic singer (Crosby) who's sunk in depression until he finally gets a chance for a come back. Songs include "The Search Is Through" and "The Land Around Us."

C: Bing Crosby, Grace Kelly, William Holden, Gene Reynolds, Anthony Ross   D: George Seaton   AA: '54 Best Actress (Kelly), Screenplay, Nom: Best Actor (Crosby), Director, Picture

DAMN YANKEES *1958 110m/C*

When a ballclub is in a serious slump one of the team's fans sells his soul to the devil in exchange for the athletic ability to take his team to the top. Verdon as Lola, the devil's assistant, is top-notch. Songs include "Whatever Lola Wants" and "You Gotta Have Heart."

C: Gwen Verdon, Ray Walston, Tab Hunter, Jean Stapleton, Russ Brown   D: George Abbott, Stanley Donen

DIRTY DANCING *1987 87m/C (PG-13)*

A young girl's early '60s Catskill vacation is going nowhere until she meets the hotel's dance instructor (Swayze) and two-steps her way into a romantic rock and roll filled summer. High energy performances and solid dance numbers. Swayze sang one of the songs on the soundtrack. Independently produced pic has become one of the most popular musicals ever made.

C: Patrick Swayze, Jennifer Grey, Cynthia Rhodes, Jerry Orbach, Jack Weston   D: Emile Ardolino

FAME *1980 133m/C (R)*

Well done engaging look at a group of students at the New York High School for the Performing Arts, following them through their four years of studying to work as actors, singers, and dancers. Intelligent script captures the pressures and self-doubt all high schoolers feel. Strong song and dance numbers include the title track and "I Sing The Body Electric."

C: Irene Cara, Barry Miller, Paul McCrane, Anne Meara   D: Alan Parker

FIDDLER ON THE ROOF *1971 184m/C (G)*

Set in the 1890s in a small village in the Ukraine, this is a musical epic about a poor Jewish milkman and his five daughters who, one by one, get married and leave the nest. Lavishly made with beautiful cinematography and a great score. One of the all-time great musicals. Songs include "If I Were A Rich Man" and "Sunrise, Sunset."

C: Chaim Topol, Norma Crane, Leonard Frey, Molly Picon   D: Norman Jewison   AA: '71 Nom: Best Actor (Topol), Director, Picture, Supporting Actor (Frey)

42ND STREET *1933 89m/B&W*

The production of a big-budget Broadway play has everybody biting their nails and an understudy realizing her chance for stardom. Songs include "Shuffle Off to Buffalo" and the title tune.

C: Warner Baxter, Ruby Keeler, Bebe Daniels, George Brent, Dick Powell   D: Lloyd Bacon

FUNNY GIRL *1968 151m/C (G)*

The early years of vaudevillian/comedienne Fanny Brice are luxuriously captured in this high-spirited pic that has Streisand in her screen debut replaying the role she made famous on Broadway. Includes the title track and "People."

C: Barbra Streisand, Omar Sharif, Walter Pidgeon, Kay Medford, Anne Francis   D: William Wyler   AA: '68 Best Actress (Streisand), Nom: Best Picture, Supporting Actress (Medford)

THE GAY DIVORCEE *1934 107m/B&W*

Sparks fly when Astaire and Rogers meet at a seaside resort in England. Songs include "Don't Let It Bother You" and "Night And Day."

C: Fred Astaire, Ginger Rogers, Edward Everett Horton, Eric Blore   D: Mark Sandrich   AA: '34 Nom: Best Picture

GIGI *1958 119m/C*

Classic tale of a young girl who's the friend of a millionaire. After realizing how beautiful a woman she has become the rich man begins to fall in love with her. Shot on location in France and loaded with rich French flavor. A classic. Songs include "Thank Heaven For Little Girls" and "The Night They Invented Champagne."

C: Leslie Caron, Louis Jourdan, Maurice Chevalier, Hermione Gingold, Eva Gabor   D: Vincente Minnelli   AA: '58 Best Picture, Director, Adapted Screenplay

GOING MY WAY 1944 126m/B&W

Crosby sang his way to an Oscar in his portrayal of a priest who comes to a down and out parish, gets it on its feet, and wins the hearts of everyone, including his tough superior. Songs include "Swinging On A Star" and "Silent Night."

C: Bing Crosby, Barry Fitzgerald, Rise Stevens, Frank McHugh, Gene Lockhart   D: Leo McCarey   AA: '44 Best Actor (Crosby), Director, Picture, Supporting Actor (Fitzgerald), Story and Screenplay

GOLD DIGGERS OF 1933 1933 96m/B&W

A group of gorgeous show girls come to the rescue of a songwriter whose show is ailing. Big budget extravaganza. Tunes include "We're In The Money" (sung in pig latin by Ginger Rogers) and "Forgotten Man."

C: Joan Blondell, Ruby Keeler, Aline MacMahon, Dick Powell, Guy Kibbee   D: Mervyn LeRoy

GREASE 1978 110m/C (PG)

Olivia Newton-John and John Travolta star as a "goody two shoes" girl and a "tough guy" gang member who go through the ups and downs of a high school romance. Filled with great songs and terrific dance numbers. Tunes include "Greased Lightning" and "Summer Nights."

C: John Travolta, Olivia Newton-John, Jeff Conaway, Stockard Channing   D: Randal Kleiser

GUYS AND DOLLS *1955 150m/C*

Two gamblers (Brando, Sinatra) make a bet on the dating possibility of a Salvation Army woman. Then they learn a lesson about life. Songs include "Luck Be A Lady" and the title track.

C: Marlon Brando, Jean Simmons, Frank Sinatra, Vivian Blaine, Stubby Kaye   D: Joseph L. Mankiewicz

HAIR *1979 122m/C (PG)*

The free-spirit '60s are perfectly captured in this musical adapted from the Broadway hit. The flower children shower themselves with love and sing about peace, war, and sunshine. Groovy, man. From the director of *One Flew Over The Cuckoo's Nest* and *Amadeus*.

C: Treat Williams, John Savage, Beverly D'Angelo, Annie Golden, Nicholas Ray   D: Milos Forman

A HARD DAY'S NIGHT *1964 90m/B&W*

A wild wacky day in the life of the mop top Beatles is the basis for this super charged, critically praised romp that never slows down and holds the distinction of containing the first music video. An important and enjoyable viewing experience.

C: John Lennon, Ringo Starr, Paul McCartney, George Harrison
D: Richard Lester

HOLLYWOOD CANTEEN *1944 124m/B&W*

Star-studded film has a love-struck GI winning a date with a girl of his dreams in a raffle held at the famed Hollywood Canteen. A rousing tribute to patriots at home and abroad. Songs include "Don't Fence Me In" and "Sweet Dreams."

C: Robert Hutton, Joan Leslie, Bette Davis, Errol Flynn, Joan Crawford, Olivia de Havilland   D: Delmer Davies

HOW TO SUCCEED IN BUSINESS WITHOUT REALLY TRYING *1967 121m/C*

Engaging musical comedy with Robert Morse playing a lowly

window washer who charms his way up the corporate ladder. Entertaining songs, top notch direction, and an excellent cast.

C: Robert Morse, Michele Lee, Rudy Vallee, Anthony Teague, George Fenneman   D: David Smith

JAILHOUSE ROCK *1957 96m/B&W*

Of all the Presley movies, this is the one that really captures the electrifying performer known as "The King." A teen is sent to prison and, while serving his time, takes up the guitar. After his release, he slowly rocks his way to the top. Songs include the title track and "I Don't Care."

C: Elvis Presley, Judy Tyler, Vaughn Taylor, Dean Jones, Mickey Shaughnessy, William Forrest   D: Richard Thorpe

JESUS CHRIST SUPERSTAR *1973 108m/C (G)*

The final seven days of Christ's life on Earth are told in this moving adaptation of the London stage play by Andrew Lloyd Weber. Very strong musical numbers include the title track and "I Don't Know How To Love Him."

C: Ted Neeley, Carl Anderson, Yrowne Elliman, Josh Mostel   D: Norman Jewison

THE KING AND I *1956 133m/C*

See "Top 100"

MEET ME IN ST. LOUIS *1944 113m/C*

Garland stars in this enchanting story about a St. Louis family's ups and downs during the 1903 World's Fair. Songs include the title track and "Have Yourself a Merry Little Christmas."

C: Judy Garland, Margaret O'Brien, Mary Astor, Lucille Brenner, Tom Drake   D: Vincente Minnelli

THE MUSIC MAN *1962 151m/C*

A con-man arrives in a small town and learns about a pool

hall soon to be built. He convinces the people that it will corrupt the young ones and they should instead start a wholesome children's marching band. His plans on splitting with the money for the uniforms is put on hold when he begins to fall for the pretty librarian. Songs include "Seventy Six Trombones" and "Trouble."

C: Robert Preston, Shirley Jones, Buddy Hackett, Hermione Gingold, Paul Ford, Pert Kelton, Ron Howard   D: Morton Da Costa
AA: '62 Nom: Best Picture

MY FAIR LADY 1964 170m/C (G)
See "Top 100"

OKLAHOMA 1955 145m/C
Partridge Family mom Shirley Jones plays a cute country gal who falls in love with a cowboy. The only problem is the evil Jud, who also wants the young lady. Uh-oh. Songs include "Oh, What A Beautiful Morning" and "Many A New Day."

C: Gordon MacRae, Shirley Jones, Rod Steiger, Gloria Grahame, Eddie Albert   D: Fred Zinneman

OLIVER! 1968 145m/C (G)
Dickens' classic rags to riches tale of an orphan who falls in with a feisty gang of pick pockets and, after a series of wild events, is sent to live with a wealthy family. High energy musical extravaganza.

C: Mark Lester, Jack Wild, Ron Moody, Shani Wallis, Oliver Reed
D: Carol Reed   AA: '68 Best Director, Picture, Nom: Best Actor
(Moody), Supporting Actor (Wild)

ON THE TOWN 1949 98m/C
Three sailors are on a 24-hour leave in New York City where they search for adventure and romance. Gene Kelly's first stint as a director. Tunes include the title song and "New York, New York."

C: Gene Kelly, Frank Sinatra, Vera-Ellen, Ann Miller, Betty Garrett
D: Gene Kelly, Stanley Donen

PAJAMA GAME *1957 101m/C*

Day plays the leader of a union committee that demands a pay hike from their pajama plant. As negotiations continue she falls in love with the leader of the opposition. Fun, high spirited pic.

C: Doris Day, John Raitt, Eddie Foy, Jr., Reta Shaw, Carol Haney
D: Stanley Donen, George Abbott

THE ROCKY HORROR PICTURE SHOW *1975 105m/C (R)*

One of the most financially successful musicals ever made, this bizarre tale is admittedly for certain tastes only. A newly-wed couple's car breaks down in front of Dr. Frankenfurter's gothic castle. They go in for help and experience a bizarre series of sexually charged events as Dr. Frankenfurter plots to use them in a twisted experiment. Great fun. Songs include "There's A Light," "Time Warp," "Rose Tint My World."

C: Tim Curry, Susan Sarandon, Barry Bostwick, Meatloaf, Little Nell, Richard O'Brien   D: Jim Sharman

THE ROSE *1979 134m/C (R)*

Midler, in her film debut, gives an electrifying performance as a wild rock and roll singer whose talents can't keep up with her self destructiveness. Strong cast, great soundtrack. Loosely based on the life of Janis Joplin. Tunes include "The Fire Down Below" and "The Rose."

C: Bette Midler, Alan Bates, Frederic Forrest, Harry Dean Stanton, David Keith   D: Mark Rydell   AA: '79 Nom: Best Actress (Midler), Supporting Actor (Forrest)

SEVEN BRIDES FOR SEVEN BROTHERS *1954 103m/C*

The oldest brother of a fur trapping family takes a bride and soon his six brothers see what a good life he has and decide they need to get married right away. A rollicking high-steppin' flick with some of the greatest choreographed dance sequences ever filmed. Tunes include "Bless Your Beautiful Hide" and "June Bride."

C: Howard Keel, Jane Powell, Russ Tamblyn, Julie Newmar, Jeff Richards   D: Stanley Donen   AA: '54 Nom: Best Picture

1776 *1972 141m/C (G)*

Rollicking re-staging of the events surrounding the writing and signing of the Declaration of Independence. Based on the Broadway play with a few actors reprising their roles. Includes "He Plays The Violin" and "The Egg."

C: William Daniels, Howard da Silva, Ken Howard, Donald Madden, Blythe Danner   D: Peter Hunt

SHOWBOAT *1936 110m/B&W*

Marvelous musical revolves around the ups, downs, loves, and adventures, of the many inhabitants of a Mississippi showboat. High energy, lavish production. Songs include "Make Believe" and "Ol' Man River."

C: Irene Dunne, Allan Jones, Paul Robeson, Helen Morgan, Hattie McDaniel   D: James Whale

SINGIN' IN THE RAIN *1952 103m/C*
See "Top 100"

SOUND OF MUSIC *1965 174m/C*
See "Top 100"

SOUTH PACIFIC *1958 167m/C*

A Rodgers and Hammerstein love story, this time set in the South Seas during WWII, involving a navy nurse who falls in love with a Frenchman. Songs include "Some Enchanted Evening" and "I'm Gonna Wash That Man Right Out Of My Hair."

C: Mitzi Gaynor, Rossano Brazzi, Ray Walston, France Nuyen, John Kerr D: Joshua Logan

A STAR IS BORN 1954 175m/C (PG)

A young talented actress is embraced by a veteran actor who helps her rise to stardom. Though they're in love, her success crushes him and leads to tragedy. A classic. Tracks include "I'll Get By" and "My Melancholy Baby."

C: Judy Garland, James Mason, Jack Carson, Tommy Noonan, Charles Bickford D: George Cukor AA: '54 Nom: Best Actor (Mason), Actress (Garland)

SWEET CHARITY 1969 148m/C

MacLaine is perfectly appealing as a prostitute looking for a man to marry. She finds a nice one who is completely oblivious to her profession. Adapted from the hit Broadway play. Songs include "Hey Big Spender" and "If My Friends Could See Me Now."

C: Shirley MacLaine, Chita Rivera, John McMartin, Paula Kelly, Sammy Davis, Jr. D: Bob Fosse

TOP HAT 1935 97m/B&W

See "Top 100"

VICTOR/VICTORIA 1982 133m/C (PG)

Andrews plays an out of work actress who decides to put on a vaudeville act playing a woman who's supposed to be a man. She's a hit with the fans, especially gangster Garner. Solid, comedic entertainment. Tunes include "Crazy World" and "You and Me."

C: Julie Andrews, James Garner, Robert Preston, Lesley Ann Warren, Alex Karras D: Blake Edwards AA: '82 Nom: Best Adapted Screenplay, Actress (Andrews), Supporting Actor (Preston), Supporting Actress (Warren)

WEST SIDE STORY *1961 151m/C*

See "Top 100"

YANKEE DOODLE DANDY *1942 126m/B&W*

See "Top 100"

MYSTERY/SUSPENSE

THE ADVENTURES OF SHERLOCK HOLMES *1939 83m/B&W*

With the crown jewels at stake, Holmes and Watson match wits against Scotland Yard to see who will be the first to stop the fiendish and cunning Professor Moriarty.

C: Basil Rathbone, Nigel Bruce, Ida Lupino, George Zucco, E. E. Clive D: Alfred Werker

ALL THE PRESIDENT'S MEN *1976 135m/C (PG)*

The true and remarkable story of Bob Woodward and Carl Bernstein, the two aggressive Washington Post reporters who dug up, uncovered, and eventually connected the criminal information that led to the Watergate scandal of the Nixon Administration. Gripping the whole way through.

C: Robert Redford, Dustin Hoffman, Jason Robards, Jr., Martin Balsam, Jane Alexander D: Alan J. Pakula AA: '76 Best Supporting Actor (Robards), Adapted Screenplay, Nom: Best Picture, Director, Supporting Actress (Alexander)

AND THEN THERE WERE NONE *1945 97m/C*

Ten people are given invitations to visit a remote mansion in England. Unfortunately for them, they don't know the real reason for the invitations: to be murdered one by one until there are none.

C: Louis Hayward, Barry Fitzgerald, Walter Huston, Roland Young, C. Aubrey Smith   D: Rene Clair

THE ASPHALT JUNGLE *1950 112m/B&W*

A veteran criminal is released from prison and decides to try one last job, a jewel heist. Director Huston lets the viewer quickly know how the scheme will end but uses this to his advantage as you find yourself constantly waiting for surprises. Considered one of the all-time top films.

C: Sterling Hayden, Louis Calhern, Jean Hagen, James Whitmore, Sam Jaffe, Marilyn Monroe   D: John Huston   AA: '50 Nom: Best Director, Supporting Actor (Jaffe), Screenplay

THE BIG EASY *1987 101m/C (R)*

A police detective (Quaid) discovers a mob drug war complete with a gruesome murder. An uptight conscientious D.A. (Barkin) gets involved with the case and the detective gets involved with her. Then the twists begin. Fast-paced pic.

C: Dennis Quaid, Ellen Barkin, Ned Beatty, John Goodman, Ebbe Roe Smith   D: Jim McBride

THE BIG HEAT *1953 90m/B&W*

A detective's sister is murdered by a bomb that was supposed to have his name on it, so he goes after the thugs responsible. He finds out who did it, opening the door to trouble and mayhem.

C: Glen Ford, Lee Marvin, Gloria Grahame, Jocelyn Brando, Alexander Scourby   D: Fritz Lang

THE BIG SLEEP *1946 114m/B&W*

See "Top 100"

BLOOD SIMPLE *1985 96m/C (R)*

The crusty owner of a redneck bar finds out his wife is double dealing with one of his employees. So what does he do? He hires an even crustier private detective to wipe both of them out. If this sounds like a standard thriller, guess again. Coen shows what he can do in this stylized, near-flawless gem.

C: Dan Hedaya, Frances McDormand, John Getz, M. Emmet Walsh
D: Joel Coen

BLUE VELVET 1986 121m/C (R)

A young man finds a severed ear in an empty lot and is thrust into the bizarre twisted underbelly of America. Darkly handled by David Lynch and containing one of Hopper's most memorable performances.

C: Kyle MacLachlan, Isabella Rossellini, Dennis Hopper, Laura Dern, Hope Lange   D: David Lynch   AA: '86 Nom: Best Director

BODY HEAT 1981 113m/C (R)

Hurt plays a lawyer who has an affair with a beautiful woman (Turner) leading to a devilish plot to kill her husband. Rourke has an unforgettable part as an arsonist. Tense pic, moves at a brisk pace.

C: William Hurt, Kathleen Turner, Richard Crenna, Ted Danson, Mickey Rourke   D: Lawrence Kasdan

CAPE FEAR 1961 106m/B&W

A prosecutor is visited by a freshly released ex-con who he was responsible for sending up the river. The criminal taunts the lawyer, becoming more and more violent. Finally, the situation explodes, and with he and his family's lives at stake, the prosecutor makes his move. Quick moving thriller, remade in 1991 by Martin Scorsese.

C: Gregory Peck, Robert Mitchum, Polly Bergen, Martin Balsam, Telly Savalas   D: J. Lee Thompson

CHARADE 1963 113m/C

When a WWII officer is murdered after stealing $250,000, his widow (Hepburn) and a stranger (Grant) try to find the hidden cash. Vicious secret agents and evil conniving thieves stand in their way. Great chemistry between Hepburn and Grant.

C: Cary Grant, Audrey Hepburn, Walter Matthau, James Coburn, George Kennedy   D: Stanely Donen

THE CHINA SYNDROME *1979 123m/C (PG)*

Lemmon plays a nuclear plant executive who tries to expose the cover up of a disastrous accident. Top-notch suspense with classic performances from Fonda, Douglas, and Lemmon. Noted for using no music in film at all. A few months after the release, the real-life "Three Mile Island" horror occurred.

C: Jane Fonda, Jack Lemmon, Michael Douglas, Scott Brady, James Hampton   D: James Bridges   AA: '79 Nom: Best Actor (Lemmon), Actress (Fonda)

CHINATOWN *1974 131m/C (R)*

See "Top 100"

CLEAR AND PRESENT DANGER *1994 120m/C (R)*

Fast-paced thriller begins with drug dealers murdering a government official's family. Ford investigates the killing and unravels a web of cover ups, killings, and a few hundred million dollars spread in bank accounts all over the world. Solid stuff.

C: Harrison Ford, Anne Archer, James Earl Jones, Willem Dafoe
D: Phillip Noyce

THE COLLECTOR *1965 119m/C*

Stamp gives a chilling performance as a butterfly collector who kidnaps a young girl and locks her in the basement of his remote farmhouse, hoping she will fall in love with him. Directed with a highly effective, unsettling style.

C: Terence Stamp, Samantha Eggar, Maurice Dallimore, Mona Washbourne   D: William Wyler   AA: '65 Nom: Best Actress (Eggar), Director

COMA *1978 113m/C (PG)*

Killings and disappearing bodies are becoming par for the course at a Boston Hospital until a female doctor sets her sights on nabbing the fiend behind the madness. From the man who brought you *Jurassic Park* and *Westworld*.

C: Genevieve Bujold, Michael Douglas, Elizabeth Ashley, Rip Torn, Richard Widmark   D: Michael Crichton

CUL DE SAC *1966 111m/C*

Pleasence plays a retired businessman who spends his days in a remote castle with his young, bored, lustful wife. When two gangsters burst into their home, a menacing, horrifying evening is in store for all. Taut, psychological sexual thriller, one of Polanski's best.

C: Donald Pleasence, Francoise Dorleac, Lionel Stander, Jack Mac-Gowran   D: Roman Polanski

DOUBLE INDEMNITY *1944 107m/B&W*

See "Top 100"

DRESSED TO KILL *1980 105m/C*

Dickinson plays a woman who's sexually unfulfilled by her husband so she beds a stranger in the back seat of a cab. She turns up dead and her son teams up with a hooker to entice the murderer into another brutal act. Praised for its style and the cab scene.

C: Angie Dickinson, Michael Caine, Keith Gordon, Nancy Allen   D: Brian DePalma

FAIL-SAFE *1964 111m/B&W*

This edge-of-your-seat pic has a nuclear attack accidentally activated against Russia, and the two countries in a desperate scramble to figure a way out.

C: Henry Fonda, Fritz Weaver, Walter Matthau, Larry Hagman   D: Sidney Lumet

FATAL ATTRACTION 1987 120m/C (R)

Douglas plays a married man who has a brief affair with a seemingly "normal" woman. After he ends the fling she doesn't want to let him go and begins to wreak bloody havoc on him and his family. Dynamite thriller adapted from a short student film.

C: Michael Douglas, Glenn Close, Anne Archer, Stuart Pankin, Ellen Hamilton   D: Adrian Lyne   AA: '87 Nom: Best Picture, Director, Actress (Close), Supporting Actress (Archer)

FIVE FINGERS 1952 108m/B&W

Mason stars as the "loyal" valet to a British Ambassador who, taking advantage of his esteemed position, sells intelligence information to the Germans during WWII. Oddly enough, the Germans believe Mason to be a double agent and, although they buy the info, never act on it. Based on a true story.

C: James Mason, Danielle Darrieux, Michael Rennie, John Wengraf, Michael Pate   D: Joseph L. Mankiewicz

FOREIGN CORRESPONDENT 1940 120m/B&W

Hitchcock delivers magnificent results in handling the story of a London reporter sent to cover a pacifist conference. Once there, he reports on the organization and falls in love with the founder's daughter. When a kidnapping takes place, he learns of the peace organization's involvement, leading to chaos.

C: Joel McCrea, Laraine Day, Herbert Marshall, George Sanders, Robert Benchley   D: Alfred Hitchcock   AA: '40 Nom: Best Picture, Supporting Actor (Albert Basserman)

FREAKS 1932 66m/B&W

A circus midget falls in love with a beautiful trapeze artist and becomes the victim in her twisted plan for money. The abuse enrages his co-working "freaks" and they dish out a very sick form of revenge. A classic.

C: Wallace Ford, Olga Baclanova, Leila Hyams, Roscoe Ates, Harry Earles   D: Tod Browning

FRENZY 1972 116m/C (R)

A man is hunted by Scotland Yard for a series of murders he didn't commit. Quick, engrossing, and at times morbidly humorous.

C: John Finch, Barry Foster, Barbara Leigh-Hunt, Anna Massey, Alec McCowen   D: Alfred Hitchcock

F/X 1986 109m/C (R)

Great cat-and-mouse pic about a special effects wizard who's hired by the government to stage a phony murder of a mob informant. It goes off like clockwork but his pay isn't what he expected, and he must use his "F/X" magic to survive.

C: Bryan Brown, Brian Dennehy, Cliff DeYoung, Diane Venora, Jerry Orbach   D: Robert Mandel

GREEN FOR DANGER 1947 91m/B&W

Sim stars as a detective trying to track down a demented doctor who's burying operating table patients. Great script, laced with black humor.

C: Trevor Howard, Alastair Sim, Leo Genn   D: Sidney Gilliat

THE GRIFTERS 1990 114m/C (R)

Stylish, moody piece about three con-artists caught up in a world of greed and deceit that may be about to bury them. Critically hailed.

C: Anjelica Huston, John Cusack, Annette Bening, Pat Hingle, J. T. Walsh   D: Stephen Frears   AA: '90 Nom: Best Director, Actress (Huston), Supporting Actress (Bening), Adapted Screenplay

HIDE IN PLAIN SIGHT *1980 96m/C (PG)*

Caan plays a tire factory worker whose ex-wife decides to marry a mobster. The thug turns informant and the new family, complete with Caan's two children, are given new identities by the government and disappear, leaving him to begin an endless search for his kids. Based on a true story.

C: James Caan, Jill Eikenberry, Robert Viharo, Kenneth McMillan, Danny Aiello D: James Caan

THE HIT *1985 105m/C (R)*

A couple of hitmen hunt down a man wanted by the mob. They find him and begin to transport the prisoner to their boss but something goes terribly wrong.

C: Terence Stamp, John Hurt, Tim Roth, Laura Del Sol D: Stephen Frears

THE HOT ROCK *1970 97m/C (PG)*

A mixture of comedy, drama, and suspense, combined with classic performances from Segal and Redford, create top notch entertainment in the form of four hilarious criminals who plan to rob a very large, very expensive, diamond. Great script sails along.

C: Robert Redford, George Segal, Ron Leibman, Zero Mostel, Moses Gunn D: Peter Yates

THE HOUND OF THE BASKERVILLES *1939 85m/B&W*

A demonic hound from Hell has been wreaking havoc on a noble family for centuries. Finally, one of the victims, Henry Baskerville, calls in Holmes and Watson to try to save him.

C: Basil Rathbone, Nigel Bruce, Lionel Atwill, John Carradine, Wendy Barrie D: Sidney Lanfield

HOUSE OF GAMES *1987 102m/C (R)*

A female psychiatrist takes a patient's gambling problem to heart and decides to try to infiltrate the con-men who took him for a ride. She is soon in a world where each road is filled with twists and turns, and everyone is a possible mark.

C: Joe Mantegna, Lindsay Crouse, Lilia Skala, J. T. Walsh, Meshach Taylor D: David Mamet

HUNT FOR RED OCTOBER *1990 137m/C (PG)*

John McTiernan expertly directs this potboiler about a Soviet nuclear sub captain who violently commands his own vehicle toward the U.S. for defection. Both sides jump into action to try to stop him. Fast, furious suspense, with some classic scenes.

C: Sean Connery, Alec Baldwin, Richard Jordan, Scott Glenn, Joss Ackland, Sam Neill D: John McTiernan

IN A LONELY PLACE *1950 93m/B&W*

Bogart is a hot tempered Hollywood screenwriter who begins an affair with a strange neighbor and soon is the chief suspect in a murder. Well made, taut thriller.

C: Humphrey Bogart, Gloria Grahame, Frank Lovejoy, Carl Benton Reid, Art Smith D: Nicholas Ray

IN COLD BLOOD *1967 133m/B&W*

A prisoner gets a tip from a cellmate about a rich farmer who keeps a load of money in his house. When the prisoner gets out, he and his friend drive hundreds of miles to steal the money and kill the farmer and his family "in cold blood." Chilling pic based on the true murder of a Kansas farming family on November 15, 1959. Adapted from Truman Capote's award winning novel.

C: Robert Blake, Scott Wilson, John Forsythe D: Richard Brooks
AA: '67 Nom: Best Director, Adapted Screenplay

IN THE HEAT OF THE NIGHT *1967 109m/C*

Poitier plays a detective who is visiting his southern home-town when a wealthy industrialist is murdered. An expert in homicide, Poitier is asked to help solve the case, even though the anti-black sheriff wants nothing to do with him. Racial prejudice is effectively explored in this tense, murder-thriller.

C: Sidney Poitier, Rod Steiger, Warren Oates, Lee Grant   D: Norman Jewison   AA: '67 Best Actor (Steiger), Picture, Adapted Screen-play, Nom: Best Director

JACOB'S LADDER *1990 116m/C (R)*

A Vietnam vet begins to have visions of ghoulish figures following him around, and his nightmare is justified when he discovers other men from his troop are experiencing the same phenomenon. His horror escalates when he learns that they all were used as government guinea pigs in a twisted drug experiment. Dark, moody pic with eerie ending.

C: Tim Robbins, Elizabeth Pena, Danny Aiello, Matt Craven, Jason Alexander   D: Adrian Lyne

JAWS *1975 124m/C (PG)*

A beach town is virtually closed down when a man-eating shark begins to devour swimmers. A bounty is put on its head and an old sea captain, along with the sheriff and an oceanographer, go after the beast. One of the best thrillers ever made, filmed off the Massachusetts' coast.

C: Roy Scheider, Robert Shaw, Richard Dreyfuss, Lorraine Gary, Murray Hamilton   D: Steven Spielberg   AA: '75 Nom: Best Picture

JUGGERNAUT *1974 109m/C (PG-13)*

Well-paced, expertly directed thriller about a lunatic who's hidden some bombs on a luxury liner and then transmits taunting remarks about the explosives over the radio. A tense race against time follows.

C: Richard Harris, Omar Sharif, David Hemmings, Anthony Hopkins, Shirley Knight   D: Richard Lester

KEY LARGO *1948 101m/B&W*

A group of people are held hostage in a shady Florida motel by a gang of crooks. Bogart plays one of the captives, a war vet who now despises violence, and tries to stay peaceful until crime boss Robinson goes a little too far.

C: Humphrey Bogart, Lauren Bacall, Claire Trevor, Edward G. Robinson, Lionel Barrymore   D: John Huston

THE KILLING *1956 93m/B&W*

Stanley Kubrick's brilliant pic about a group of men who decide to rob a racetrack and the brutal, tragic events that precede and follow the heist. The story is superbly told in a flashback/flash forward style that's combined with a strange technique of revisiting complete scenes from a different camera angle, creating a strange tension.

C: Sterling Hayden, Marie Windsor, Elisha Cook, Jr., Jay C. Flippen, Vince Edwards   D: Stanley Kubrick

KISS ME DEADLY *1955 105m/B&W*

Private eye Mike Hammer picks up a hitchhiking blonde. The next thing he knows, she's dead. Being a detective, he needs to get to the bottom of this, but not without murder, chaos, and a nuclear conspiracy coming into play. Heralded by the French upon its release, and considered the inspiration for the French New Wave that gave us Godard, Truffaut, and Louis Malle.

C: Ralph Meeker, Albert Dekker, Paul Stewart, Wesley Addy, Cloris Leachman   D: Robert Aldrich

KLUTE *1971 114m/C (R)*

Sutherland plays John Klute, a cop whose friend may have been murdered. He comes to New York City to find out, and his only lead is Bree (Fonda), an intelligent, hard edged call girl. She's reluctant to help him, but when her own life is in danger, she suddenly befriends him. Great performances by Fonda and Sutherland.

C: Jane Fonda, Donald Sutherland, Charles Cioffi, Roy Scheider, Rita Gam   D: Alan J. Pakula   AA: '74 Best Actress (Fonda)

THE LADY FROM SHANGHAI *1948 87m/B&W*

Welles filmed this imaginative pic on Errol Flynn's yacht. The story involves a woman who hires a young man to work on her crippled husband's boat. Before long, murder comes into play. Famous climactic scene in amusement park "hall of mirrors."

C: Orson Welles, Rita Hayworth, Everett Sloane, Glen Anders, Ted de Corsia   D: Orson Welles

THE LADY VANISHES *1938 99m/B&W*

A woman suddenly disappears during a train ride and her young friend, trying to find out what happened, enters a bizarre world of mystery, intrigue, and deception. A solid, top notch thriller.

C: Margaret Lockwood, Paul Lukas, Michael Redgrave, May Whitty   D: Alfred Hitchcock

LAURA *1944 85m/B&W*

See "Top 100"

THE LETTER *1940 96m/B&W*

W. Somerset Maugham's famous story about a plantation owner's wife who shoots and kills a man. She claims self-defense, but her case begins to unravel, opening up a dreadful secret.

C: Bette Davis, Herbert Marshall, James Stephenson, Gale Sondergaard, Bruce Lester   D: William Wyler   AA: '40 Nom: Best Picture, Director, Actress (Davis), Supporting Actor (Stephenson)

LIFEBOAT *1944 96m/B&W*

A freighter is sunk by a German war vessel and eight survivors climb into a lifeboat. The crowded tension builds as a Nazi makes it nine. Days pass and lack of food and the struggle to live force choices to be made as who can stay and who must go.

C: Tallulah Bankhead, William Bendix, John Hodiak, Walter Slezak, Henry Hull   D: Alfred Hitchcock   AA: '44 Nom: Best Director

LIST OF ADRIAN MESSENGER *1963 98m/B&W*

A group of people, all in line to inherit a bundle of money, are slowly disappearing in this quick paced star-studded thriller. Famous pic due in part to make-up that makes big stars unrecognizable.

C: Kirk Douglas, George C. Scott, Dana Wynter, Robert Mitchum, Burt Lancaster, Frank Sinatra   D: John Huston

THE MALTESE FALCON *1941 101m/B&W*
See "Top 100"

THE MAN WHO KNEW TOO MUCH *1934 77m/B&W*

A man vacationing in Switzerland is thrown into a web of foreign intrigue when he is given secret information by a dying spy and then his daughter is kidnapped to ensure his silence. Hitchcock remade his own movie in 1956.

C: Leslie Banks, Edna Best, Peter Lorre, Nova Pilbeam   D: Alfred Hitchcock

THE MANCHURIAN CANDIDATE *1961 126m/B&W*
See "Top 100"

MANHUNTER *1986 100m/C (R)*

An FBI agent who quits the service after a brutal manhunt for a serial killer returns to the squad when a new monster starts to leave a trail of dismembered corpses. Based on *Red Dragon* by Thomas Harris, who also wrote *Silence Of The Lambs*.

C: William L. Peterson, Kim Greist, Joan Allen, Brian Cox, Dennis Farina   D: Michael Mann

MARATHON MAN *1976 125m/C (R)*

Hoffman plays a New York City grad student who's training for the Olympic Marathon. When his secret agent brother (unknown to Hoffman) pays him a visit, Hoffman gets unwittingly caught up in a diamond smuggling ring headed by a Nazi war criminal who took the jewels from concentration camp prisoners. This is the film that contains the infamous dentist torture scene . . . "is it safe?" A classic.

C: Dustin Hoffman, Laurence Olivier, Marthe Keller, Roy Scheider, William Devane   D: John Schlesinger   AA: '76 Nom: Best Supporting Actor (Olivier)

MILLER'S CROSSING *1990 115m/C (R)*

State of the art style combines with an excellent story in this tale of an Irish hood and his "boss" who part ways when a woman comes between them. Violence and deceit follow. The scene of Finney's attempted assassination is awesome.

C: Albert Finney, Gabriel Byrne, Marcia Gay Harden, John Turturro, Jon Polito   D: Joel Coen

MURDER MY SWEET *1944 95m/B&W*

Classic film noir has singer Powell playing hard edged detective Phillip Marlowe. The P.I. travels down a crooked road filled with danger, mayhem, and no speed limit, as he tries to find an ex-convict's girlfriend who has vanished.

C: Dick Powell, Claire Trevor, Otto Kruger, Mike Mazurki   D: Edward Dmytryk

MURDER ON THE ORIENT EXPRESS 1974 128m/C (PG)

During a train ride from Istanbul to Calais, one of the passengers turns up dead. It's up to super-sleuth Hercule Poirot to find out which one of the passengers is responsible. All star cast.

C: Albert Finney, Martin Balsam, Ingrid Bergman, Lauren Bacall, Sean Connery, Jacqueline Bisset   D: Sidney Lumet   AA: '74 Best Supporting Actress (Bergman), Nom: Best Actor (Finney)

THE NAKED CITY 1948 96m/B&W

When a beautiful lady winds up murdered, two detectives question lead after lead, but get no solid answer. When they finally do get a break, it takes them to the killer and a terrific showdown on the Brooklyn Bridge.

C: Barry Fitzgerald, Don Taylor, Howard Duff, Ted de Corsia, Dorothy Hart   D: Jules Dassin   AA: '48 Best Story

NIGHT OF THE HUNTER 1955 93m/B&W

A classic tale of a psychotic preacher who marries a distraught widow who he believes is hiding a load of cash from a robbery. Actually, it's her children who have the money. When the preacher (played to eerie perfection by Mitchum) learns the truth, a long and fiendish chase begins. Laughton's only pic as director.

C: Robert Mitchum, Shelley Winters, Lillian Gish, Don Beddoe, Evelyn Varden   D: Charles Laughton

NO WAY OUT 1987 114m/C (R)

A Navy officer (Costner) has an affair with a woman who he later finds out is also having an affair with the Secretary of Defense. When she winds up dead, Costner is handed the case and soon becomes the chief suspect.

C: Kevin Costner, Sean Young, Gene Hackman, Will Patton, Howard Duff   D: Roger Donaldson

NORTH BY NORTHWEST *1959 136m/C*
See "Top 100"

NOTORIOUS *1946 101m/B&W*
Bergman is a playgirl recruited as an American spy and sent to infiltrate some Nazis the U.S. Government has been watching in Brazil. Grant is her superior, and Bergman, who is in love with Grant, is finding it difficult to follow the orders of feigning love with one of the German leaders. Classic romantic thriller.

C: Cary Grant, Ingrid Bergman, Claude Rains, Louis Calhern, Madame Konstantin   D: Alfred Hitchcock

ONE FALSE MOVE *1991 105m/C (R)*
Three low-life thugs (two men and one woman), get involved in a drug deal that goes awry. With two Los Angeles detectives hot on their heels, they head out of the city for the safety of the girl's quiet Arkansas hometown. What the male crooks don't realize is that their paradise isn't what it seems. The girl and the sheriff have a deep dark secret that could bury everybody. Masterfully handled.

C: Michael Beach, Billy Bob Thornton, Bill Paxton, Jim Metzler, Cynda Williams   D: Carl Franklin

THE ONION FIELD *1979 126m/C (R)*
True story of a cop who saw his partner get murdered and the mental downfall this horrific experience had on his life. Woods' and Seales' greasy portrayal of the two killers bring this film to another level.

C: John Savage, James Woods, Ronny Cox, Franklyn Seales, Ted Danson   D: Harold Becker

PARALLAX VIEW 1974 102m/C (R)

Tense, well-made pic about a reporter who begins uncovering evidence that a senator's assassination was a conspiracy. The people responsible are not too pleased with his progress and decide to stop him.

C: Warren Beatty, Hume Cronyn, William Daniels, Paula Prentiss, Kenneth Mars   D: Alan J. Pakula

PEEPING TOM 1963 88m/C

This pic would be exploitative trash if it wasn't done so amazingly well. A photographer takes pictures of beautiful women and then keeps his camera rolling as he kills them. In 1979, Martin Scorsese helped bring this film to the U.S.

C: Karl-Heinze Boehm, Moira Shearer, Anna Massey, Maxine Audley, Esmond Knight   D: Michael Powell

THE POSTMAN ALWAYS RINGS TWICE 1946 113m/B&W

Garfield plays the drifter who's all over Turner like hot fudge on a sundae. Turner plays the lusty housewife who conspires with Garfield to do away with the third wheel. It gets hotter and hotter until it finally explodes. Remade in '81 with Jack Nicholson and Jessica Lange.

C: Lana Turner, John Garfield, Cecil Kellaway, Hume Cronyn, Leon Ames   D: Tay Garnett

PRESUMED INNOCENT 1990 127m/C (R)

Ford plays a deputy prosecutor who is a chief suspect in the brutal murder of a beautiful colleague. As the plot unfolds, his friends become his enemies and his co-workers accusers, creating a harrowing nightmare to escape from. Tight script, and on the mark direction make it fly by.

C: Harrison Ford, Brian Dennehy, Bonnie Bedelia, Greta Scacchi, Raul Julia   D: Alan J. Pakula

REAR WINDOW *1954 112m/C*
See "Top 100"

REBECCA *1940 130m/B&W*
A truly bizarre love triangle exists between a man, his new bride, and his first wife, who died under mysterious circumstances and who he still longs for. A gothic, moody romance that takes you to an eerie place. Hitchcock's only Best Picture Oscar.

C: Joan Fontaine, Laurence Olivier, Judith Anderson, George Sanders
D: Alfred Hitchcock   AA: '40 Best Picture, Nom: Best Director, Actor (Olivier), Actress (Fontaine), Supporting Actress (Anderson)

REPULSION *1965 105m/B&W*
A sexually repressed, mentally unstable girl is left alone for a weekend and slips into a mode of madness that ultimately turns extremely violent. One of Polanski's best.

C: Catherine Deneuve, Yvonne Furneaux, Ian Hendry, John Fraser, Patrick Wymark   D: Roman Polanski

ROPE *1948 90m/B&W*
Two college friends murder a peer and then, for an added thrill, put him in a trunk and invite friends over for a party, serving food on the unknown tomb. One of their old professors (Stewart) begins to sense something is amiss. Based on the real life, 1920s Leopold-Loeb murder.

C: James Stewart, John Dall, Farley Granger, Cedric Hardwicke
D: Alfred Hitchcock

RUNAWAY TRAIN *1985 112m/C (R)*
Two criminals break out of prison (the warden was hoping they would because he wants to kill them) and sneak aboard a freight train for a ride to freedom. When the engineer dies, and they learn there are no brakes, they come to the harrow-

ing realization they're hurtling toward disaster. Based on a screenplay by Akira Kurosawa. Riveting.

C: Jon Voight, Eric Roberts, Rebecca DeMornay, John P. Ryan   D: Andrei Konchalovsky   AA: '85 Nom: Best Actor (Voight), Supporting Actor (Roberts)

SABOTAGE *1936 81m/B&W*

A woman grows increasingly fearful that the quaint, reserved man she is married to is the same person who is setting off bombs all over London.

C: Oscar Homolka, Sylvia Sydney, John Loder   D: Alfred Hitchcock

SEANCE ON A WET AFTERNOON *1964 111m/B&W*

A woman who performs seances convinces her husband to kidnap their child so she can gain fame by using her "powers" to discover the child's whereabouts. Their perfect plan runs into some major problems. Critically lauded.

C: Kim Stanley, Richard Attenborough, Margaret Lacey, Maria Kazan, Mark Eden   D: Bryan Forbes   AA: '64 Nom: Best Actress (Stanley)

SHADOW OF A DOUBT *1943 108m/B&W*
See "Top 100"

SILENCE OF THE LAMBS *1991 118m/C (R)*
See "Top 100"

SISTERS *1973 93m/C (R)*

Considered by some to be DePalma's best film, this pic revolves around siamese twins separated at birth, and the surviving one's split personality which has a pleasant side and a very, very, very, bad side.

C: Margot Kidder, Charles Durning, Barnard Hughes   D: Brian DePalma

SLEUTH 1972 138m/C (PG)

A mystery writer, sickened by the prospect of losing his wife to hairdresser Caine, begins a game of cat and mouse, but he may have underestimated his opponent. Top notch thriller, even more amazing since the entire film has only two actors.

C: Laurence Olivier, Michael Caine D: Joseph L. Mankiewicz
AA: '72 Nom: Best Director, Actor (Caine, Olivier)

A SOLDIER'S STORY 1984 101m/C (PG)

Rollins plays a black army attorney who's sent to the southern base of Fort Neal, Louisiana to investigate the killing of a hated officer. This story of murder and racism is told in flashbacks, creating a tense, first-rate mystery drama. Based on Charles Fuller's Pulitzer Prize winning play.

C: Howard E. Rollins, Jr., Adolph Caesar, Denzel Washington, Patti LaBelle, Robert Townsend D: Norman Jewison AA: '84 Nom: Best Picture, Supporting Actor (Caesar)

THE SPY WHO CAME IN FROM THE COLD 1965 110m/B&W

Burton plays an aging, disillusioned spy who tries to crack an East German network. Famous for its gritty, realistic look at espionage, the opposite of "James Bond."

C: Richard Burton, Oskar Werner, Claire Bloom, Sam Wanamaker, Peter Van Eyck D: Martin Ritt AA: '65 Nom; Best Actor (Burton)

STRANGERS ON A TRAIN 1951 101m/B&W

Two strangers meet on a train and, after an odd conversation, they decide to exchange murders, one killing the other's father and one killing the other's wife. While one of the strangers takes the conversation as a joke, the other was serious and leaves the train with a plan already in his mind. This leads to a nail-biting, edge-of-your-seat thriller.

C: Farley Granger, Robert Walker, Ruth Roman, Leo G. Carroll, Patricia Hitchcock   D: Alfred Hitchcock

THE STUNT MAN 1980 129m/C (R)

Wicked pic about a guy on the lam who happens upon a movie set and accidentally causes the death of a stunt man. The director agrees to hide the fugitive if he'll take over the dangerous stunt duties, making the criminal wonder what the director's true motives are. An excellent movie that took nine years to get made.

C: Peter O'Toole, Steve Railsback, Barbara Hershey, Chuck Ball, Alex Rocco   D: Richard Rush   AA: '80 Nom: Best Director, Actor (O'Toole)

SUSPICION 1941 99m/B&W

Great chiller has Fontaine slowly coming to the horrific realization that her loving husband is a cold blooded killer. As if that's not enough, she begins to fear she's his next victim.

C: Cary Grant, Joan Fontaine, Cedric Hardwicke, Nigel Bruce, May Whitty   D: Alfred Hitchcock   AA: '41 Best Actress (Fontaine), Nom: Best Picture

THE TAKING OF PELHAM ONE, TWO, THREE 1974 105m/C (R)

Shaw plays the head of a team of villains who take over a subway car and demand one million dollars to be delivered in one hour or the hostages begin dying one by one. Matthau plays the transit official who tries to keep Shaw from pulling the trigger. A winner.

C: Robert Shaw, Walter Matthau, Martin Balsam, Hector Elizondo, James Broderick   D: Joseph Sargent

THEY DRIVE BY NIGHT 1940 97m/B&W

Plot twists abound in this thriller about two brothers who quit a big trucking corporation to start their own driving business.

An accident forces one to return to his old paycheck, and the boss's wife takes a very strong liking to him. Murder and chaos follow.

C: Humphrey Bogart, Ann Sheridan, George Raft, Ida Lupino, Alan Hale, Jr.   D: Raoul Walsh

THE THIN MAN *1934 90m/B&W*

Husband and wife team Nick and Nora Charles investigate the murder of an inventor (The Thin Man) in what has become the blueprint for the enormous amount of married private detective pictures and television shows that followed. Inspired five sequels.

C: William Powell, Myrna Loy, Maureen O'Sullivan, Cesar Romero, Porter Hall   D: Woodbridge S. Van Dyke   AA: '34 Nom: Best Picture, Director, Actor (Powell)

THE THIRD MAN *1949 104m/B&W*

See "Top 100"

THE 39 STEPS *1935 80m/B&W*

Classic Hitchcock about an average Canadian citizen who innocently travels to England and is targeted as a spy trying to gain top secret information. Remade in 1959 and 1979.

C: Robert Donat, Madeleine Carroll, Godfrey Tearle, Lucie Manheim
D: Alfred Hitchcock

TO HAVE AND HAVE NOT *1944 100m/B&W*

Action, suspense and foreign intrigue combine with Bacall's film debut to tell the story of a sea captain's tangled trouble with a sexy lady and French resistance fighters.

C: Humphrey Bogart, Lauren Bacall, Walter Brennan, Hoagy Carmichael   D: Howard Hawks

TOPKAPI *1964 122m/C*

A gang of thieves plan a daring heist of a priceless jeweled dagger from the Topkapi palace museum in Istanbul. Played partly tongue-in-cheek with great performances from the entire cast.

C: Melina Mercouri, Maximillian Schell, Peter Ustinov, Robert Morley, Akim Tamiroff   D: Jules Dassin

TOUCH OF EVIL *1958 108m/B&W*

See "Top 100"

THE TRAIN *1965 133m/C*

It's 1943 in German occupied Paris. The Nazi forces have loaded a train with priceless French art they plan on bringing back to Germany. A group of French Resistance soldiers learn about the trip and decide to do something about it. Exciting, expertly made pic.

C: Burt Lancaster, Paul Scofield, Jeanne Moreau, Michael Simon, Suzanne Flon   D: John Frankenheimer

VERTIGO *1958 126m/C (PG)*

See "Top 100"

WHAT EVER HAPPENED TO BABY JANE? *1962 132m/B&W*

Two aging sisters, one in a wheelchair, the other on the edge of sanity, live together in an old mansion. When the demented one learns of her sister's plan to institutionalize her, she begins a series of mind cracking ruthless tortures. Davis is a classic psycho.

C: Bette Davis, Joan Crawford, Victor Buono, Anna Lee, B. D. Merrill
D: Robert Aldrich   AA: '62 Nom: Best Actress (Davis), Supporting Actor (Buono)

THE WINDOW *1949 73m/B&W*

A small boy witnesses a murder, but when he tells his parents, they don't believe him. The tension mounts when the killers kidnap the tyke. Child star Driscoll was given a special Oscar for his performance.

C: Bobby Driscoll, Barbara Hale, Arthur Kennedy, Ruth Roman
D: Ted Tetzlaff

WITNESS *1985 112m/C (R)*

Ford plays a cop who, on his own undertaking, guards a boy who witnessed a murder that involves a major police cover up. Ford follows the boy and his single mother, both Amish, to their home in Pennsylvania, and contacts a friend at the police department, hoping to expose the crime. The bad element soon learns of Ford's whereabouts and, in an incredibly tense, violent scene, visits Amish country to silence Ford, the boy, and his mother, forever. Beautifully paced, riveting pic.

C: Harrison Ford, Kelly McGillis, Alexander Godunov, Lukas Haas, Josef Sommer, Danny Glover   D: Peter Weir   AA: '85 Best Original Screenplay, Nom: Best Picture, Director, Actor (Ford)

WITNESS FOR THE PROSECUTION *1957 115m/B&W*

Agatha Christie classic about an aging lawyer who takes on the seemingly straight forward case of a man charged with murdering a wealthy widow. It soon unwinds into the strangest case he's ever had.

C: Charles Laughton, Marlene Dietrich, Tyrone Power, Elsa Lanchester   D: Billy Wilder   AA: '57 Nom: Best Picture, Director, Actor (Laughton), Supporting Actress (Lanchester)

ALIEN 1979 116m/C (R)

A spaceship's mission takes a wrong turn when a slimey, razor-toothed alien goes on a rampage. What could have been just another "monster terrorizes humans" story is stepped up a few levels with tense, stylistic direction, imaginative sets, great special effects, and an energized cast.

C: Tom Skerritt, Sigourney Weaver, Veronica Cartwright, Yaphet Kotto, Harry Dean Stanton   D: Ridley Scott

ALIENS 1986 138m/C (R)

"Alien" sequel has Ripley and her cohorts investigating a colonized planet that has mysteriously cut off all communication. She quickly finds out it's her old nemesis and the high tech, gore-filled rollercoaster ride begins.

C: Sigourney Weaver, Michael Biehn, Lance Henriksen, Bill Paxton, Paul Reiser   D: James Cameron

ALTERED STATES 1980 103m/C (R)

Hurt plays an overly devoted scientist who's trying to get inside the inner workings of man's mind. He does this by downing strong drugs while in an immersion tank. His experiment works but, unfortunately, its side effect is madness.

C: William Hurt, Blair Brown, Bob Balaban, Charles Haid, Dori Brenner   D: Ken Russell

ANDROID 1982 80m/C (PG)

A strange scientist is conducing experiments in space, assisted by an android. When the android learns that his is soon to be terminated, he has no choice but to stage a violent revolt. Worth seeing just for Kinski's performance.

C: Klaus Kinski, Dan Opper, Brie Howard   D: Aaron Lipstadt

THE ANDROMEDA STRAIN *1971 131m/C (G)*

Based on the bestseller by Michael Crichton (*Westworld, Jurassic Park*), this story centers around a satellite that has returned to earth, unknowingly bringing along a deadly virus that could virtually obliterate the planet overnight. A team of scientists jump into action to try to destroy it.

C: Arthur Hill, David Wayne, James Olson, Kate Reid, Paula Kelly
D: Robert Wise

BLADE RUNNER *1982 122m/C (R)*

Ford plays a 21st century detective/exterminator going after alien robots who kill to extend their life cycle. He runs into a major stumbling block when he falls in love with one of the mechanical murderers. Highly stylized direction with visually stunning sets.

C: Harrison Ford, Rutger Hauer, Sean Young, Daryl Hannah, M. Emmet Walsh   D: Ridley Scott

THE BROTHER FROM ANOTHER PLANET *1984 109m/C*

A black alien, being pursued by space police, crash lands in the New York harbor and winds up in Harlem. Two bounty hunters soon arrive and the chase is on. More social commentary than action.

C: Joe Morton, Dee Dee Brigewater, Ron Woods, Steve James, Maggie Renzi   D: John Sayles

A CLOCKWORK ORANGE *1971 137m/C (R)*

See "Top 100"

CLOSE ENCOUNTERS OF THE THIRD KIND *1977 152m/C (PG)*

A family man gets a strange telephone call from an alien force. He leaves his wife and kids and follows the "voice," meeting up with hundreds of other earthlings and, finally, the force.

C: Richard Dreyfuss, Teri Garr, Melinda Dillon, Francois Truffaut, Bob Balaban   D: Steven Spielberg

DAY OF THE TRIFFIDS *1963 94m/C*

An enormous meteor shower spreads a blinding agent over much of the earth's population. It also drops plants which grow and turn into carnivorous creatures. Classic '50s sci-fi.

C: Howard Keel, Janet Scott, Nicole Maurey, Kiernon Moore, Mervyn Johns   D: Steve Sekely

THE DAY THE EARTH STOOD STILL *1951 92m/B&W*

The planet earth is visited by a peaceful alien who offers a polite warning against experimenting with nuclear power. Although many humans agree, the powerful figures of the planet don't, causing a big problem with the alien and his large robot, Gort. Considered one of the all-time great sci-fi films.

C: Michael Rennie, Patricia Neal, Hugh Marlowe, Sam Jaffe, Francis Bavier   D: Robert Wise

DEAD ZONE *1983 104m/C (R)*

A man is severely injured in a car accident and when he wakes up in the hospital he has incredible psychic powers. The harrowing visions he feels frighten him and he remains in seclusion until he starts receiving strong signs of a political assassination. Tense.

C: Christopher Walken, Brooke Adams, Tom Skerritt, Martin Sheen, Herbert Lom   D: David Cronenberg

THE DEVIL AND DANIEL WEBSTER *1941 106m/B&W*

Truly bizarre *Twilight Zone*-ish pic about an 1840s farmer who cuts a deal with the devil to get rich, and then hires a lawyer, Daniel Webster, to get him out of it. Startling images and witty dialogue.

C: James Craig, Edward Arnold, Simone Simon, Walter Huston
D: William Dieterle

THE EMPIRE STRIKES BACK *1980 124m/C (PG)*

It's good vs. evil once again as Luke and the gang wage war against Darth Vadar and crew. This is the sequel that introduces Jabba the Hut and also contains Darth Vader's shocking secret.

C: Mark Hamill, Carrie Fisher, Harrison Ford, Billy Dee Williams, Alec Guinness   D: Irvin Kershner

EXCALIBUR *1981 140m/C (R)*

A mini epic, lushly produced, on the life of King Arthur. Begins with his famous pulling of the sword from the stone, then moves through his battles, controversial romances, search for the Holy Grail, and war against Mordred.

C: Nigel Terry, Nicol Williamson, Nicolas Clay, Helen Mirren, Cherie Lunghi   D: John Boorman

FAHRENHEIT 451 *1966 112m/C*

Ray Bradbury's absorbing story about a futuristic society which bans all reading. The central character is a fireman whose job is to man the furnaces where the paper's burned. Trouble begins when he meets a well-read, pretty girl and starts to question the morality of his job.

C: Oskar Werner, Julie Christie, Cyril Cusack, Anton Diffring   D: Francois Truffaut

FANTASTIC VOYAGE *1966 100m/C*

A world renowned scientist on a top secret mission is severely wounded by the enemy. Conventional operation procedures are useless so a medical team is shrunk to microscopic size, injected into his body, and fights to save his life. Highly original and entertaining.

C: Stephen Boyd, Edmond O'Brien, Raquel Welch, Arthur Kennedy,

Donald Pleasence   D: Richard Fleischer

THE FLY 1958 94m/C

The highly original and bizarre tale of a scientist who unknowingly lets a house fly in on the electronic waves of one of his experiments, resulting in the scientist's slow torturous transformation into the bug. Worth it just for the "help me, help me" finale. Writer Clavell went on to pen *The Great Escape* and write and direct *To Sir With Love*.

C: Vincent Price, David Hedison, Patricia Owens, Herbert Marshall
D: Kurt Neumann

THE FLY 1986 94m/C (R)

A scientist is conducting experiments in something that looks like a futuristic phone booth with cables and wires shooting out of it. As he begins another try, he climbs into the machine but so, unfortunately, does a house fly. A few zaps and electronic jolts later, he is on his way to a slow gruesome transformation into the winged insect.

C: Jeff Goldblum, Geena Davis, John Getz, Jay Baushel   D: David Cronenberg

FORBIDDEN PLANET 1956 98m/C

Famous pic about a mission from Earth to Planet Altair-4 to find out what happened to members of a previous excursion. They're greeted by the only survivors, a doctor and his daughter, and soon discover that some other force is present and doesn't want them around.

C: Walter Pidgeon, Anne Francis, Leslie Nielson, Warren Stevens, Jack Kelly   D: Fred M. Wilcox

GODZILLA, KING OF THE MONSTERS 1956 80m/B&W

Some nuclear testing wakes up a stone-age monster and the angry beast from the sea lashes out at the city of Tokyo.

C: Takashi Shimura, Raymond Burr   D: Terry Morse

THE INCREDIBLE SHRINKING MAN *1957 81m/B&W*

A man is exposed to a radiation cloud which causes him to get smaller and smaller and smaller. Doctors are baffled, his wife is distraught, and he is soon alone battling spiders and cats to survive. Terrifyingly real with great special effects. One of the best sci-fi films ever made.

C: Grant Williams, Randy Stuart, April Kent, Paul Langton, Raymond Bailey   D: Jack Arnold

INVASION OF THE BODY SNATCHERS *1956 80m/B&W*

A ruthless force comes to earth in the form of pods that enter humans and "duplicate" them for their own sinful purpose. Truly believable script, excellent direction and disturbing atmosphere.

C: Kevin McCarthy, Dana Wynter, Larry Gates, Carolyn Jones, King Donovan   D: Don Siegel

THE INVISIBLE MAN *1933 71m/B&W*

A scientist has devised an incredible serum that can transform a person into a state of invisibility. He tests it on himself and it works perfectly except for one small drawback: it slowly drives him mad and soon he wants to take over the world. Sci-fi classic.

C: Claude Rains, Gloria Stuart, Dudley Diggs, William Harrigan, Una O'Connor   D: James Whale

JOURNEY TO THE CENTER OF THE EARTH *1959 132m/C*

Mason leads an adventurous expedition to find the center of the earth. His eccentric entourage includes Gertrude the goose. Loads of fun with music by the same man (Bernard Hermann) who gave us the shrieking notes of *Psycho*.

C: James Mason, Arlene Dahl, Pat Boone, Diane Baker, Thayer David   D: Henry Levin

JURASSIC PARK *1993 126m/C (PG-13)*

An entrepreneur plans to open up an amusement park filled with real live dinosaurs he's scientifically created. He invites a few big shots for a preview and something goes terribly wrong. State-of-the-art effects (you get what you pay for) make for great entertainment.

C: Sam Neill, Jeff Goldblum, Laura Dern, Richard Attenborough, Samuel L. Jackson   D: Steven Spielberg

THE MAN WHO FELL TO EARTH *1976 118m/C (R)*

Roughly resembling Fyodor Dostoyevsky's *The Dream Of A Ridiculous Man*, this story centers around an alien visiting Earth in order to bring much needed water back to his dying family. Unfortunately he begins to like Earth a little too much, makes some big money, and gets sucked into the fast lane.

C: David Bowie, Candy Clark, Rip Torn, Buck Henry, Bernie Casey   D: Nicolas Roeg

MYSTERIOUS ISLAND *1961 101m/C*

Some Civil War prisoners escape their captors by commandeering an observation balloon. Blown off course, they wind up on an island populated by gigantic animals. Ray Harryhausen outdoes himself with the effects.

C: Michael Craig, Joan Greenwood, Michael Callan, Gary Merrill, Herbert Lom   D: Cy Endfield

1984 *1984 117m/C (R)*

Great film version of Orwell's classic novel about a government worker who falls in love with a woman in a futuristic society where emotions are outlawed. "Big Brother is watching." Suspenseful sci-fi.

C: John Hurt, Richard Burton, Suzanna Hamilton, Cyril Cusack, Gregory Fisher   D. Michael Radford

THE OMEGA MAN *1971 98m/C (PG)*

The apocalypse has passed leaving one normal man on earth surrounded by a tribe of sick violent albinos who want him dead. They sleep by day, he sleeps by night, and the battle rages on. A twisted nightmare come true.

C: Charlton Heston, Anthony Zerbe, Rosalind Cash, Paul Kosio
D: Boris Sagal

PLANET OF THE APES *1968 112m/C (G)*

Classic picture about a group of astronauts who run off course, land on a planet controlled by human-like apes, and are soon taken prisoner. Complete with that famous mind-bending ending that will make your jaw drop.

C: Charlton Heston, Roddy McDowall, Kim Hunter, Maurice Evans, Linda Harrison   D: Franklin J. Schaffner

PREDATOR *1987 107m/C (R)*

A group of hostages are being held in a Central American jungle so the government activates a team of highly trained mercenaries, led by Schwarzenegger, to get them out. Once there, they start dropping like flies but it's not the enemy they counted on, it's an alien killing machine. Tense, fast-paced spectacle.

C: Arnold Schwarzenegger, Jesse Ventura, Sonny Landham, Bill Duke, Elpidia Carrillo   D: John McTiernan

THE PRINCESS BRIDE *1987 98m/C (PG)*

The tongue-in-cheek tale following a young warrior as he meets crazy characters and engages in swashbuckling battles, all the while trying to rescue his fair maiden from the fiendish grasp of Prince Humperdink. A smooth ride with zany performances from everyone.

C: Cary Elwes, Mandy Patinkin, Robin Wright, Chris Sarandon, Carol Kane, Wallace Shawn, Peter Falk   D: Rob Reiner

ROBOCOP *1987 103m/C (R)*

An officer of the law is beaten, brutalized, and left for dead. A group of "surgeons" fix him up ("Six Million Dollar Man"-style) and he returns to the streets as a one man police force. Some great scenes, great special effects.

C: Peter Weller, Nancy Allen, Ronny Cox, Kurtwood Smith, Ray Wise
D: Paul Verhoeven

ROLLERBALL *1975 123m/C (R)*

An action packed philosophical sci-fi flick about a futuristic society run by corporate giants. There's no war or other violent activity, only rollerball, an aggressive combination of basketball, ice hockey, and roller derby. Trouble begins when an industrial bigwig thinks it's best for business if the top player quits.

C: James Caan, John Houseman, Maud Adams, Moses Gunn
D: Norman Jewison

STARMAN *1984 115m/C (PG)*

Bridges plays an intellectually advanced alien stranded on Earth. He meets a woman and they drive cross-country so he can find his spacecraft and return home. Film succeeds in strangely reversing normal alien/human differences and violence.

C: Jeff Bridges, Karen Allen, Charles Martin Smith, Richard Jaeckel
D: John Carpenter   AA: '84 Nom: Best Actor (Bridges)

STAR TREK 2: THE WRATH OF KHAN *1982 113m/C (PG)*

Those space pioneers are back and do battle with old nemesis Khan in the best-to-date of the *Star Trek* movie series. Plot includes a few surprises like Kirk's old flame, his mysterious son, and the "death" of Spock.

C: William Shatner, Leonard Nimoy, Ricardo Montalban, DeForest Kelley   D: Nicholas Meyer

STAR WARS *1977 121m/C (PG)*
See "Top 100"

THE TERMINATOR *1984 108m/C (R)*
Schwarzenegger, in the pic that made him a household name, is a robotic killing machine sent from the future to murder a woman who, unless she is stopped, will someday give birth to a child that will change the course of history. Non-stop "I'll be back" action.

C: Arnold Schwarzenegger, Michael Biehn, Linda Hamilton, Paul Winfield   D: James Cameron

THEM! *1954 93m/B&W*
Something strange is going on in the desert so a group of scientists decide to check it out. What they find are a race of gigantic mutant ants who, unfortunately, are not very friendly. One of the first "big bug" movies of the '50s with classic sci-fi thrills.

C: James Whitmore, Edmund Gwenn, Fess Parker, James Arness, Onslow Stevens   D: Gordon Douglas

THE THIEF OF BAGHDAD *1940 106m/C*
The classic tale of a young king who's tricked out of his kingdom by the evil Grand Vizier and enlists the aid of a magical genie to get it back. Brought to the screen with wit, charm, style, and fantastic special effects. The flying carpet and Rex Ingram's genie are crowd pleasers.

C: Sabu, Conrad Veidt, Rex Ingram, June Duprez, Tim Whelan   D: Ludwig Berger

THE THING *1951 87m/B&W*
Classic '50s sci-fi thriller about an arctic research team that

discovers a snow covered spaceship and a frozen alien. The beast thaws out and, one by one, brutally eliminates the group of scientists. Perfectly directed with a great '50s sci-fi creature.

C: James Arness, Kenneth Tobey, Margaret Sheridan, Dewey Martin
D: Christian Nyby, Howard Hawks

THE TIME MACHINE *1960 103m/C*

H. G. Wells classic about a scientist in the 1890s who invents a machine that can transport him into the future. His adventures bring him to the year 802701 where he finds a world much unlike the one he was living on. A sci-fi buff favorite.

C: Rod Taylor, Yvette Mimieux, Whit Bissell, Sebastian Cabot, Alan Young   D: George Pal

TOTAL RECALL *1990 113m/C (R)*

Schwarzenegger plays a futuristic construction worker who dreams of the building boom on Mars. He goes to a strange tourist agency that lets you travel without leaving your seat; they implant a chip into your brain. Something goes wrong with the implant and violent, pulse-pounding action follows.

C: Arnold Schwarzenegger, Rachel Ticotin, Sharon Stone, Michael Ironside, Ronny Cox   D: Paul Verhoeven

12 MONKEYS *1995 130m/C (R)*

Bizarre story and rich images round out this pic about a man from the future (Willis) sent back to the past to locate and stop the producers of a deadly virus that will wipe out most life forms and send everyone else underground. Artfully directed with a great, surreal ending. Pitt's portrayal of a mental patient stands out.

C: Bruce Willis, Madeline Stowe, Brad Pitt   D: Terry Gilliam
AA: '95 Nom: Best Supporting Actor (Pitt)

20,000 LEAGUES UNDER THE SEA *1954 127m/C*

Great sci-fi adventure about Captain Nemo and his submarine trying to take over the world and the good guys who try to stop his diabolical plan.

C: Kirk Douglas, James Mason, Peter Lorre, Paul Lukas, Robert J. Wilke   D: Richard Fleischner

2001: A SPACE ODYSSEY *1968 139m/C*
See "Top 100"

VILLAGE OF THE DAMNED *1960 78m/B&W*

A dozen children are born simultaneously in a small English village. As they grow they reject interaction with their fathers and any other men except for their male teacher. It's soon learned that they are the first wave of an evil alien invasion. Top-notch thriller.

C: George Sanders, Barbara Shelley, Martin Stephens, Laurence Naismith, Michael C. Goetz   D: Wolf Rilla

VOYAGE TO THE BOTTOM OF THE SEA *1961 106m/C*

A submarine has to take on an Earth destructing belt of radiation that is burning through the Arctic icebergs. A rollicking adventure with fun special effects.

C: Walter Pidgeon, Joan Fontaine, Barbara Eden, Peter Lorre, Robert Sterling   D: Irwin Allen

WESTWORLD *1973 90m/C (PG)*

Two friends visit a futuristic vacation resort where you can act out your fantasies with the robot employees. In *Westworld* a mechanical gunslinger malfunctions, shoots one of the friends, and goes off in a relentless pursuit of the other. Great stuff. Director Crichton later penned *Jurassic Park*.

C: Yul Brynner, Richard Benjamin, James Brolin, Dick Van Patten, Majel Barrett   D: Michael Crichton

YELLOW SUBMARINE 1968 87m/C (G)

Classic animated musical fantasy has the legendary band battling the Blue Meanies to save Pepperland. Awesome pop art imagery as effective as any Disney pic and loaded with great songs like "All You Need Is Love" and "Lucy In The Sky With Diamonds." Surprisingly, Beatles did not provide their own speaking voices.

V: John Clive (John), Geoff Hughes (Paul), Peter Batten (George), Paul Angelis (Ringo) D: George Dunning, Dick Emery

SLEEPERS

BAD LIEUTENANT 1992 98m/C (NC-17)

Harvey Keitel, in what may be his greatest role, plays a strung out, gambling addicted New York City cop who would rather score a fix than arrest a criminal. After a nun is brutally raped on a church altar, Keitel is obsessed with capturing the slime, not because he cares but because the reward money will pay a serious debt he owes to a ruthless bookie. Redemption, in bizarre form, soon follows. A sleeper classic.

C: Harvey Keitel, Frankie Acciario, Brian McElroy, Peggy Gormley, Stella Keitel D: Abel Ferrara

THE BEGUILED 1970 109m/C (R)

A wounded union soldier (Eastwood) is taken into a southern all-girl school where he's subjected to love starved females whose desire makes them hide him from passing southern troops. But their jealousy among themselves leads to a twisted harrowing series of events. Overlooked excellence.

C: Clint Eastwood, Geraldine Page, Elizabeth Hartman D: Don Siegel

THE BIG BLUE 1988 122m/C (PG)

Beautifully photographed story exploring the friendly but deep rivalry between two athletes, one Italian, one French. The sport, free-diving, has the competitors seeing how far they can descend in the deep sea without any type of breathing apparatus.

C: Jean Reno, Jean-Marc Barr, Rosanna Arquette,   D: Luc Besson

THE BIG PICTURE 1989 95m/C (PG-13)

After he wins an esteemed film festival, recent graduate Bacon is offered a big time deal with a studio. Ditching his friends and girl, he trades in his jalopy for a Porsche and gets ready for Hollywood. Then the studio head who hired him is fired, and Bacon is dropped into "nobody land." But later, when a burning grilled cheese sandwich forces him to refuse a studio exec's phone call, he's transformed into a "very busy" genius. Hilarious satire with a classic cameo by Martin Short.

C: Kevin Bacon, Jennifer Jason Leigh, Michael McKean, Emily Longstreth, Richard Belzer, Teri Hatcher   D: Christopher Guest

BILLY LIAR 1963 96m/B&W

Well crafted story about a young Englishman who dreams of becoming a successful writer/entertainer. He's stuck in a dull job and can't afford to move out of his unsympathetic parents' home and so he frequently escapes into a "Walter Mitty"-like existence. Great look at ambition and fear of success. Schlesinger's (*Marathon Man*, *Falcon And The Snowman*) debut.

C: Tom Courtenay, Julie Christie, Wilfred Pickles, Finlay Currie
D: John Schlesinger

BIRDY 1984 120m/C (R)

An intelligent, positive, and somehow uplifting journey into madness about two teenagers who go to Vietnam. One comes back insane, and the other, now physically handicapped, tries desperately to bring him back to reality. A compelling, engrossing pic.

C: Nicholas Cage, Matthew Modine, Sandy Baron, John Harkins, Bruno Kirby   D: Alan Parker

BITE THE BULLET *1975 131m/C (PG)*

A grueling 600-mile horse race is the center of attention as the contestants, over a long period of time, brutally learn that respect for one another is just as important as winning.

C: Gene Hackman, James Coburn, Candice Bergen, Dabney Coleman, Jan-Michael Vincent   D: Richard Brooks

BLACK RAINBOW *1991 103m/C (R)*

A father/daughter team of scamming clairvoyants takes a wicked turn when the daughter begins to have visions of murders which actually soon take place. Well-paced thriller.

C: Jason Robards, Jr., Tom Hulce, Rosanna Arquette   D: Mike Hodges

BLUE COLLAR *1978 114m/C (R)*

Great story about three factory workers in an autoplant who discover they're being ripped-off by their bosses and their union. They ban together and plan a crime. Elevated high above the common "heist" film by strong characters and "working man's" message.

C: Richard Pryor, Harvey Keitel, Yaphet Kotto, Ed Begley, Jr.   D: Paul Schrader

BLUME IN LOVE *1973 115m/C (R)*

George Segal plays a man who's dumped by his wife after she finds out about an affair. He is destroyed and begins a relentless obsessive quest to win her back, but she's taken up with a drifter. Includes great little song by Kristofferson ("Sittin' Around Doin' Nothin', Nothin' But Sittin' Around").

C: George Segal, Susan Anspach, Kris Kristofferson   D: Paul Mazursky

CALIFORNIA SPLIT *1974 108m/C (PG)*

Elliott Gould and George Segal play two compulsive gamblers addicted to life on the edge and the lure of the big score. In-depth study of the desperation and emptiness of the gambling addict, whether it's a win or loss. Classic ending—one of Altman's best.

C: George Segal, Elliott Gould, Gwen Welles, Ann Prentiss
D: Robert Altman

CHAMPION *1949 99m/B&W*

Douglas gives an unforgettable performance as a win-at-all-costs boxer who sacrifices everyone around him in his relentless pursuit of success. Considered one of the best boxing films ever made.

C: Kirk Douglas, Arthur Kennedy, Ruth Roman   D: Mark Robson
AA: '49 Nom: Best Actor (Douglas), Supporting Actor (Kennedy)

CHIMES AT MIDNIGHT *1967 115m/B&W*

Orson Welles combined pieces of five Shakespeare plays and came up with this story about the relationship between a snob and a prince. Some great scenes of battles and love. Much of the budget came from Welles' own pocket, shooting scenes after acting paydays.

C: Orson Welles, Jeanne Moreau, Margaret Rutherford, John Gielgud   D: Orson Welles

CHOOSE ME *1984 106m/C (R)*

Dr. Love, a radio sex-talk host, moves in with one of her listeners, a former prostitute who owns a bar. Neither one knows the other's "secret" identity. A seedy drifter enters the picture, along with strange situations of sex, love, and desire.

C: Keith Carradine, Genevieve Bujold, Lesley Ann Warren, Rae

Dawn Chong, John Larroquette   D: Alan Rudolph

CITY OF HOPE *1991 132m/C (R)*

John Sayles' look at the morals of city politics and family values is like a cynical Norman Rockwell painting, but it's on target. The story centers around Spano's problems with the police and his father's dirty deal with a politician to get his resentful son off the hook.

C: Vincent Spano, Joe Morton, Tony LoBianco, Todd Graff, David Strathairn, Angela Bassett, Barbara Williams   D: John Sayles

CLEAN AND SOBER *1988 124m/C (R)*

Caron, who started his career as a television writer (*Taxi*) and later created *Moonlighting*, hits a home run with this beautifully crafted drama about a drug addict who signs into a rehab to hide from the police. After he's in, he learns he can hide from the law but he can't hide from himself. One of Keaton's best.

C: Michael Keaton, Kathy Baker, Morgan Freeman, Claudia Christian
D: Glenn Gordon Caron

THE COCA-COLA KID *1984 94m/C (R)*

Roberts plays an American soft drink executive who travels to Australia to convince a company that owns a valuable stretch of land to sell his soft drink there. Sex and business politics soon take their toll.

C: Eric Roberts, Greta Scacchi, Bill Kerr   D: Dusan Makavejev

COMFORT AND JOY *1984 93m/C (PG)*

A Scottish disc jockey is dumped by his girlfriend and, after a strange series of events, becomes dangerously entangled in an underworld mob war over ice cream. Wacky treasure from the director of *Local Hero*.

C: Bill Paterson, Eleanor David, C. P. Grogan, Alex Norton, Patrick Malahide   D: Bill Forsyth

THE CONNECTION 1961 105m/B&W

Engrossing film about heroin junkies who are eagerly await-ing the arrival of their "connection" and a documentary film-maker who's standing by, camera ready, for the drug deal to consummate.

C: William Redfield, Garry Goodrow, Warren Finnerty, Carl Lee, Roscoe Lee Browne   D: Shirley Clarke

COOLEY HIGH 1975 107m/C (PG)

A group of black high schoolers in Chicago struggle to sur-vive the adventures and misadventures of senior year. Smart, fast-paced, well acted/directed pic. What Spike Lee's *Crook-lyn* tried to be.

C: Glynn Turman, Lawrence Hilton-Jacobs, Garrett Morris, Cynthia Davis   D: Michael A. Schultz

CRISS CROSS 1948 98m/B&W

An armored car driver returns to his hometown and is manip-ulated by his ex-wife into a robbery she and her thug husband have planned. Wicked twists and turns follow in this stylish thriller considered a classic of grade B film noir.

C: Burt Lancaster, Yvonne DeCarlo, Dan Duryea, Stephen McNally D: Robert Siodmak

CROSSING DELANCEY 1988 97m/C (PG)

A thirtyish New York City woman (Irving) who works in a literary bookstore and considers herself an intellectual, reluctantly goes on a date set up by her grandmother with a lowly pickle salesman. Charming sentimental story with music by The Roches and a performance by Suzy Roche as Irving's friend.

C: Amy Irving, Peter Riegert, Reizi Bozyk, Jeroen Krabbe, Sylvia Miles   D: Joan Micklin Silver

CRUSOE 1989 94m/C (PG-13)

The famous story of the shipwrecked slave trader is masterfully told and acted in this beautifully photographed, expertly directed film. After Crusoe is stranded he befriends a native. As their relationship strengthens his views of buying and selling human beings drastically changes. When he is rescued with his new friend his morals are tested. A must see.

C: Aidan Quinn, Ade Sapara, Jimmy Nail, Timothy Spall   D: Caleb Deschanel

A CRY IN THE DARK *1988 120m/C (PG-13)*

An intense retelling of the Australian murder trail in which Lindy Chamberlain was accused of killing her own child. She claimed that the child was mauled to death by a wild dog. Riveting.

C: Meryl Streep, Sam Neill, Bruce Myles, Charles Tingwell   D: Fred Schepisi   AA: '88 Best Actress (Streep)

THE DEAD *1987 82m/C (PG)*

A Christmas dinner party in 1904 creates an intense confrontation between a man and his wife when she begins to talk about a love she once had. Excellent characterizations, based on a James Joyce short story. John Huston's last film.

C: Anjelica Huston, Donal McCann, Marie Kean, Donal Donnelly   D: John Huston

DEATH AND THE MAIDEN *1994 100m/C (R)*

Weaver plays a woman who was once repeatedly raped and tortured by a doctor during a military coup. Years have passed and she's tried to put her life back together. When her husband brings home a friend who she believes is the same demented medic, she goes crazy, takes rule of the house with a gun, and begins to decide on a fitting revenge.

C: Sigourney Weaver, Ben Kinglsey   D: Roman Polanski

DOGFIGHT *1991 94m/C (R)*

Phoenix plays a marine who makes a bet with a group of his

buddies as to who can go out with the ugliest girl. He gets his date (Taylor in a great performance) but soon finds out there's more to love than meets the eye. Beautifully poignant.

C: River Phoenix, Lili Taylor, Richard Panebianco, Anthony Clark
D: Nancy Savoca

DOG STAR MAN 1964 80m/C

Brakhage is the king of avant-garde/experimental filmmaking and if you're into that type of experience then you shouldn't miss this pic which, through strange collages and lab effects, details the war between spiritual man and physical man.

D: Stan Brakhage

DOWN BY LAW 1986 105m/B&W (R)

A trio of mismatched cons break out of prison and sluggishly make their way through the swamplands of Louisiana. Besieged by wacky mishaps and clashing personalities they begin to believe jail wasn't so bad after all. Slick, offbeat, with classic Jarmusch style.

C: John Lurie, Tom Waits, Robert Benigni, Ellen Barkin, Rockets Redglare   D: Jim Jarmusch

DOWNHILL RACER 1969 102m/C (PG)

Lesser known Redford flick has him playing a rebellious olympic skiing hopeful from a small town who has a one track mind for winning. Filled with some great scenes like a talk with his farmer father who doesn't understand Redford's disdain for the simple life and a classic ending that asks the questions, "does winning really make you a winner?"

C: Robert Redford, Gene Hackman, Dabney Coleman, Camilla Sparv   D: Michael Ritchie

DROWNING BY NUMBERS 1987 121m/C (R)

Strange story about three women in three different time periods, all with the same name, who murder their husbands by drowning them and then cover their tracks by striking an arrangement with an odd coroner. Greenaway, known for his visual style, delivers an eyeful.

C: Joan Plowright, Juliet Stevenson, Joely Richardson, Bernard Hill
D: Peter Greenaway

EATING RAOUL *1982 83m/C (R)*

The Blands want to open their own country restaurant and serve up home made dishes like "The Bland Taco," but they haven't got the cash. So they put an ad in a sex magazine, lure kinky perverts with the promise of lusty Mary Bland, kill them, and sell their bodies to fast food hustler Raoul. Hilarious film festival favorite.

C: Paul Bartel, Mary Woronov, Robert Beltran, Ed Begley, Jr., Buck Henry D: Paul Bartel

84 CHARING CROSS ROAD *1986 100m/C (PG)*

A book collector has a 20 year relationship through the mail with a book seller that begins as a business dealing, grows into friendship, then blossoms into love. A warm, tender story, based on the real life memoirs of Helen Hanff. Hopkins and Bancroft are perfect in the leads.

C: Anne Bancroft, Anthony Hopkins, Judi Dench, Jean DeBaer, Mercedes Ruehl D: David Jones

EXOTICA *1995 103m/C (R)*

Bizarrely intoxicating journey into the strange world of lushly atmosphered strip clubs and the "relationship" between a dancer and her fan. See it for the mood and style.

C: Mia Kirshner, Bruce Greenwood D: Atom Egoyan

FAT MAN AND LITTLE BOY *1989 127m/C (PG-13)*

Engrossing story of the development of the atomic bomb with J. Robert Oppenheimer putting together some of the top minds on the planet, most of whom ended up seriously ill from the testing and regretting what they created. Cusack is outstanding.

C: Paul Newman, John Cusack, Bonnie Bedelia, Dwight Schultz
D: Roland Joffe

FINGERS 1978 89m/C (R)

An aspiring concert pianist (Harvey Keitel) is forced to work for his father, a mobster, collecting debts. This doesn't stop him from dreaming about success in music and the two, dreams and reality, crash. Excellent, tight knit drama.

C: Harvey Keitel, Jim Brown, Tisa Farrow, Danny Aiello, Tanya Roberts   D: James Toback

THE FIVE HEARTBEATS 1991 122m/C (R)

Solid, well told story of a black quintets ups and downs in and out of the music business. The direction is tight, the story breezes along, and the acting is excellent.

C: Robert Townsend, Tressa Thomas, Michael Wright, Harry J. Lennix, Diahann Carroll   D: Robert Townsend

THE 5000 FINGERS OF DR. T 1953 88m/C

A young boy flees his piano lesson only to wind up at the castle of fiendish Dr. Terwilliger, where hundreds of other naughty boys are being held. Darkly magical with great sets and characters, including the infamous "skating brothers." Co-scripted by Dr. Seuss.

C: Peter Lind Hays, Mary Healy, Tommy Rettig, Hans Conried
D: Roy Rowland

THE FRESHMAN 1990 102m/C (PG)

Broderick takes a job from a friend that eventually puts him in the middle of a seemingly mob run business that captures, kills, and cooks endangered animals for wealthy eccentric tastes. An offbeat story that's filled with hilarious twists and turns.

C: Marlon Brando, Matthew Broderick, Bruno Kirby, Penelope Ann Miller, Maximilian Schell   D: Andrew Bergman

THE FRONT *1976 95m/C (PG)*

One of the few films Woody Allen starred in, which he didn't direct, has him playing the front for a group of 1950s screenwriters who have been blacklisted by the insane senate communist hearings which were headed by Joe McCarthy. Classic satire based on a true story with a few of the actors being the actual screenwriters who were blacklisted. Great scene where Allen gives the panel a piece of his mind.

C: Woody Allen, Zero Mostel, Michael Murphy, Herschel Bernardi, Danny Aiello   D: Martin Ritt   AA: '76 Nom: Best Original Screenplay

THE GAMBLER *1974 111m/C (R)*

Caan plays a NYU professor with a serious gambling addiction. He goes through all his friends' money, takes his mother to the cleaners, and has one of his students throw a college basketball game, always believing he's one roll of the dice away from the good life. Expertly crafted character study.

C: James Caan, Paul Sorvino, Lauren Hutton, Burt Young, James Woods   D: Karel Reisz

GREGORY'S GIRL *1980 91m/C*

An English schoolboy tries out for the soccer team and loses his spot to a superior athlete. When he finds out the player is a girl he's crestfallen. But when he sees her, his anger turns to love, and he decides she must be his. Gordon John Sinclair, as the love struck boy, gives a performance worthy of an Academy Award. An engaging heartfelt comedy.

C: Gordon John Sinclair, Dee Hepburn, Chic Murray, Alex Norton D: Bill Forsyth

---

THE GREY FOX *1983 92m/C (PG)*

An old-timer is released from prison after spending 30 years behind bars for a "stagecoach" robbery. Thrust into a modernized world he must switch to a new form of crime, train robbery. Based on the real-life exploits of charismatic Canadian thief, Bill Miner.

C: Richard Farnsworth, Jackie Burroughs, Wayne Robson   D: Philip Borsos

HEAR MY SONG *1991 104m/C (R)*

Crazy night club owner Mickey O'Neill does his best to bring in the customers by booking talent like Franc Cinatra. But a phone call leads him to believe he's got the real legend, Josef Locke, set to perform. When the singer proves to be a phony, O'Neil must redeem himself by tracking down the reclusive Locke and bring him to sing at the club. A beautifully told, acclaimed comedy.

C: Ned Beatty, Adrian Dunbar, Tara Fitzgerald, Shirley Anne Field   D: Peter Chelsom

HEAVENLY CREATURES *1994 100m/C (R)*

Two 13-year-old girls form a strong relationship that goes beyond friendship, but ultimately leads to a murder that neither one can stop. Directed in a darkly surreal style that transforms the normal drama. Based on a true story.

C: Melanie Lynskey, Kate Winslet, Sarah Pierse, Clive Merrison   D: Peter Jackson   AA: '94 Nom: Best Original Screenplay

HIGH HOPES *1989 110m/C*

A pair of hippies, living in modern England, face the day-to-day numbness of progress and their yuppie neighbors. A seething satire from the man who brought us *Naked*.

C: Ruth Sheen, Philip Davis, Edna Dore, Philip Jackson   D: Mike Leigh

HI MOM! *1970 87m/C (R)*

Strange, effective second film from DePalma (he doesn't make them like this anymore) has DeNiro playing a peeping tom who becomes a porno filmmaker, falls in love with one of his stars, and turns him into a violent, bomb wielding anarchist. Wacky.

C: Robert DeNiro, Allen Garfield, Jennifer Salt, Lara Parker
D: Brian DePalma

THE HOT SPOT *1990 120m/C (R)*

Johnson gives what is undoubtedly his best performance in this stylish story about a con-man/drifter who takes a job at a used car lot, gets involved with the boss's wife, and is sucked into a pulse-pounding bank job. Madsen plays the femme-fatale and Connelly is great as the innocent temptress who works at the lot.

C: Don Johnson, Virginia Madsen, Charles Martin Smith, Jennifer Connelly, William Sadler   D: Dennis Hopper

HOURS AND THE TIMES *1993 60m/B&W*

Possible fact, possible fiction pic about a short vacation John Lennon and Beatle manager, Brian Epstein, took together in which homosexual Epstein declared his love for Lennon.

C: David Angus, Ian Hart, Stephanie Pack   D: Christopher Munch

HUMORESQUE *1946 123m/B&W*

A young, broke musician takes up with a wealthy married older woman but she soon slowly realizes her money can't buy her love. She's a bit unstable to begin with and the ending is a classic.

C: John Garfield, Joan Crawford, Oscar Levant, Joan Chandler, J. Carroll Naish   D: Jean Negulesco

I NEVER SANG FOR MY FATHER *1970 90m/C (PG)*

Heartfelt story of a man (Hackman) who must decide whether

to care for his sick, mean father (Douglas) or leave to marry the woman he loves. His mother wants him to stay but his sister, who cut her ties with the family, tells him to live his own life and go.

C: Gene Hackman, Melvyn Douglas, Estelle Parsons, Dorothy Stickney D: Gilbert Cates AA: '70 Nom: Best Actor (Hackman), Supporting Actor (Douglas), Adapted Screenplay

IMAGINARY CRIMES *1994 106m/C (PG)*

The delicately written character study of a widowed dreamer who continuously gambles his family's life in his neverending get rich quick schemes, never realizing the damage he's causing. His daughter, with her own dreams of becoming a writer, copes with his strained lifestyle by confiding in a sympathetic caring English teacher who guides her out of the mess.

C: Harvey Keitel, Fairuza Balk, Elisabeth Moss, Kelly Lynch, Vincent D'Onofrio D: Anthony Drazan

THE INTRUDER *1961 82m/B&W*

Pre-Star Trek Shatner plays a drifter who roams from southern town to town and riles people to fight against the new laws of integration in their schools. Roger Corman, usually responsible for pics like *Little Shop of Horrors*, brought us this effective "message" film.

C: William Shatner, Jeanne Cooper, Frank Maxwell, Leo Gordon D: Roger Corman

THE KILLING OF A CHINESE BOOKIE *1976 109m/C (R)*

A nightclub owner gets in debt way over his head and is offered a deal by the local thugs he owes the money to; sneak onto the estate of a Chinese bookie and kill him or lose his nightclub and, possibly, his life. Excellent, painfully realistic pic.

C: Ben Gazzara, Seymour Cassel, Zizi Johari, Robert Phillips, Soto Joe Hugh D: John Cassavetes

KING OF THE HILL *1993 102m/C (PG-13)*

Touching story of a Depression era St. Louis boy whose travelling father and hospitalized mother force him to survive on his own, using only his wit and tenacity to get by. From the director of *sex, lies, and videotape*. Based on the real life memoirs of writer A. E. Hotchner.

C: Jesse Bradford, Lisa Eichorn, Jeroen Krabbe, Spalding Gray, Elizabeth McGovern D: Steven Soderbergh

THE LAST SEDUCTION *1994 110m/C (R)*

A sadistic man-eating woman steals $700,000 from her husband and tries to get her new unknowing "boyfriend" to murder him. A stylish, twisted thriller with great performances.

C: Linda Fiorentino, Bill Pullman, Peter Berg D: John Dahl

LAWS OF GRAVITY *1992 100m/C (R)*

Critically hailed pic made for $38,000 details three days in the life of wild Brooklynite Jon (Trese) as he double-crosses a loan shark and a gun dealer. The results of his actions are brutal. Expertly made.

C: Peter Greene, Adam Trese, Edie Falco, Arabella Field D: Nick Gomez

LET HIM HAVE IT *1991 115m/C (R)*

A rooftop confrontation between police and burglars results in a dead officer when one of the thieves yells to the other, "let him have it." Did he mean "shoot the officer" or "give him the gun"? Though he didn't pull the trigger, the boy who shouted, Dereck Bentley (with an IQ of 66), was sentenced to death by the British Courts. Based on a true story.

C: Christopher Eccleston, Paul Reynolds, Tom Bell, Eileen Atkins, Tom Courtenay D: Peter Medak

LONELINESS OF THE LONG DISTANCE RUNNER
1962 104m/B&W

A rebellious young track star at a boys reformatory is the only one on the team who can win the most prestigious race of the year. Trouble is, he doesn't know if he wants to give the warden the satisfaction. Considered by some the best coming-of-age film ever made.

C: Tom Courtenay, Michael Redgrave, Avis Bunnage, Peter Madden, Topsy Jane   D: Tony Richardson

LUCAS *1986 100m/C (PG-13)*

Haim plays a high school whiz kid who falls for the pretty girl in town and tries to win her heart by trying out for the football team. Very good, non-sugar coated coming-of-age pic.

C: Corey Haim, Kerri Green, Charlie Sheen, Winona Ryder, Courtney Thorne-Smith   D: David Seltzer

THE MADNESS OF KING GEORGE *1994 103m/C (NR)*

A beautifully produced pic about King George III and how, when he seemed to be slipping into a state of insanity, his son (the Prince of Wales) tried to legally and deceitfully take the throne from him.

C: Nigel Hawthorne, Helen Mirren, Ian Holm, Rupert Everett, Rupert Graves   D: Nicholas Hytner   AA: '94 Nom: Best Actor (Hawthorne), Supporting Actress (Mirren)

MALCOLM *1986 86m/C (PG-13)*

A strange little comedy about a "slow" young man who has a genius ability when dealing with mechanical objects. After he loses his job for tinkering with some of the company's parts, he happily enters a life of crime.

C: Colin Friels, Lindy Davies, John Hargreaves, Beverly Phillips   D: Nadia Tass

MAN IN THE MOON *1991 100m/C (PG-13)*

In a small farm town, two sisters grow increasingly apart as they fight for the affection of a local boy. This simple plot is turned into a sensitive endearing film by a beautiful script and the genuine, innocent feelings between the boy and the two girls.

C: Reese Witherspoon, Emily Warfield, Jason London, Sam Waterston, Tess Harper   D: Robert Mulligan

MELVIN AND HOWARD *1980 95m/C (R)*

Melvin Dummar, a gas station owner, was riding in his pick-up when he pulled off to the side of the road to relieve himself. He found an old man, semi-delirious, lying in the brush. He gave him a ride and twenty five cents. A while later, after Howard Hughes died, someone came into Dummar's gas station and handed him Hughes' will which allegedly left him $156 million. The resulting onslaught of press conferences and media coverage rocketed Dummar into national fame. Engrossing, entertaining pic.

C: Paul LeMat, Jason Robards, Jr., Mary Steenburgen, Michael J. Pollard, Dabney Coleman   D: Jonathan Demme   AA: Best Original Screenplay, Supporting Actress (Steenburgen), Nom: Best Supporting Actor (Robards)

MISTRESS *1991 100m/C (R)*

A hustling producer and artistic director finally get the money for their film. Only one catch; all the investors want their mistresses in the picture and the ensuing problems this creates sends all of their lives into madness.

C: Robert Wuhl, Martin Landau, Robert DeNiro, Tuesday Weld, Eli Wallach   D: Barry Primus

MONA LISA *1986 104m/C (R)*

An involving story about a petty crook who's hired to chauffeur a high priced call girl. The more they ride the deeper involved they get.

C: Bob Hoskins, Michael Caine, Cathy Tyson, Clarke Peters, Kate Hardie   D: Neil Jordan   AA: '86 Nom: Best Actor (Hoskins)

MOONLIGHTING *1982 97m/C (PG)*

A cinematic essay on morals has Jeremy Irons the English speaking leader of a crew of Polish workers doing an illegal construction job in London. When a law is passed that affects the workers, Irons keeps them in the dark, pushing them harder.

C: Jeremy Irons, Eugene Lipinski, Jiri Stanislay, Eugeniusz Haczkiewicz   D: Jerzy Skolimowski

MOUNTAINS OF THE MOON *1990 104m/C (R)*

The story of Sir Richard Burton and John Hanning Speke's late 1800's trek across East Africa to find the source of the Nile River. Burton was one of the most talked about figures of the 19th century (he was also a poet and linguist) and he and Speke saw land never before seen by man. Ultimately the two were split apart by their own differences. Lushly photographed.

C: Patrick Bergin, Iain Glen, Richard E. Grant, Fiona Shaw, Peter Vaughan   D: Bob Rafelson

MS. 45 *1981 85m/C (R)*

A deaf mute girl is raped and beaten two times in one evening. Something in her mind snaps and she becomes a vigilante, hunting down slime. But what easily could have been a slasher/trasher is transformed into something special, with a classic ending.

C: Zoe Tamerlis, Steve Singer, Jack Thibeau, Peter Yellen   D: Abel Ferrara

THE MUSIC OF CHANCE *1993 98m/C (R)*

Offbeat story about a fireman (Patinkin) who quits his job, hits the road, and picks up a hitchhiking gambler (Spader) who's on his way to a high stakes "easy mark" card game. Patinkin backs the gambler and when they lose more than they can pay, the strange winning duo (Grey, Durning) make Patinkin and Spader build a giant wall on their property. Very strange, but very good.

C: Mandy Patinkin, James Spader, Joel Grey, Charles Durning, M. Emmet Walsh   D: Philip Haas

NAKED *1993 131m/C (R)*

A drifter travels to London to visit an old girlfriend. They have an argument and he spends the next few days wandering the streets, waxing philosophical with a wide assortment of characters. He drifts back to his girlfriend's apartment where she gives him the opportunity to leave his difficult, unsettled lifestyle and stay with her. A critically hailed, classic character study.

C: David Thewlis, Katrin Cartlidge, Lesley Sharp, Greg Cruttwell D: Mike Leigh

NOBODY'S FOOL *1994 101m/C (R)*

Newman, in one of his best roles, plays an upstate New York carpenter who was never able to get his life together. Director Benton perfectly captures the nuances and mood of this small town life and how Newman, who could have left long ago to chase success, decided it wasn't worth the effort.

C: Paul Newman, Jessica Tandy, Bruce Willis, Melanie Griffith, Dylan Walsh   D: Robert Benton   AA: '94 Nom: Best Actor (Newman)

ON THE BEACH *1959 135m/B&W*

Captivating story about a group of people who have survived an apocalypse and how they struggle to stay sane knowing a radioactive mist is headed their way.

C: Gregory Peck, Anthony Perkins, Ava Gardner, Donna Anderson, Fred Astaire   D: Stanley Kramer

ONCE AROUND 1991 115m/C (R)

Holly Hunter plays a young woman told by her long time boyfriend that he has no plans of ever marrying her. Distraught, she goes on a trip and meets Richard Dreyfuss, an uproarious lover-of-life whose rowdy brash attitude both intrigues and puts off Hunter's family. They get married and his outlandish behavior culminates in an experience that changes their lives forever.

C: Holly Hunter, Richard Dreyfuss, Danny Aiello, Laura San Giacomo, Gena Rowlands   D: Lasse Hallstrom

PARTING GLANCES 1986 90m/C (R)

A final day between two gay roommates before one leaves on a job transfer. Touching realistic story revolves around their learning of a friend's contraction of the AIDS virus and the effect it has on their lives. Director/writer Bill Sherwood died of AIDS in 1990.

C: Steve Buscemi, John Bolger, Richard Ganoung, Adam Nathan   D: Bill Sherwood

PASSION FISH 1992 135m/C (R)

A televison star suffers a brutal car accident which confines her to a wheelchair. She returns to her hometown in Louisiana to start a new life and meets a nurse who warms her heart.

C: Mary McDonnell, Alfre Woodard, David Strathairn   D: John Sayles
AA: '92 Nom: Best Actress (McDonnell), Original Screenplay

POPE OF GREENWICH VILLAGE 1984 122m/C (R)

Rourke stars as a young con man working his wares in the Little Italy section of New York City. He's fairly successful at what he does until he teams up with his cousin (Roberts) whose bad luck steers them into big trouble.

C: Mickey Rourke, Eric Roberts, Geraldine Page, Daryl Hannah, Tony Musante   D: Stuart Rosenberg

PROOF *1991 90m/C (R)*

A blind photographer who takes pictures so someone can describe them and give him proof of the world around him becomes the object of desire of his housekeeper. This situation is endangered by a new friend he makes. Great performances with a clever blend of comedy and drama.

C: Hugo Weaving, Genevieve Picot, Russell Crowe, Jeffrey Walker, Heather Mitchell D: Jocelyn Moorhouse

PUTNEY SWOPE *1969 84m/B&W (R)*

When a black man is mistakenly named the head of an ad agency he sets in motion a series of events that sets the company on its ear. Contains famous commercial spoofs. Overlooked for years, but now getting its due on home video.

C: Arnold Johnson, Laura Greene, Stanley Gottlieb, Mel Brooks D: Robert Downey

RED ROCK WEST *1994 98m/C (R)*

A bar owner mistakes a drifter (Cage) for the hit man he hired to kill his wife. The drifter takes the cash but when he arrives at the house the wife doubles the offer to kill her husband. Meanwhile, the real hit man (Hopper) has met up with the bar owner, taking this thriller around another twisted turn on a non-stop road to madness.

C: Nicolas Cage, Lara Flynn Boyle, Dennis Hopper, J. T. Walsh, Dwight Yoakam D: John Dahl

REPO MAN *1983 93m/C (R)*

An average guy is annoyed with his idiotic best friend, catches his girlfriend sleeping with another guy, and is told by his parents that they have given his college money to a TV evangelist. So he gets a job repossessing cars, becomes involved in an alien plot, and learns the secret of life from a burned-out bum. Classic, whacked out pic, with Estevez as the kid and Stanton ("people . . . I hate 'em") as his repo partner. Executive produced by ex-Monkee Mike Nesmith.

C: Emilio Estevez, Harry Dean Stanton, Sy Richardson, Tracy Walter, Olivia Barash   D: Alex Cox

RESTORATION 1995 118m/C (R)

It's England, the late 1600s. Downey is Marivel, a womanizing doctor who may have the ability to find a cure for the plague but would rather chase females and drink gallons of wine. The witnessing of a medical miracle sends him on a road of wild success, failure, tragedy, and ultimately, redemption. Downey is excellent as is Neill as King Charles II.

C: Robert Downey, Jr., Sam Neill, David Thewlis, Meg Ryan
D: Michael Hoffman

RETURN OF THE SECAUCUS 7 1980 110m/C

Where does Hollywood get its ideas for movies? Probably from small independent films like this one. Low budget *Big Chill* has seven friends, all 30, reuniting for a weekend of life reflection. Director Sayles appears in the film as "Howie."

C: David Strathairn, Mark Arnott, John Sayles, Gordon Clapp, Maggie Cousineau-Arndt   D: John Sayles

RIVER'S EDGE 1987 99m/C (R)

Based on a true murder in the early '80s, this pic tells the story of a high school student who murders his girlfriend and leaves her on the bank of a river. He then brings his friends to view the corpse which becomes their own gruesome secret. Dennis Hopper has a great role as a whacked out recluse.

C: Keanu Reeves, Crispin Glover, Dennis Hopper, Daniel Roebuck, Ione Skye   D: Tim Hunter

ROUND MIDNIGHT 1986 131m/C (R)

Alcoholic jazzman Dale Turner, getting on in years, decides to go to Paris, hoping to sober up and start anew. Once there he meets a young man who thinks Dale's the greatest sax player who ever lived and rekindles the fire that had almost gone out. Dexter Gordon is brilliant as the musician and the jazz score is as cool as it gets.

C: Dexter Gordon, Lonette McKee, Martin Scorsese, Francois Cluzet
D: Bertrand Tavernier   AA: '86 Nom: Best Actor (Gordon)

SAINT JACK 1979 112m/C (R)

Gazzara is great as Jack Flowers, an American who winds up in Singapore working as a successful pimp. Trouble begins when a group of Singapore thugs get a little jealous, but this film isn't about action or revenge, it's about the study of character. Director Peter Bogdanovich helmed *Paper Moon* and *The Last Picture Show*.

C: Ben Gazzara, Denholm Elliot, Joss Ackland   D: Peter Bogdanovich

SERIAL 1980 90m/C (R)

Mull plays the head of a shaky household in flaky Northern California where his kid joins a religious cult, his wife is "finding herself," his best friend is going through a mid-life crisis with an 18-year-old, and his boss is the leader of a gay motorcycle gang. Hilarious, overlooked flick.

C: Martin Mull, Tuesday Weld, Sally Kellerman, Bill Macy, Tom Smothers   D: Bill Persky

SEX, LIES, AND VIDEOTAPE 1989 100m/C (R)

Gallagher plays a "loving" husband with a lustful mistress. His old college buddy, who has a strange habit of videotaping women talking about sex, arrives and changes everyone's lives.

C: James Spader, Andie MacDowell, Peter Gallagher, Laura San Giacomo   D: Steven Soderbergh

SHE'S GOTTA HAVE IT 1986 84m/B&W (R)

Spike Lee's second film (his first was *Joe's Bed-Stuy Barber-*

shop: We Cut Heads) is a funny look at a free-spirited girl who has three guys dying to be her one and only. Spike stars as one of the boys and his "please baby, please baby, please baby, baby, baby, please" is one of the comic high points of the flick.

C: Spike Lee, Tracy Camilla Johns, Tommy Redmond Hicks
D: Spike Lee

THE SNAPPER *1993 90m/C (R)*

After his big budget Hollywood outing with *Hero*, director Stephen Frears returned to his England home to helm this low budget comedic treasure about a girl who accidentally becomes pregnant and won't divulge the name of the father to her family or friends. When they do find out who it is, a neighborhood scandal erupts. Great script about family loyalty and morals, with an incredible performance by Colm Meaney as the father.

C: Colm Meaney, Tina Kellegher, Ruth McCabe, Pat Laffan, Colm O'Bryne   D: Stephen Frears

STRAIGHT TIME *1978 114m/C (R)*

After six years in prison, a convict enters the outside world. The pressure of trying to stay clean proves too much for him and he is sucked back into a life of crime. Hoffman's great in this pic that he originally was slated to direct. Rock solid cast.

C: Dustin Hoffman, Harry Dean Stanton, Theresa Russell, Gary Busey, M. Emmet Walsh   D: Ulu Grosbard

STRANGER THAN PARADISE *1984 90m/B&W (R)*

Two deadbeats go on a road trip to Cleveland to see their Hungarian cousin who's working at a fast food joint. They pick her up and head to Florida in search of paradise, only to lose their money at the dog races. But then a miracle happens. Offbeat gold.

C: Richard Edson, John Lurie, Eszter Balint   D: Jim Jarmusch

STRICTLY BALLROOM *1992 94m/C (PG)*

A surprise independent hit which has a flashy unconventional dancer training for the "olympics of dancing" since he was a child. His partner leaves him and he's forced to take up with a new girl who teaches him a few steps of her own.

C: Paul Mercurio, Tara Morice, Bill Hunter, Pat Thomson, Barry Otto
D: Baz Luhrmann

THE TENANT *1976 126m/C (R)*

A twisted eerie tale about a shy office worker who rents an apartment that has a disturbing history: the former tenant committed suicide. Soon the new boarder feels like he's under a spell.

C: Roman Polanski, Isabelle Adjani, Melvyn Douglas, Jo Van Fleet, Shelley Winters   D: Roman Polanski

THEY SHOOT HORSES DON'T THEY? *1969 121m/C (R)*

Symbolism rings true in this story about a Depression era dance marathon where the contestants are two-stepping for a big cash prize but are dropping like flies from exhaustion.

C: Jane Fonda, Michael Sarrazin, Gig Young, Susannah York
D: Sydney Pollack AA: '69 Best Supporting Actor (Young), Nom: Best Screenplay, Actress (Fonda), Supporting Actress (York), Director

TICKET TO HEAVEN *1981 109m/C (PG)*

A young comedian learns that his friend has been sucked into a religious cult and flies to California to help him before he's completely "programmed" and mentally unable to come back to his life. Insightful, disturbing film with great performances all around.

C: Nick Mancuso, Saul Rubinek, Meg Foster, Kim Cattrall, R. H. Thomson   D: Ralph L. Thomas

THE TWELVE CHAIRS *1970 94m/C (PG)*

Fast paced comedy about a wealthy woman who hid her family jewels in the upholstery of one of twelve chairs that are presently floating around Russia. Langella and Moody play the desperate duo who have to track down the booty before arch rival DeLuise.

C: Frank Langella, Ron Moody, Mel Brooks, Dom DeLuise   D: Mel Brooks

29TH STREET *1992 110m/C (R)*

A young NYC man has one of fifty tickets to a six million dollar lottery drawing but must decide whether to sell it to thugs, use it to bail his dad out of mob trouble, or go for the big bucks. Frank Capra-like story is set against Christmas Eve. Great stuff.

C: Danny Aiello, Anthony LaPaglia, Frank Pesce, Lainie Kazan
D: George Gallo

UNTAMED HEART *1993 102m/C (PG-13)*

A poignant, moving tale of a young waitress who finds love where she's not looking for it; in a bus boy (Slater) thought of by all the other employees as an oddball. A beautiful, tender tearjerker.

C: Marisa Tomei, Christian Slater, Rosie Perez, Kyle Secor   D: Tony Bill

USED CARS *1980 113m/C (R)*

Russell owns a car lot and is in danger of losing it so he concocts a number of plans to crush his competitors, including breaking into the televised Superbowl game with a low budget commercial. What could have been a silly idea that goes nowhere is given life by Robert Zemeckis (*Back To The Future, Forrest Gump*) and energized performances from all involved.

C: Kurt Russell, Deborah Harmon, Jack Warden, Michael McKean, Joe Flaherty   D: Robert Zemeckis

VERNON, FLORIDA 1982 73m/C

Errol Morris's portrait of a small town in the southern state inhabited by plain, simple folks who talk about their lives and philosophies. Morris's camera captures them in their day to day activities, whether it's a turkey hunter searching for his prize or a policeman explaining his town's speed trap. Mellow gold.

D: Erroll Morris

THE YEAR MY VOICE BROKE 1987 103m/C (PG-13)

Touching heartfelt story of a young boy in love with an older girl and the hope and pain this causes. Critically hailed.

C: Noah Taylor, Ben Mendelsohn, Loene Carmen, Graeme Blundell, Lynette Curran   D: John Duigan

---

WAR

ALL QUIET ON THE WESTERN FRONT 1930 103m/B&W

Masterfully produced epic about the horrors of war, focusing on one soldier's change from enthusiastic gung-ho soldier to emotionally torn, battle fatigued, anti-war veteran. Controversial with graphic fight scenes and strong anti-war message. Contains one of the most famous final shots ever filmed, which must be seen to be appreciated.

C: Lew Ayres, Louis Wolheim, John Wray, Slim Sommerville, Russell Gleason   D: Lewis Milestone   AA: '30 Best Director, Picture

APOCALYPSE NOW 1979 153m/C (R)

See "Top 100"

BEAU GESTE *1939 114m/B&W*

Unforgettable classic about three brothers who join the Foreign Legion after confessing to a jewel heist they didn't commit. Brutal battles, the harsh desert, and a sadistic commander are just three of the elements they have to put up with in order to clear their family's name.

C: Gary Cooper, Ray Milland, Robert Preston, Brian Donlevy, Donald O'Connor, Susan Hayward   D: William A. Wellman

THE BEST YEARS OF OUR LIVES *1946 170m/B&W*
See "Top 100"

THE BIG PARADE *1925 141/B&W*

Just how harrowing war can be on and off the battle field is exemplified to perfection in this masterpiece, considered one of the best war films ever made. Gilbert plays the soldier and Adoree the beautiful love of his life, until the brutal war comes between them. Some of the best combat footage ever put on screen.

C: John Gilbert, Renee Adoree, Hobart Bosworth, Claire McDowell
D: King Vidor

BIRTH OF A NATION *1915 175m/B&W*

The granddaddy of cinema, D. W. Griffith, made this epic about the Civil War, which is considered the first full length feature film. A masterpiece in camera movement, storytelling and battle choreography. Pic set the stage for endless imitations of style. Stars actress Lillian Gish, whose film career spanned nine decades.

C: Lillian Gish, Mae Marsh, Henry B. Walthall, Robert Harron, Wallace Reid   D: D. W. Griffith

BORN ON THE 4TH OF JULY *1989 145m/C (R)*

Ron Kovic's experience during and after the Vietnam War is brought to the screen in this powerful film that begins with his innocent induction into the service and ends with his post-war life as a paralyzed anti-war activist. Cruise has never been better and Kovic appears in the film as a veteran in a parade.

C: Tom Cruise, Kyra Sedgwick, Raymond Barry, Tom Berenger, Jerry Levine   D: Oliver Stone   AA: '89 Best Director (Stone), Nom: Best Actor (Cruise), Adapted Screenplay, Picture

BREAKER MORANT 1980 107m/C (PG)

True story of three soldiers whose war efforts lead them to a court martial. The pic examines whether the trial deals with justice or political gameplay, or whether justice is political gameplay.

C: Edward Woodward, Jack Thompson, Bryan Brown, John Waters
D: Bruce Beresford

BRIDGE ON THE RIVER KWAI 1957 161m/C

See "Top 100"

BURN! 1970 112m/C (PG)

Brando gives a tour-de-force performance as William Walker, a man sent to incite a slave revolt on a Caribbean sugar plantation owned by the Portuguese. Walker does his job a little too well and when the new leader becomes power obsessed, Walker is sent back to do him in.

C: Marlon Brando, Evarist Marquez, Renato Salvatori   D: Gillo Pontecorvo

CATCH-22 1970 121m/C (R)

Satire on the insanity of war follows a group of pilots flying missions around the Mediterranean, and the resulting physical and mental madness this causes. Based on Joseph Heller's award winning novel.

C: Alan Arkin, Art Garfunkel, Martin Balsam, Jon Voight, Richard Benjamin, Charles Grodin, Martin Sheen, Orson Welles, Buck Henry, Paula Prentiss   D: Mike Nichols

THE CHARGE OF THE LIGHT BRIGADE *1936*
116m/B&W

Tennyson's poem is brought to the screen in this lavish production which includes the famous thundering troops gallantly charging into the Valley Of Death. Spectacular battle scene was state of the art for the day.

C: Errol Flynn, Olivia de Havilland, Nigel Bruce, Patrick Knowles, Henry Stephenson   D: Michael Curtiz

COMING HOME *1978 130m/C (R)*

Beautifully told, realistic story about a woman (Fonda) whose war loving Marine husband (Dern) goes off to fight while she volunteers at a veteran's hospital. There she meets a bitter, but caring, paralyzed soldier (Voight) and slowly falls in love.

C: Jane Fonda, Jon Voight, Bruce Dern, Penelope Milford, Robert Carradine, Robert Ginty   D: Hal Ashby   AA: '78 Best Actor (Voight), Actress (Fonda), Nom: Best Director, Picture, Supporting Actor (Dern), Supporting Actress (Milford)

THE DEER HUNTER *1978 183m/C (R)*
See "Top 100"

THE DIRTY DOZEN *1967 149m/C (PG)*

A group of soldiers/convicts volunteer for a suicide mission into Nazi Germany under the arrangement that if they succeed they're granted immunity. Marvin plays the hardcore Major who must win the outcasts' respect and whip them into shape. Fast-moving action with all-star cast.

C: Lee Marvin, Charles Bronson, Jim Brown, Ernest Borgnine, John Cassavetes, Telly Savalas, Donald Sutherland   D: Robert Aldrich   AA: '67 Nom: Best Supporting Actor (Cassavetes)

THE DUELLISTS *1977 101m/C (PG)*

The long mental feud between two French officers during the Napoleonic War serves as the center of drama for this pic which is one of the most beautifully photographed films of the last twenty years. The directorial debut of Ridley Scott (*Blade Runner, Alien*).

C: Keith Carradine, Harvey Keitel, Albert Finney, Edward Fox
D: Ridley Scott

THE FIGHTING SULLIVANS 1942 110m/B&W

The heart wrenching true story of the Sullivan Brothers, five siblings who enlisted in WWII after the bombing of Pearl Harbor and died together when the ship they were on, Juneau, was torpedoed. A tragic, powerful tribute.

C: Anne Baxter, Thomas Mitchell, Selena Royle, Eddie Ryan, Trudy Marshall   D: Lloyd Brown

THE FOUR FEATHERS 1939 99m/C

A young man decides against going to war but his family and fiance reject his decision and give him four white feathers as a symbol of his cowardliness. Angered, he enlists and becomes a major war hero, saving the lives of three of the men who scorned him. Highly acclaimed.

C: John Clements, Ralph Richardson, C. Aubrey Smith, June Duprez, Donald Gray   D: Zoltan Korda

FROM HERE TO ETERNITY 1953 118m/B&W

The lives of three soldiers stationed in Honolulu just prior to the attack on Pearl Harbor are followed in this gripping, perfectly made pic. Contains the famous Burt Lancaster/Deborah Kerr love scene amidst the beach crashing waves.

C: Burt Lancaster, Montgomery Clift, Frank Sinatra, Deborah Kerr, Donna Reed   D: Fred Zinneman   AA: '53 Best Picture, Director, Screenplay, Supporting Actor (Sinatra), Supporting Actress (Reed), Nom: Best Actor (Clift, Lancaster), Actress (Kerr)

FULL METAL JACKET 1987 116m/C (R)

One man's journey into Vietnam is followed from boot camp

to front line duty and we witness the effect this senseless war has on his outlook on life. Considered by many critics to be the most realistic war film ever made.

C: Matthew Modine, Lee Ermey, Vincent D'Onofrio, Adam Baldwin, Dorian Harewood   D: Stanley Kubrick

GALLIPOLI *1981 111m/C (PG)*

Unknown Mel Gibson stars as one of two Australian friends who become soldiers in WWI and fight side by side with tragic results. Compelling, powerful anti-war flick, one of the best of its kind. Director Weir later helmed *Green Card* and *Witness*.

C: Mel Gibson, Mark Lee, Bill Kerr, David Argue, Tim McKenzie
D: Peter Weir

GLORY *1989 122m/C (R)*

Broderick (in his best role) stars as Robert Gould Shaw, commander of the first black Civil War Volunteer Infantry Unit, the 54th Massachusetts. The unit took part in one of the bloodiest battles of the war and proved to the Northern military leaders that blacks were excellent soldiers, opening up a new area of recruitment that may have been responsible for the North's victory. A sweeping, historical production with lavish costumes and beautiful photography.

C: Matthew Broderick, Morgan Freeman, Denzel Washington, Cary Elwes   D: Edward Zwick   AA: '89 Best Supporting Actor (Washington)

GO TELL THE SPARTANS *1978 114m/C (R)*

Lancaster plays an Army Major who's ordered to Muc Wa to command a platoon of soldiers made up of mentally and physically fatigued Americans and Vietnamese mercenaries. A strong anti-war message with Lancaster's character knowing the war is a lost cause even before he leaves.

C: Burt Lancaster, David Clennon, Craig Wasson, Marc Singer
D: Ted Post

THE GREAT ESCAPE *1963 170m/C*

It's WWII and the Germans have just put the most notorious POW's into one escape-proof camp. They immediately set to work building three tunnels, "Tom," "Dick," and "Harry," planning the largest single escape attempt in the history of the war. From a true story.

C: Steve McQueen, James Garner, Richard Attenborough, Charles Bronson, James Coburn D: John Sturges

GUNGA DIN *1939 117m/B&W*

One of the best films ever, this pic centers around three 18th century British soldiers who, in India, attempt to quell a native uprising. In classic style, it's their water boy who saves the day. Great action sequences and tongue-in-cheek humor.

C: Cary Grant, Victor McLaglen, Douglas Fairbanks, Jr., Sam Jaffe, Eduardo Ciannelli D: George Stevens

THE GUNS OF NAVARONE *1961 159m/C*

The Germans have set up a troop of armed soldiers on an island off the coast of Greece. Allied transport ships will soon be sailing into an ambush. British Intelligence finds out about it and sends a group of military combat experts to do away with the guns and soldiers. Highly regarded WWII action pic.

C: Gregory Peck, David Niven, Anthony Quinn, Richard Harris, Stanley Baker D: J. Lee Thompson AA: '61 Nom: Best Director

HELL IN THE PACIFIC *1968 101m/C (PG)*

Well paced pic about two soldiers, one American, one Japanese, who are stranded on an island and the resulting battle that erupts between them.

C: Lee Marvin, Toshiro Mifune D: John Boorman

HELL IS FOR HEROES *1962 90m/B&W*

A small group of soldiers, led by Steve McQueen, must hold

off the large German force that will seemingly crush them. Tense, fast moving drama leads to a classic climax. Director Siegel went on to direct the *Dirty Harry* movies.

C: Steve McQueen, James Coburn, Fess Parker, Bobby Darin, Bob Newhart   D: Don Siegel

HELL'S ANGELS *1930 135m/B&W*

The notoriety behind this film is as famous as the film itself: financier/billionaire Howard Hughes fired three directors and ended up getting the director credit, and three pilots died while shooting the incredible flying sequences. The story centers around two brothers, one gung-ho, the other cowardly, and how the war affects them. Pic made a sex symbol of Harlow.

C: Jean Harlow, Ben Lyon, James Hall, John Darrow, Lucien Prival
D: Howard Hughes

THE KILLING FIELDS *1984 142m/C*

True story of a U.S. reporter's harrowing search for his Cambodian assistant during the fall of Saigon and the brutal reign of terror known as "Zero Hour." Powerfully made.

C: Sam Waterston, Haing S. Ngor, John Malkovich, Julian Sands
D: Roland Joffe   AA: '84 Best Supporting Actor (Ngor), Nom: Best Picture, Director

LAST OF THE MOHICANS *1992 114m/C (R)*

Richly textured, lush adoption of James Fenimore Cooper's novel about an Indian who tries to stay out of the French American War but ultimately becomes involved due to his love of a beautiful woman. Lavishly produced with incredibly realistic battle scenes.

C: Daniel Day-Lewis, Madeleine Stowe, Wes Studi, Russell Means, Eric Schweig   D: Michael Mann

LAWRENCE OF ARABIA *1962 221m/C (PG)*

See "Top 100"

THE LIFE AND DEATH OF COLONEL BLIMP *1943 115m/C*

The sensitively handled, intelligent story of a British soldier who fights in three wars (The Boer War, WWI, WWII) and loves three women.

C: Roger Livesey, Deborah Kerr, Anton Walbrook, Ursula Jeans, Albert Lieven   D: Michael Powell, Emeric Pressburger

THE LONGEST DAY *1962 179m/C*

An all-star cast recreates the events of D-Day, June 6, 1944, when the allied troops landed at Normandy. A huge budget brought this film to epic proportions and no cost was spared attending to historical detail.

C: John Wayne, Richard Burton, Red Buttons, Robert Mitchum, Henry Fonda   D: Ken Annakin   AA: '62 Nom: Best Picture

A MIDNIGHT CLEAR *1992 107m/C (PG)*

It's Christmas time in WWII. A group of American soldiers, sent on a dangerous mission to check out an abandoned house near the German border, undergo an experience that changes their lives forever.

C: Gary Sinise, Kevin Dillon, Ethan Hawke, Peter Berg, Ayre Gross   D: Keith Gordon

OBJECTIVE BURMA! *1945 142m/B&W*

A command of paratroopers descend on Burma where the Japanese have a strategic radar post that the troops are going to destroy. They are successful in removing the station but are trapped by enemy troops and are faced with brutal attacks, starvation and fatigue as they desperately wait for a rescue unit.

C: Errol Flynn, James Brown, William Prince, George Tobias, Henry Hull   D: Raoul Walsh

PATHS OF GLORY *1957 86m/B&W*
See "Top 100"

PATTON *1970 171m/C (PG)*
See "Top 100"

PLATOON *1986 113m/C*
A young man gets a brutal blast of the harrowing realities of war as a soldier in Vietnam. Director Stone based the pic on his own experiences.

C: Charlie Sheen, Tom Berenger, Willem Dafoe, Francesco Quinn   D: Oliver Stone   AA: '86 Best Picture, Director, Nom: Best Original Screenplay, Supporting Actor (Berenger, Dafoe)

PORK CHOP HILL *1959 97m/B&W*
A brutally realistic look at the closing hours of the Korean war with Peck as an officer who tries to hold his own as the relentless Chinese troops attack.

C: Gregory Peck, Harry Guardino, Rip Torn, George Peppard, James Edwards   D: Lewis Milestone

THE RED BADGE OF COURAGE *1951 70m/B&W*
A Civil War soldier runs from a battle, becomes riddled with guilt, and begins a mental war of whether or not he's a coward. Incredible battle scenes, based on the Stephen Crane classic.

C: Audie Murphy, Bill Mauldin, Douglas Dick, Royal Dano   D: John Huston

SALVADOR *1986 123m/C (R)*
A great performance by Woods propels this fascinating pic that depicts the real life journey of photojournalist Richard

Boyle through wartorn El Salvador during 1980-81.

C: James Woods, James Belushi, John Savage, Michael Murphy, Elpidia Carrillo   D: Oliver Stone   AA: '86 Nom: Best Actor (Woods), Original Screenplay

SANDS OF IWO JIMA 1949 104m/B&W

Wayne stars as a hard-core sergeant who is hated by most of his troop for his brutal demeanor. When the outfit is sent to capture Iwo Jima from the Japanese (in what was one of WWII's most difficult and heroic battles), they realize the sergeant's toughness had an important meaning. Some real footage of the war was used in the film.

C: John Wayne, Forrest Tucker, John Agar, Richard Jaeckel D: Allan Dwan

SERGEANT YORK 1941 134m/B&W

Cooper is Alvin York, the Tennessee farm boy who tried to avoid the WWI draft because it conflicted terribly with his religious beliefs. But a series of events led him into battle and he became one of the war's most decorated heroes.

C: Gary Cooper, Joan Leslie, Walter Brennan, Dickie Moore, Margaret Wycherly   D: Howard Hawks   AA: '41 Best Actor (Cooper), Nom: Best Picture, Director, Screenplay, Supporting Actor (Brennan), Supporting Actress (Wycherly)

STALAG 17 1953 120m/B&W

American prisoners in a German POW camp are convinced one of them is a spy. Compelling, strongly acted and directed pic.

C: William Holden, Don Taylor, Peter Graves, Otto Preminger D: Billy Wilder   AA: '53 Best Actor (Holden), Nom: Best Director, Supporting Actor (Robert Strauss)

THEY WERE EXPENDABLE 1945 135m/B&W

Small American PT boats go up against a Japanese Navy

fleet in this first rate WWII pic based on an actual incident.

C: Robert Montgomery, Donna Reed, John Wayne, Jack Holt
D: John Ford

TWELVE O'CLOCK HIGH *1949 132m/B&W*

Gregory Peck plays a WWII officer who replaces a bad egg, only to begin to feel the pressure of the war himself. Intelligent examination of the horrific strain of combat.

C: Gregory Peck, Hugh Marlowe, Gary Merrill, Millard Mitchell
D: Henry King   AA: '49 Best Supporting Actor (Dean Jagger), Nom: Best Actor (Peck), Picture

VIVA ZAPATA! *1952 112m/B&W*

Marlon Brando is Emiliano Zapata, the famed Mexican revolutionary who, after the turn of the century, led the peasants into a brutal, successful war. Soon after, Zapata became obsessed with his own power and began a downward spiral into madness.

C: Marlon Brando, Anthony Quinn, Jean Peters, Margo, Arnold Moss, Joseph Wiseman   D: Elia Kazan   AA: '52 Best Supporting Actor (Quinn), Nom: Best Actor (Brando)

WHERE EAGLES DARE *1968 158m/C (PG)*

Edge of your seat war/action pic has Burton and Eastwood heading a WWII allied troop that must free a General being held in a Nazi infested Bavarian Alps castle. Top-notch suspense pic.

C: Clint Eastwood, Richard Burton, Mary Ure, Michael Hordern
D: Brian G. Hutton

WESTERN

ANGEL AND THE BADMAN *1947 100m/B&W*

A gunfighter is struck down and a peace loving family rescues him and gives him a place to stay. The daughter of the clan ends up falling in love with him and tries to dissuade his revenge seeking gun-slinging ways.

C: John Wayne, Gail Russell, Irene Rich, Harry Carey, Sr., Bruce Cabot D: James Edward Grant

THE BALLAD OF GREGORIO CORTEZ *1983 104m/C (PG)*

A Mexican ranch hand has a violent confrontation with a sheriff and kills him in self-defense, beginning the biggest manhunt in the history of Texas. All of this takes place because of a misinterpretation of the Spanish language. Based on a true story.

C: Edward James Olmos, James Gammon, Tom Bower, Alan Vint, Barry Corbin D: Robert M. Young

BUTCH CASSIDY AND THE SUNDANCE KID *1969 110m/C (PG)*

See "Top 100"

CAT BALLOU *1965 96m/C*

Fonda plays a turn-of-the-century school teacher who drops her books and picks up a pair of six guns to avenge her father's death. Lively tongue-in-cheek take of traditional western.

C: Jane Fonda, Lee Marvin, Michael Callan, Dwayne Hickman, Reginald Denny D: Elliot Silverstein AA: '65 Best Actor (Marvin), Nom: Best Adapted Screenplay

THE COWBOYS *1972 128m/C (PG)*

Wayne plays a rancher whose workers leave for the gold rush. Wayne still must take his cattle over 400 miles and is forced to hire eleven school boys to help him with the task. Included is a famous battle scene between an outlaw (Dern) and the Duke.

C: John Wayne, Roscoe Lee Browne, A. Martinez, Bruce Dern, Colleen Dewhurst D: Mark Rydell

DANCES WITH WOLVES *1990 181m/C (PG-13)*

Costner plays a decorated U.S. Civil War soldier who chooses to be transferred to a remote post in the Dakotas near a tribe of Lakota Sioux. He befriends the Indians, gains their trust, and eventually becomes accepted as a member. Stunning cinematography and a beautiful score.

C: Kevin Costner, Mary McDonnell, Graham Greene, Rodney Grant, Floyd "Red Crow" Westerman D: Kevin Costner AA: '90 Best Director, Picture, Adapted Screenplay, Nom: Best Actor (Costner), Supporting Actor (Greene), Supporting Actress McDonnell)

DARK COMMAND *1940 95m/B&W*

The true story of a once upright citizen who formed a band of outlaws known as Quantrell's Raiders and wreaked havoc on the Kansas territory. Wayne plays the man who finally went up against the rogue and his bandits.

C: John Wayne, Walter Pidgeon, Claire Trevor, Roy Rogers, Marjorie Main D: Raoul Walsh

DESTRY RIDES AGAIN *1939 94m/B&W*

Stewart plays an ordinary citizen pushed into the role of town sheriff. Not one for violence, he amazingly succeeds in beating the bad guys without firing one bullet. Look for Dietrich singing "See What the Boys In the Back Room Will Have."

C: James Stewart, Marlene Dietrich, Brian Donlevy, Charles Winninger, Misha Auer D: George Marshall

EL DORADO *1967 126m/C*

Wayne plays a hired gunman who travels to town to help a

cattle baron fight off some farmers. After he talks with his old friend, who happens to be the town's drunken sheriff, Wayne decides to switch sides and fight on the side of the farmers. Remake of *Rio Bravo* with Wayne in the same role.

C: John Wayne, Robert Mitchum, James Caan, Charlene Holt, Ed Asner   D: Howard Hawks

A FISTFUL OF DOLLARS *1964 101m/C (R)*
Eastwood was turned into an international star in this film about a drifter who walks into the middle of a war between two families over a piece of land.

C: Clint Eastwood, Gian Marie Volante, Marianne Koch   D: Sergio Leone

FORT APACHE *1948 125m/B&W*
Fonda plays an officer who seeks some glory and will start a war with the Apache Indians to get it. Wayne plays the soldier who lets Fonda know this may not be a good idea. First film in John Ford's famous trilogy followed by *She Wore A Yellow Ribbon* and *Rio Grande*.

C: John Wayne, Henry Fonda, Shirley Temple, John Agar, Pedro Armendariz, Sr.   D: John Ford

THE GOOD, THE BAD, AND THE UGLY *1966 161m/C*
The stylistic final installment of great Italian master Sergio Leone's "Dollars" trilogy has three gunslingers going up against each other for a stash of gold buried in a grave. Solid action with some rowdy gunfights.

C: Clint Eastwood, Eli Wallach, Lee Van Cleef, Chelo Alonso, Luigi Pistill   D: Sergio Leone

GUNFIGHT AT THE O.K. CORRAL *1957 122m/C*
Star-studded cast adds power to the tension building story of Wyatt Earp and Doc Holliday going up against the Clanton gang on a dreary 1881 day in Tombstone, Arizona.

Watch for Dennis Hopper.

C: Burt Lancaster, Kirk Douglas, Rhonda Fleming, Jo Van Fleet, John Ireland   D: John Sturges

THE GUNFIGHTER *1950 84m/B*

A magnificent character study of a legendary gunfighter who tries to settle down and live a life of peace. Unfortunately, he can't escape his reputation and is constantly approached and challenged by men who want to dethrone him.

C: Gregory Peck, Helen Westcott, Millard Mitchell, Jean Parker, Karl Malden   D: Henry King

HIGH NOON *1952 85m/B&W*

See "Top 100"

HIGH PLAINS DRIFTER *1973 105m/C (R)*

Eastwood directed and stars in this eerie and effective tale of a gunslinger hired to protect a town from three escaped outlaws who are on their way to wreak some wild west violence. Famous "Welcome to Hell" scene. Best line happens when one of the townspeople asks Clint, "what are you gonna do after you kill them?" to which Clint replies, "live with it."

C: Clint Eastwood, Verna Bloom, Mitchell Ryan, Marianna Hill
D: Clint Eastwood

JEREMIAH JOHNSON *1972 107m/C (PG)*

Redford plays the title character, a man whose distaste for cities and people leads him to the mountains where he must face the hazards of weather, rival trappers, and Indians. He overcomes all these obstacles to find his peace of mind.

C: Robert Redford, Will Greer   D: Sydney Pollack

LITTLE BIG MAN *1970 135m/C (PG)*

Hoffmann gives an inspired performance as Jack Crabbe, a

121-year-old westerner who, through flashbacks, tells of his drinking days with Wild Bill Hickock, his stint as a medicine show con-man, his days living with an Indian family, his amazing survival of Custer's last stand, and other adventures. Epic-like and thoroughly satisfying.

C: Dustin Hoffman, Faye Dunaway, Chief Dan George, Richard Mulligan, Martin Balsam   D: Arthur Penn

THE LONG RIDERS *1980 100m/C (R)*

Well crafted story follows the James and Younger gangs as they make money the violent way in late 1800's Missouri. Four pairs of outlaw brothers are portrayed by four pairs of real-life acting brothers. Includes a great slow motion shootout and smooth score by slide guitarist Ry Cooder.

C: Stacy Keach, James Keach, Dennis Quaid, Randy Quaid, David Carradine, Keith Carradine, Robert Carradine, Christopher Guest, Nicholas Guest   D: Walter Hill

THE MAGNIFICENT SEVEN *1960 126m/C*

A Mexican town turns to hiring seven expert gunslingers to save them from a band of outlaws who are terrorizing their village. An all-star remake of Akira Kurosawa's classic *The Seven Samurai.*

C: Yul Brynner, Steve McQueen, Robert Vaughn, James Coburn, Charles Bronson   D: John Sturges

THE MAN FROM LARAMIE *1955 104m/C*

An aging rancher must decide which son to leave his business to. This dilemma is doubled by a new problem in the form of Stewart, a cowboy obsessed with finding out who sold rifles to the Indians who murdered his kin. Excellent, tension building pic.

C: James Stewart, Arthur Kennedy, Donald Crisp, Alex Nicol, Cathy O'Donnell   D: Anthony Mann

THE MAN WHO SHOT LIBERTY VALANCE *1962 123m/B&W*

Great character study of a man who becomes a hero after shooting a ruthless gunfighter named Liberty Valance. Stewart is the man who takes his popularity all the way to a seat in the Senate while Wayne is the tough cowboy and friend who tries to comfort Stewart's feeling of guilt. One of Ford's best.

C: James Stewart, John Wayne, Vera Miles, Lee Marvin, Edmund O'Brien   D: John Ford

MCCABE AND MRS. MILLER *1972 121m/C (R)*

Beatty plays a small time bragging businessman who opens up a brothel in a turn-of-the-century western town. The business takes off, resulting in a group of bandits making an offer he better not refuse. All of his bragging must be put to the test as his day of truth is at hand. Beautifully done.

C: Warren Beatty, Julie Christie, William Devane, Keith Carradine, John Schuck   D: Robert Altman

MY DARLING CLEMENTINE *1946 97m/B&W*

Director John Ford was a friend of Wyatt Earp's and used his stories in making this film which retells the exact events that led up the famous gunfight at the O.K. Corral. One of the best westerns ever made.

C: Henry Fonda, Victor Mature, Walter Brennan, Linda Darnell, Tim Holt, Ward Bond, John Ireland   D: John Ford

THE NAKED SPUR *1953 93m/C*

Jimmy Stewart plays a bounty hunter tracking outlaw Robert Ryan through the Rocky Mountains. Once caught, a psychological twist enters the script as Ryan tries to break apart Stewart and his "posse." Nice mountain photography is an added plus.

C: Jimmy Stewart, Robert Ryan, Janet Leigh, Millard Mitchell   D: Anthony Mann

ONCE UPON A TIME IN THE WEST *1968 165m/C (PG)*

Henry Fonda, in a reversal of his normal roles, is the ruthless leader of a gang of outlaws who plan on murdering a female landowner who's waiting for the railroad to come through. Taut thriller.

C: Henry Fonda, Jason Robards, Jr., Charles Bronson, Claudia Cardinale, Keenan Wynn   D: Sergio Leone

ONE-EYED JACKS *1961 141m/C*

Fantastic story about an outlaw (Brando) who is double crossed by his partner. Later the partner becomes a sheriff and the bad man decides it's time for revenge. Stanley Kubrick began as director but was replaced by Brando.

C: Marlon Brando, Karl Malden, Katy Jurado, Elisha Cook, Jr.
D: Marlon Brando

THE OUTLAW JOSEY WALES *1976 135m/C (PG)*

A blistering story about a farmer whose family is brutally killed by Red Legs, a gang of murderers who join the Union Army. Josey Wales (Eastwood) also joins the army to avenge their deaths. First rate story and characters make this one of the great westerns.

C: Clint Eastwood, Chief Dan George, Sandra Locke, Matt Clark, John Vernon   D: Clint Eastwood

THE OX-BOW INCIDENT *1943 75m/B&W*

A rancher is murdered and the angry townspeople, lusting for revenge, hang the first three men they can find. Two drifters (Fonda, Morgan) try to stop them. One of the greatest westerns ever made and a brilliant study of "mob" mentality. Based on a true story.

C: Henry Fonda, Harry Morgan, Dana Andrews, Anthony Quinn, Frank Conroy   D: William A. Wellman   AA: '43 Nom: Best Picture

PAT GARRETT & BILLY THE KID *1973 106m/C*

Kristofferson is the outlaw and Coburn his partner turned sheriff who must hunt him down. Dylan sang "Knockin' On Heaven's Door" for the soundtrack.

C: Kris Kristofferson, James Coburn, Bob Dylan, Richard Jaeckel, Katy Jurado D: Sam Peckinpah

RED RIVER *1948 133m/B&W*

A western version of *Mutiny On The Bounty* with a father and son caught in a taut emotional war while leading a cattle drive.

C: John Wayne, Montgomery Clift, Walter Brennan, Joanne Dru, John Ireland D: Howard Hawks

RIDE THE HIGH COUNTRY *1962 93m/C*

Two old-time gunslingers team up to guard a gold shipment. One, honest and law abiding, wants to get it to its destination no matter what. The other has plans of stealing the loot. Gorgeously photographed.

C: Randolph Scott, Joel McCrea, Mariette Hartley, Edgar Buchanan, R. G. Armstrong, Warren Oates D: Sam Peckinpah

RIO BRAVO *1959 140m/C*

Wayne plays a sheriff who captures a notorious outlaw and must bring him to justice. The only problem is the relentless onslaught of bandits who are hell bent on stopping him. Tense, expertly directed pic. Remade, see *El Dorado*.

C: John Wayne, Dean Martin, Angie Dickinson, Ricky Nelson, Walter Brennan D: Howard Hawks

THE SEARCHERS *1956 119m/C*
See "Top 100"

SHANE *1953 117m/C*
See "Top 100"

SHE WORE A YELLOW RIBBON *1949 93m/C*

In one of his most memorable performances, Wayne plays an Army Captain who puts off retirement when his post is targeted for attack by a band of blood thirsty Apache Indians.

C: John Wayne, Joanne Dru, John Agar, Ben Johnson, Harry Carey, Jr. D: John Ford

THE SHOOTIST *1976 100m/C (PG)*

Wayne's final film has him in the role of a legendary gunfighter who, stricken with cancer, wishes to be left alone so he can die in peace. Unfortunately, a couple of outlaws are still seeking revenge against him, so he may not be going peacefully.

C: John Wayne, Lauren Bacall, Ron Howard, James Stewart, Richard Boone D: Don Siegel

SILVERADO *1985 132m/C (PG-13)*

A group of righteous cowboys decide to rid a town of a dishonest lawman, even if it means getting violent, which it does. Big budget Hollywood western, the first in years, provides solid entertainment.

C: Kevin Kline, Scott Glenn, Kevin Costner, Danny Glover, Jeff Goldblum, Brian Dennehy D: Lawrence Kasdan

STAGECOACH *1939 100m/B&W*

See "Top 100"

TELL THEM WILLIE BOY IS HERE *1969 98m/C (PG)*

Blake plays an Indian who kills his white wife's father in self-defense. Redford plays the sheriff who's forced against his will to go after him. A tight script with solid performances

C: Robert Redford, Katharine Ross, Robert Blake, Susan Clark, Barry Sullivan D: Abraham Polonsky

---

THERE WAS A CROOKED MAN *1970 123m/C (R)*

There's a new warden at the Arizona prison and he makes the old one look like Mr. Rogers. But this doesn't stop one determined inmate's (Douglas) obsessive desire to escape. Great script and cast.

C: Kirk Douglas, Henry Fonda, Warren Oates, Burgess Meredith
D: Joseph L. Mankiewicz

TOMBSTONE *1993 127m/C (R)*

Russell plays Wyatt Earp in this retelling of the famous showdown in Tombstone, Arizona. Some great scenes and probably the best Doc Holliday portrayal (Kilmer) ever on film raise this above the average western.

C: Kurt Russell, Val Kilmer, Michael Biehn, Sam Elliott, Dana Delany, Powers Boothe   D: George P. Cosmatos

TRUE GRIT *1969 128m/C (G)*

A young girl hires the heavy drinking town sheriff (John Wayne) to hunt down the man who killed her father. Wayne's great, and the pic includes the famous shootout at the end between the sheriff and Ned Pepper (Robert Duvall).

C: Wayne, Glen Campbell, Kim Darby, Duvall   D: Henry Hathaway
AA: '69 Best Actor (Wayne)

ULZANA'S RAID *1972 103m/C (R)*

A calvary officer and an Indian scout team up to take on a ruthless Apache Chief and his tribe. Unfortunately, they're first going to have to get over a war that erupts between themselves. A violent western that's gained wide acclaim over the years.

C: Burt Lancaster, Bruce Davidson, Richard Jaeckel, Lloyd Bochner, Jorge Luke   D: Robert Aldrich

UNFORGIVEN *1992 130m/C (R)*

A ruthless gunfighter (Eastwood), who has since tried to put his past behind him, is financially forced to bounty hunt two men who sliced up a prostitute. The gunfighter believes he can kill the men and come back home without returning to his old lifestyle. But a sadistic sheriff poses a physical and psychological road block.

C: Clint Eastwood, Gene Hackman, Morgan Freeman, Richard Harris, Jaimz Woolvet   D: Clint Eastwood   AA: '92 Best Director, Picture, Supporting Actor (Hackman), Nom: Best Actor (Eastwood), Original Screenplay

THE WAGON MASTER *1950 85m/B&W*

A group of Mormons are heading west and convince two cowboys to help them on their trek. Problems arise including some vicious thugs who join the passengers in order to hide out from the law.

C: Ben Johnson, Joanne Dru, Harry Carey, Jr., Ward Bond, Jane Darwell, James Arness   D: John Ford

WESTERN UNION *1941 94m/C*

The linking of the Western Union Telegraph line from Omaha to Utah during the Civil War serves as the backdrop to Indian violence, romance, adventure, and an outlaw trying to reform himself. One of Fritz Lang's early American films.

C: Randolph Scott, Robert Young, Dean Jagger, Slim Sommerville, Virginia Gilmore   D: Fritz Lang

THE WILD BUNCH *1969 145m/C (R)*

See "Top 100"

WILL PENNY *1967 109m/C*

Heston's personal favorite performance has him playing a drifter who makes a bad move by getting on the wrong side of a family of outlaws. His trouble is followed by a woman who wants him in a very bad way. Classic lone cowboy pic.

C: Charlton Heston, Joan Hackett, Donald Pleasence, Lee Majors, Bruce Dern   D: Tom Gries

WINCHESTER 73 *1950 82m/C*

Stewart is a cowpoke who purchases a beautiful Winchester 73 rifle and then, after it's stolen, has to track it down as it goes from person to person. Fast paced, tongue-in-cheek gem includes a classic shoot-out finale.

C: James Stewart, Shelley Winters, Stephen McNally, Dan Duryea, Millard Mitchell, Rock Hudson   D: Anthony Mann

---

DECADE BY DECADE

BEST OF THE 1920s

THE BIG PARADE *1925 141m/B&W*
See "War"

BIRTH OF A NATION *1915 175m/B&W*
See "War"

THE BLACK PIRATE *1926 121m/B&W*
See "Action Adventure"

THE CAMERAMAN *1928 78m/B&W*
See "Comedy"

CHANG: A DRAMA OF THE WILDERNESS *1927 69m/B&W*
Compelling study of a family living at the edge of the Siam jungle in Thailand, and the day to day hardships they must endure to survive. "Chang" is Siamese for "elephant" and the title comes to life in an incredibly filmed stampede of the mammoth animals. Directors Cooper and Schoedsack later made *King Kong*.

C: Bimbo, Kru, Ladah, Nah, Chantui   D: Merian C. Cooper, Ernest B. Schoedsack

THE CIRCUS *1928 105m/B&W*

Chaplin joins the "Big Top" and a series of wild adventures ensue, including the "Little Tramp" falling in love with the bareback rider. Chaplin was awarded a special Academy Award for this one, a "versatility and genius in writing, directing, acting, and producing" trophy.

C: Charlie Chaplin, Merna Kennedy   D: Charlie Chaplin

THE DOCKS OF NEW YORK *1928 60m/B&W*

A woman tries to kill herself but is saved by a dockworker who marries her. Though the marriage is not based on love, he sees her for the beautiful person she is and their hearts soon interlock.

C: George Bancroft, Betty Compson, Olga Baclanova   D: Josef von Sternberg

DON JUAN *1926 90m/B&W*

See "Action/Adventure"

THE FOUR HORSEMEN OF THE APOCALYPSE
1921 110m/B&W

Valentino plays a young man talked into joining the army by a recruiter who conjures up visions of the biblical Horsemen Of The Apocalypse. He enlists with pride, but it's not what he thought.

C: Rudolph Valentino, Alice Terry, Pomeroy Cannon, Josef Swickard
D: Rex Ingram

THE FRESHMAN *1925 75m/B&W*

A favorite among audiences, this pic has comedian Lloyd playing a fresh-from-the-farm college boy who gets in major madcap hijinx as he tries to win the girl of his dreams and become a member of the football team. Classic, big game finale.

C: Harold Lloyd, Jobyna Ralston, Brooks Benedict, James Andersen
D: Sam Taylor

THE GENERAL 1927 79m/B&W
See "Comedy"

THE GOLD RUSH 1925 85m/B&W
See "Comedy"

THE GOLEM 1920 80m/B&W
Not only is this one of the best films of the '20s, it's also one of the weirdest plots of any film ever made. A medieval Rabbi uses his "powers" to bring a statue to life so it can protect a Jewish village in Prague. Classic effects add to a truly bizarre, but excellent pic.

C: Paul Wegener, Albert Steinruck, Ernst Deutsch, Syda Salmonava
D: Paul Wegener

GREED 1924 140m/B&W
See "Drama"

HALLELUJAH 1929 90m/B&W
A simple caring southern man goes from cotton picker to preacher but ultimately cannot resist the temptation of a sultry, deceitful woman. This was the first all-black film ever made and the soundtrack showcases some beautiful high-energy gospel music.

C: Daniel L. Haynes, Nina Mae McKinney, William Fountaine, Everett McGarrity   D: King Vidor

INTOLERANCE 1916 175m/B&W
A D. W. Griffith masterpiece which weaves together four stories of morals, humanity, and intolerance. Beautifully paced with a brilliant climax.

C: Lillian Gish, Mae Marsh, Robert Harron, Bessie Love, Constance Talmadge   D: D. W. Griffith

THE LAST COMMAND *1928 88m/B&W*

A once powerful Russian military figure, now living a hard life in the U.S., must eke out a meager living as a Hollywood extra. To add insult to injury, he is hired as an extra in a tinsletown pic about the Russian Revolution. Considered a masterpiece.

C: Emil Jannings, Evelyn Brent, William Powell, Nicholas Soussanin
D: Josef von Sternberg   AA: '28 Nom: Best Screenplay, Picture

NANOOK OF THE NORTH *1922 55m/B&W*

See "Documentary"

PHANTOM OF THE OPERA *1925 79m/B&W*

See "Horror"

SEVEN CHANCES *1925 60m/B&W*

Keaton plays a man who is going to inherit seven million dollars as long as he can get married by 7:00 PM. He thinks he's got it made until he proposes to his girlfriend and she says no. As the clock ticks, he goes on a frantic search. Keaton came close to turning this film down and passing it on to fellow comedian Harold Lloyd.

C: Buster Keaton, T. Roy Barnes, Snitz Edwards   D: Buster Keaton

SUNRISE *1927 110m/B&W*

Gaynor is great as a sultry city girl who seduces a simple young man from the country into trying to kill his wife.

C: George O'Brien, Janet Gaynor, Bodil Rosing, Margaret Livingston
D: F. W. Murnau

THE UNHOLY THREE *1925 70m/B&W*

Chaney plays a carnival ventriloquist who teams up with the strongman and a midget to form a gang of house robbers.

Trouble begins when his two partners decide to break from the pack and go into business for themselves. Eerie, atmospheric mayhem. From the same man who brought you the other circus classic, *Freaks*.

C: Lon Chaney, Sr., Mae Busch, Matt Moore, Victor McLaglen, Harry Earles   D: Tod Browning

THE UNKNOWN *1927 60m/B&W*

Director Tod Browning again uses the underbelly of the circus world as his twisted backdrop for mayhem. Chaney plays a freak in a circus sideshow who falls in love with one of the performers. When she fails to return his fiery emotions, he decides to murder the man she does have her eye on. Creepy, but highly effective.

C: Lon Chaney, Sr., Norman Kerry, Joan Crawford, Nick DeRuiz   D: Tod Browning

WHEN THE CLOUDS ROLL BY *1919 77m/B&W*

One of the great silent comedies has Douglas Fairbanks, Sr. as a wacky doctor's wacky patient engulfed in hypochondria. From the director of *Gone With The Wind* and *The Wizard Of Oz*.

C: Douglas Fairbanks, Sr., Herbert Grimwood, Kathleen Clifford, Frank Campeau   D: Victor Fleming

BEST OF THE 1930s

BEAU GESTE *1939 114m/B&W*
See "War"

BRINGING UP BABY *1938 103m/B&W*
See "Comedy"

CITY LIGHTS *1931 86m/B&W*
See "Comedy"

DESTRY RIDES AGAIN *1939 94m/B&W*
See "Western"

DRACULA *1931 75m/B&W*
See "Horror"

DUCK SOUP *1935 70m/B&W*
See "Comedy"

FRANKENSTEIN *1931 71m/B&W*
See "Horror"

GONE WITH THE WIND *1939 231m/C*
See "Drama"

GOODBYE MR. CHIPS *1939 115m/B&W*
See "Drama"

GUNGA DIN *1939 117m/B&W*
See "War"

HUNCHBACK OF NOTRE DAME *1939 117m/B&W*
See "Drama"

I AM A FUGITIVE FROM A CHAIN GANG *1932*
93m/B&W
See "Drama"

IT HAPPENED ONE NIGHT *1934 105m/B&W*
See "Comedy"

KING KING *1933 105m/B&W*
See "Action/Adventure"

MR. SMITH GOES TO WASHINGTON *1939*
130m/B&W
See "Drama"

MUTINY ON THE BOUNTY *1935 132m/B&W*
See "Drama"

OF MICE AND MEN *1939 107m/C*
See "Drama"

MODERN TIMES *1936 87m/B&W*
See "Comedy"

PRIVATE LIFE OF HENRY VIII *1933 97m/B&W*
See "Biography"

RUGGLES OF RED GAP *1935 92m/B&W*
See "Comedy"

SNOW WHITE AND THE SEVEN DWARFS *1937
83m/C*
See "Children/Family"

STAGECOACH *1939 100m/B&W*
See "Western"

THE WIZARD OF OZ *1939 101m/C/B&W*
See "Children/Family"

TOP HAT *1935 97m/B&W*
See "Musical"

WUTHERING HEIGHTS *1939 104m/B&W*
See "Drama"

BEST OF THE 1940s

ADAM'S RIB *1949 101m/B&W*
See "Comedy"

THE BEST YEARS OF OUR LIVES *1946 170m/B&W*
See "War"

THE BIG SLEEP *1946 114m/B&W*
See "Mystery/Suspense"

CASABLANCA *1942 102m/B&W*
See "Drama"

CITIZEN KANE *1941 119m/B&W*
See "Drama"

DOUBLE INDEMNITY *1944 107m/B&W*
See "Mystery/Suspense"

THE GRAPES OF WRATH *1940 129m/B&W*
See "Drama"

HAMLET *1948 153m/B&W*
See "Drama"

HOW GREEN WAS MY VALLEY *1941 118m/C*
See "Drama"

IT'S A WONDERFUL LIFE *1946 125m/B&W*
See "Holiday"

THE LADY EVE *1941 93m/B&W*
See "Comedy"

LAURA *1944 85m/B 100m/B&W*
See "Mystery/Suspense"

LOST WEEKEND *1945 100m/B&W*
See "Drama"

THE MAGNIFICENT AMBERSONS *1942 88m/B&W*
See "Drama"

THE MALTESE FALCON *1941 101m/B&W*
See "Mystery/Suspense"

MIRACLE ON 34TH STREET *1947 97m/B&W*
See "Holiday"

NATIONAL VELVET *1944 124m/B*
See "Children"

THE OX-BOW INCIDENT *1943 75m/B&W*
See "Western"

THE PHILADELPHIA STORY *1940 112m/B&W*
See "Comedy"

REBECCA *1940 130m/B&W*
See "Mystery/Suspense"

SHADOW OF A DOUBT *1943 108mB&W*
See "Mystery/Suspense"

SULLIVAN'S TRAVELS *1941 90m/B&W*
See "Comedy"

THE THIRD MAN *1949 104m/B&W*
See "Mystery/Suspense"

TREASURE OF THE SIERRA MADRE *1949*
104m/B&W
See "Mystery/Suspense"

YANKEE DOODLE DANDY *1942 126m/B&W*
See "Musical"

BEST OF THE 1950s

THE AFRICAN QUEEN *1951 105m/C*
See "Action/Adventure"

ALL ABOUT EVE *1950 138m/B&W*
See "Comedy"

AN AMERICAN IN PARIS *1951 113m/C*
See "Musical"

THE ASPHALT JUNGLE *1950 112m/B&W*
See " Mystery/Suspense"

BAD DAY AT BLACK ROCK *1954 81m/C*
See "Drama"

BEN HUR *1959 212m/C*
See "Action/Adventure"

BRIDGE ON THE RIVER KWAI *1957 161m/C*
See "Action/Adventure"

THE CAINE MUTINY *1954 125m/C*
See "Drama"

EAST OF EDEN *1954 115m/C*
See "Drama"

HIGH NOON *1952 85m/B&W*
See "Western"

THE KING AND I *1956 133m/C*
See "Musical"

THE LAVENDER HILL MOB *1951 78m/B&W*
See "Comedy"

LILI *1953 81m/C*
See "Children/Family"

NORTH BY NORTHWEST *1959 136m/C*
See "Mystery/Suspense"

ON THE WATERFRONT *1954 108m/B&W*
See "Drama"

PATHS OF GLORY *1957 86m/B&W*
See "War"

REAR WINDOW *1954 112m/C*
See "Mystery/Suspense"

THE SEARCHERS *1956 119m/C*
See "Western"

SHANE *1954 117m/C*
See "Western"

SINGIN' IN THE RAIN *1952 103m/C*
See "Musical"

A STREETCAR NAMED DESIRE *1951 122/B&W (PG)*
See "Drama"

TEN COMMANDMENTS *1956 219m/C*
See "Drama"

TOUCH OF EVIL *1958 108m/B&W*
See "Mystery/Suspense"

TWELVE ANGRY MEN *1957 95m/B&W*
See "Drama"

VERTIGO *1958 126m/C*
See "Mystery/Suspense"

BEST OF THE 1960s

THE APARTMENT *1960 125m/B&W*
See "Comedy"

THE BIRDS *1963 120m/C*
See "Horror"

BONNIE AND CLYDE *1967 111m/C*
See "Biography"

BUTCH CASSIDY AND THE SUNDANCE KID *1969 110m/C (PG)*
See "Western"

COOL HAND LUKE *1967 126m/C*
See "Drama"

DR. STRANGELOVE OR HOW I LEARNED TO STOP WORRYING AND LOVE THE BOMB *1964 93m/B&W*
See "Comedy"

EASY RIDER *1969 94m/C (R)*
See "Drama"

THE GRADUATE *1967 106m/C (PG)*
See "Comedy"

THE GREAT ESCAPE *1963 170m/C*
See "War"

A HARD DAY'S NIGHT *1964 90m/C*
See "Musicals"

HUD *1963 112m/B&W*
See "Drama"

JUDGEMENT AT NUREMBERG *1961 178m/B&W*
See "Drama"

LAWRENCE OF ARABIA *1962 221m/C (PG)*
See "War"

A MAN FOR ALL SEASONS *1966 120m/C (G)*
See "Drama"

MIDNIGHT COWBOY *1969 113m/C (X)*
See "Drama"

MY FAIR LADY *1964 170m/C (G)*
See "Musical"

OLIVER! *1965 120m/B&W*
See "Drama"

THE PAWNBROKER *1965 120m/B&W*
See "Drama"

PSYCHO *1960 109m/B&W*
See "Horror"

THE SOUND OF MUSIC *1965 174m/C*
See "Musical"

TO SIR, WITH LOVE *1967 105m/C*
See "Drama"

TOM JONES *1963 121m/C*
See "Comedy"

2001: A SPACE ODYSSEY *1968 139m/C*
See "Sci-Fi"

WEST SIDE STORY *1961 151m/C*
See "Musical"

THE WILD BUNCH *1969 145m/C*
See "Western"

BEST OF THE 1970s

ANNIE HALL *1977 94m/B&W (PG)*
See "Comedy"

APOCALYPSE NOW *1979 155m/C (R)*
See "War"

BREAKING AWAY *1979 100m/C (PG)*
See "Drama"

CHINATOWN *1974 131m/C (R)*
See "Mystery/Suspense"

A CLOCKWORK ORANGE *1971 137m/C (R)*
See "Sci-Fi"

THE DEER HUNTER *1978 183m/C (R)*
See "War"

DELIVERANCE *1972 109m/C (R)*
See "Drama"

DOG DAY AFTERNOON *1975 124m/C (R)*
See "Drama"

THE EXORCIST *1973 120m/C (R)*
See "Horror"

FIVE EASY PIECES *1970 98m/C (R)*
See "Drama"

THE FRENCH CONNECTION *1971 102m/C (R)*
See "Action/Adventure"

THE GODFATHER *1972 171m/C (R)*
See "Drama"

THE GODFATHER, PART 2 *1974 200m/C*
See "Drama"

HAROLD AND MAUDE *1971 92m/C (PG)*
See "Drama"

JAWS *1975 124m/C*
See "Mystery/Suspense"

THE LAST PICTURE SHOW *1971 118m/C (R)*
See "Drama"

MANHATTAN *1979 96m/B&W (R)*
See "Comedy"

M*A*S*H *1970 116m/C (R)*
See "War"

ONE FLEW OVER THE CUCKOO'S NEST *1975 129m/C (R)*
See "Drama"

PAPILLON *1973 150m/C (PG)*
See "Biography"

PATTON *1970 171m/C (PG)*
See "Biography"

ROCKY *1976 125m/C (PG)*
See "Drama"

STAR WARS *1977 121m/C (PG)*
See "Sci-Fi"

THE STING *1973 129m/C (PG)*
See "Comedy"

TAXI DRIVER *1976 112m/C (R)*
See "Drama"

BEST OF THE 1980s

AMADEUS *1984 158m/C (PG)*
See "Biography"

ATLANTIC CITY *1981 104m/C (R)*
See "Drama"

BLADE RUNNER *1982 122m/C (R)*
See "Sci-Fi"

BLOOD SIMPLE *1985 96m/C (R)*
See "Thriller"

BLUE VELVET *1986 121m/C (R)*
See "Mystery/Suspense"

CRIMES AND MISDEMEANORS *1989 104m/C (PG-13)*
See "Drama"

E.T.: THE EXTRA-TERRESTRIAL *1982 115m/C*
See "Children/Family"

THE ELEPHANT MAN *1980 125m/B&W (PG)*
See "Biography"

THE FALCON AND THE SNOWMAN *1985 110m/C (R)*
See "Biography"

FULL METAL JACKET *1987 116m/C (R)*
See "War"

GANDHI *1982 188m/C (PG)*
See "Biography"

HANNAH AND HER SISTERS *1986 103m/C (PG)*
See "Comedy"

KING OF COMEDY *1982 101m/C (PG)*
See "Drama"

THE LAST EMPEROR *1987 140m/C (PG-13)*
See "Biography"

LOCAL HERO *1983 112m/C (PG)*
See "Drama"

THE LONG GOOD FRIDAY *1980 119m/C*
See "Action/Adventure"

MISSING *1982 122m/C (PG)*
See "Drama"

ORDINARY PEOPLE *1980 124m/C (R)*
See "Drama"

RAGING BULL *1980 128m/B&W(R)*
See "Biography"

RAIDERS OF THE LOST ARK *1981 115m/C (PG)*
See "Action/Adventure"

ROAD WARRIOR *1982 95m/C (PG)*
See "Action/Adventure"

ROOM WITH A VIEW *1986 117m/C*
See "Drama"

THE TERMINATOR *1984 108m/C (R)*
See "Sci-Fi"

TERMS OF ENDEARMENT *1983 132m/C (PG)*
See "Drama"

THIS IS SPINAL TAP *1984 82m/C*
See "Comedy"

BEST OF THE 1990s

BARTON FINK *1991 116m/C (R)*
See "Comedy"

BEAUTY AND THE BEAST *1991 84m/C (G)*
See "Children"

BRAVEHEART *1995 120m/C*
See "Biography"

BULLETS OVER BROADWAY *1994 85m/C (R)*
See "Comedy"

DANCES WITH WOLVES *1990 181m/C (PG-13)*
See "Western"

THE FISHER KING *1991 138m/C (R)*
See "Drama"

FORREST GUMP *1994 142m/C (PG)*
"See Drama"

THE FUGITIVE *1993 127m/C (PG-13)*
See "Drama"

GLENGARRY GLENN ROSS *1992 100m/C (R)*
See "Drama"

GLORY *1990 122m/C (R)*
See "War"

GOODFELLAS *1990 146m/C (R)*
See "Drama"

HEARTS OF DARKNESS *1991 96m/C (R)*
See "Documentary"

HOWARDS END *1992 143m/C (PG)*
See "Drama"

IN THE LINE OF FIRE *1993 128m/C (R)*
See "Mystery/Suspense"

JURASSIC PARK *1993 127m/C (PG-13)*
See "Sci-Fi"

MILLER'S CROSSING *1990 115m/C (R)*
See "Mystery/Suspense"

THE PLAYER *1992 123m/C (R)*
See "Comedy"

PULP FICTION *1994 153m/C (R)*
See "Drama"

RESERVOIR DOGS *1992 100m/C (R)*
See "Action/Adventure"

REVERSAL OF FORTUNE *1990 112m/C (R)*
See "Drama"

SCHINDLER'S LIST *1993 195m/B&W (R)*
See "Biography"

SHAWSHANK REDEMPTION *1994 112m/C (PG)*
See "Drama"

SILENCE OF THE LAMBS *1991 118m/C (R)*
See "Mystery/Suspense"

UNFORGIVEN *1992 131m/C (R)*
See "Western"

VINCENT AND THEO *1990 138m/C (PG-13)*
See "Biography"

INDEX/CHECKLIST

ISBN 0-88001-542-X

50595 >

EAN

9 780880 015424